The Inflammation- Free Diet Plan

The Scientific Way to Lose Weight, Banish Pain, Prevent Disease, and Slow Aging

P9-EGM-215

Monica Reinagel

WITH CONSULTING EDITOR

Julius Torelli, M.D.

A LYNN SONBERG BOOK

New York   Chicago   San Francisco   Lisbon   London   Madrid   Mexico City
Milan   New Delhi   San Juan   Seoul   Singapore   Sydney   Toronto

Library of Congress Cataloging-in-Publication Data

Reinagel, Monica.
    The inflammation-free diet plan : the scientific way to lose weight, banish pain, prevent
disease, and slow aging / by Monica Reinagel, with a foreword by Julius Torelli.
        p.   cm.
    "A Lynn Sonberg Book."
    Includes bibliographical references and index.
    ISBN 0-07-146471-9 (hardcover) — ISBN 0-07-148601-1 (paperback)
        1. Inflammation—Alternative treatment.   2. Inflammation—Diet therapy.
    3. Self-care, Health.   I. Title.

    RB131.R45   2006
    616'.0473—dc22   2005022619

    2 3 4 5 6 7 8 9 10 11 12 13 14 15 16 17 18 19 20   FGR/FGR   0 9 8

ISBN-13: 978-0-07-148601-9
ISBN-10:   0-07-148601-1

McGraw-Hill books are available at special quantity discounts to use as premiums and sales
promotions, or for use in corporate training programs. For more information, please write to
the Director of Special Sales, Professional Publishing, McGraw-Hill, Two Penn Plaza, New York,
NY 10121-2298. Or contact your local bookstore.

This book is for informational purposes only. It is not intended to take the place of medical
advice from a trained medical professional. Readers are advised to consult a physician or other
qualified health professional regarding any and all health concerns. The reader assumes all
responsibility for the consequences of any actions taken based on the information presented in
this book.

This information is based on the author's research and experience. Every attempt has been
made to ensure that the information is accurate; however, the author cannot accept liability for
any errors that may exist. The facts and theories on diet, inflammation, and health are subject to
interpretation, and the conclusions and recommendations presented here may not agree with
other interpretations. There is also the possibility that new information may emerge subsequent
to publication that could modify the interpretations presented here.

This book is printed on acid-free paper.

Contents

Tables and Figures

Foreword

The more we learn about the role inflammation plays in heart disease, Alzheimer's disease, diabetes, depression, osteoporosis, and cancer, the more clearly we see that inflammation is a serious threat affecting millions of people. Headlines like "The Silent Epidemic," "The Hidden Killer," and "The Cause of All Disease" are appearing on major newspapers, magazines, network news shows, and bestselling books.

As exciting as it is for researchers to have a new handle on today's most serious diseases, the recent media blitz on inflammation hasn't translated into a practical solution for a public that is frankly overwhelmed by a nonstop barrage of contradictory or confusing advice about health, nutrition, and diet.

That's why I am so delighted about the publication of *The Inflammation-Free Diet Plan*. This book offers a simple, easy-to-understand, and above all, *practical* tool for reducing excessive inflammation and avoiding the risks and symptoms that go with it. But it is more than a targeted solution for a specific problem. *The Inflammation-Free Diet Plan* synthesizes the best of the current nutrition and dietary concepts into a single program for good nutrition, weight loss, and disease prevention. I don't have a single patient—or friend—who wouldn't benefit from and thrive on this program.

A few days before sitting down to write this foreword, I was seeing patients at my medical center in High Point, North Carolina. One of my new patients had an appointment to discuss the results of her initial blood work. Shannon is in her forties, diabetic, and had been referred to me by her endocrinologist for preventive cardiology care.

Looking over her test results earlier that morning, I was glad to see that her LDL cholesterol was 79, comfortably within the acceptable range. Her blood sugar levels indicated that her diabetes was under control. But there was another test result that concerned me a great deal. As part of her workup, I had ordered a test for C-reactive protein (CRP), which is a compound in the blood that signals the presence of nonspecific systemic inflammation. Elevated levels of CRP are a serious warning sign, indicating an increased risk of cardiovascular disease.

Shannon's level of C-reactive protein was 16.9 milligrams per liter, more than eight times what I would consider to be a safe level. I put in a quick call to her endocrinologist, who had also received a copy of the test results. "Yeah," he sighed, when I got him on the phone, "I saw the report. I frequently see those kinds of CRP levels in my diabetic patients. But, frankly, I'm not sure what to suggest or what drugs to put her on. She has worked with my staff nutritionist to change her diet, and she's obviously doing a good job of managing her diabetes. What more can we tell her to do?"

I looked at the manuscript sitting on the corner of my desk—the manuscript for this book—and realized that with the publication of *The Inflammation-Free Diet Plan*, there would finally be a natural and practical solution for Shannon and the countless others who are at risk of inflammation-related illness.

Western medicine has underemphasized the importance of nutrition. Although there is no question that proper diet and nutrition can prevent and often treat disease, most medical students spend only a few hours out of their many years of training learning about nutrition. As a result, many doctors tend to view nutrition as a lifestyle issue, not a medical one.

In truth, it takes time to educate people about the complex role of foods and health—more time than many doctors feel they are able to spend with their patients. There are excellent nutritionists and dietitians who can fill this role, but with the exception of dia-

betes care, few health insurance companies are willing to reim-
burse costs associated with nutrition education. Sadly, our medical system has evolved in a way that has taken one of our most
powerful healing tools out of our medicine bags. Those of us in
the medical profession who value nutrition as a preventive and
therapeutic agent are in need of tools that can help bridge the gap
between what our medical system provides and what our patients
need to be truly healthy. *The Inflammation-Free Diet Plan* is just
that tool.

On the day of Shannon's appointment, the printing of this
book was still many months away, and she obviously needed to
take immediate action. With the permission of the author and
publisher, I made Shannon a copy of the manuscript and sent her
home to start her own Inflammation-Free Diet. Now that the
book is printed and bound, the inflammation-free solution for
optimal wellness is in your hands as well. Use it in good health.

Julius N. Torelli, M.D., FACC
Director, Integrative Cardiology Center
High Point, North Carolina

Acknowledgments

I'm grateful to the many colleagues and friends who supported me in this work. Thanks especially to Drs. Randy Wilkinson, Al Sears, and Julius Torelli for their clinical experience and input; to Drs. Hyla Cass and Ann Louise Gittleman for guidance and advice; to Fred Reinagel for help in developing the formula algorithms for the IF Rating system; to Ed Prestwood and folks at Nutribase for technical and software support above and beyond the call of duty; to Lynn Sonberg and Judith McCarthy, who believed that this book needed to be written; to Marcia Reinagel for invaluable assistance with the proofreading of the manuscript; and to Michelle Humphreys for everything.

Introduction

Do You Need to Read This Book?

If you are not concerned about inflammation, you should be. That may sound a bit extreme, but the fact is that virtually all of us are affected to some degree by *systemic inflammation*, a cellular type of inflammation that you can neither see nor feel. This silent threat has now emerged as one of the primary, preventable causes of serious diseases such as heart disease, cancer, Alzheimer's disease, osteoporosis, and diabetes. Even our crow's-feet and laugh lines are due to an inflammatory process in the skin!

That's the bad news. But there's also good news. Excessive inflammation can be prevented with a completely natural, drug-free approach—and this book will tell you exactly how to do it. The Inflammation-Free Diet is for anyone who wants to reduce the risk of heart disease, cancer, Alzheimer's disease, osteoporosis, diabetes, and other serious diseases. If you are looking for a safe and effective way to lose weight, the Inflammation-Free Diet is the ideal solution. And for the millions who suffer from allergies, asthma, or arthritis, the program in this book will help reduce pain and other symptoms. The Inflammation-Free Diet will even help slow the aging process—inside and out.

In Chapter 1, I'll go into more detail about how inflammation is connected with aging and disease and discuss why inflammation has become such a pervasive problem. But I won't spend too much time discussing the problem, because this book focuses primarily on the solution. (If you are interested in reading more about inflammation and disease, several recent books go into more depth on this topic, including *Inflammation Nation* by Floyd

Chilton, Ph.D., and *The Life Extension Revolution*, a book I wrote with Philip Miller, M.D.)

What can be done to prevent and reverse the damage caused by systemic inflammation? Healthy lifestyle habits such as exercising regularly, not smoking, maintaining a healthy weight, and minimizing stress all help to reduce inflammation. But the most important factor in fighting inflammation is the food we eat every day. Dietary choices have a dramatic impact on the inflammation process—often in ways that you might not suspect. You already may be careful about what you eat, avoiding refined carbohydrates, minimizing saturated fats, and so on. But other popular diet and nutrition concepts—even the best of them—do not adequately protect you against inflammation.

If you are already savvy about nutrition, you may only need to make a few minor (but often surprising) adjustments to your diet. And if you are not the healthiest eater right now, don't worry. You may need to make more substantial changes in your eating habits, but the IF Rating system makes it easy for anyone to follow a healthful, balanced, *and* inflammation-reducing diet.

The IF Rating System

The research that ultimately led to this book began as the result of an unusually bad hay fever season. Despite its many charms, the city in which I live is known to be one of the worst places for allergy sufferers. Sure enough, after living here for several years, I noticed that I was having more and more allergy symptoms.

My allergies were not severe. I could easily have managed the symptoms with over-the-counter drugs. But I didn't like the idea of taking medications on a daily basis. At the same time, I knew that even minor allergies can, over time, exhaust the adrenal system, accelerate the aging process, and weaken the immune response. I was looking for a more natural and permanent solution to what had become a chronic problem. Knowing that allergies are an inflammatory condition, I began to research ways of reducing inflammation through diet.

As a nutrition researcher and health food junkie, I already had fairly good eating habits. But as my research progressed, I was surprised to learn that a healthful diet is not automatically an anti-inflammatory diet. (However, the opposite is true: an anti-inflammatory diet is in every other respect a very healthful way to eat.)

Foods affect the body's inflammatory response in surprising and complex ways. Some foods have a combination of inflammatory and anti-inflammatory effects. Others have different effects depending on what you are eating them with. There are at least two dozen different factors that determine whether a particular food contributes to inflammation in the body—most of which you won't find listed on the standard nutritional label. Maybe this is why the dietary guidelines outlined in previous books on inflammation have tended to be overly restrictive, convoluted, unclear, or hard to follow. It is a complicated problem.

The IF Rating™ system was developed to make it easier for a nonspecialist to understand the inflammatory effects of a wide variety of foods. Each food is given an IF Rating number, which represents the net inflammatory or anti-inflammatory effects of that food. This rating takes into account over twenty different nutritional factors that affect inflammation. The science behind the IF Rating system is detailed in Chapter 2.

While the formula used to calculate the IF Rating is complex, the rating itself couldn't be simpler to use. Foods with a positive IF Rating are anti-inflammatory, and those with a negative IF Rating are considered inflammatory. The higher the number, the more powerful the effect.

As you'll see, the IF Rating system tends to favor foods that are low in sugar, rich in vitamins, lower in saturated fat, and higher in monounsaturated fat. Lean protein, fruits and vegetables, cold-water fish, and whole grains are naturally emphasized, while highly processed foods, hydrogenated oils, and empty calories are minimized.

But the IF Ratings also reveal some surprising truths about foods we typically think of as healthful. For example, low-fat dairy products are promoted as being a good source of calcium, which they are. But they are also slightly inflammatory due in part to their fatty acid composition. This doesn't mean that dairy products are bad for you. But like almost anything, too much of a good thing can be not so good. The IF Rating helps you keep track of the cumulative impact of your dietary choices and allows you to balance the inflammatory effects of negative-IF foods with positive-IF foods.

The IF Rating also allows you to see how similar foods stack up in terms of their inflammatory effects. For example, you'll see why almonds are a better choice than walnuts, strawberries may be better for you than apples, and tuna is sometimes preferable to salmon. And if you're looking for a good source of calcium, you'll see that calcium-rich vegetables such as broccoli and kale have much higher IF Ratings than milk. Simply put, IF Ratings help you make better dietary choices based on a wide range of factors. Beginning on page 137, you'll find the complete IF Rating tables. These tables list the IF Rating for over 1,600 foods, along with the amount of fat and carbohydrate they contain.

The Inflammation-Free Diet

The IF Rating system, in turn, forms the foundation of the Inflammation-Free Diet. In Chapter 3, an inflammation self-assessment will help you establish target values for each day's IF Rating total, along with guidelines for daily fat and carbohydrate intake. Reducing the symptoms and dangers of inflammation—and taking off excess weight—then becomes a matter of simple arithmetic.

Using the IF Rating tables found in the second half of this book, you tally up your food intake and keep the totals in line with the target values for your plan. Beyond that, the plan is the ultimate in flexibility. You cook, order, and eat the foods and recipes that you and your family enjoy. Chapter 3 includes some sample meal plans and recipes to get you started, along with easy instructions for developing your own inflammation-reducing meal plans and recipes.

The benefits of reducing inflammation are immediate as well as long term. You'll notice improvements in joint pain and stiffness, allergy symptoms, and the health and appearance of your skin. At the same time, when you reduce inflammation, you also reduce your risk of heart disease, Alzheimer's disease, cancer, osteoporosis, diabetes, and other complications of aging.

The Inflammation-Free Diet does more than reduce inflammation. It is a comprehensive approach to diet and nutrition. You no longer need to worry about "good" or "bad" carbohydrates or fats, and you don't need to count calories, blocks, points, or servings. The IF Rating integrates all of these factors into one holistic system. For vibrant health and youthful energy, weight management, disease prevention, and inflammation-free living, the Inflammation-Free Diet is the ideal nutritional solution for every member of the family.

CHAPTER 1

The Silent Enemy: Determining Your Risk

Some kinds of chronic inflammation are more obvious than others. If you suffer from arthritis, asthma, or allergies, you are already painfully aware of the presence of inflammation in your body. (Take heart; help is on the way!) But there is another, more dangerous form of inflammation—a silent, invisible inflammation that can attack your cells, blood vessels, and organs for years without causing the slightest symptom. Eventually, however, the damage may reveal itself in the form of heart disease, Alzheimer's disease, or cancer.

Everyone is at risk of this type of inflammation, for reasons we'll go into shortly. And if you are even slightly overweight, your risk is increased. In this chapter, you'll learn how to determine your level of systemic inflammation. More important, you'll learn what you can do to reduce the risk of inflammation-related disease.

At the right time and place, of course, inflammation is a good and necessary thing—an ingenious system that the body has for protecting itself from infection and healing from injury. If you've ever sprained your ankle, you have probably witnessed an impressive display of the body's inflammatory response. An injured ankle can swell to the size of a melon within minutes. This inflammation has a purpose.

Pain is a signal to stop what you are doing, thereby avoiding further damage. The rush of blood and fluid to the injured area acts as a natural splint to immobilize the area, while nutrients carried to the site by the blood begin the repair process. As any orthopedist will tell you, doctors don't heal sprained ankles. They just supervise while nature and time do the job.

Inflammation also comes to the rescue when your body's surveillance system detects that a foreign body—such as a bacterium or virus—has invaded its territory. The redness and swelling around an infected wound are caused by millions of white blood cells that have sped to the site to overpower the intruder. When you have a fever, which is a sort of whole-body inflammation, your immune system is working to overcome a virus or bacteria by raising the temperature of the body so high that the bug succumbs to heatstroke.

Obviously, we don't want to diminish the body's protective and healing powers. But we do want to eliminate excessive, chronic, and inappropriate inflammation. All kinds of arthritis, for example—whether they are caused by age, wear and tear, or diseases like rheumatoid arthritis—are characterized by painful swelling and stiffness in the joints. The inflammation of arthritis, however, is neither healing nor protective. Allergies are another sort of nonproductive inflammatory response in which the immune system tries to attack otherwise harmless substances like pollen or animal dander. These sorts of inflammation serve no useful purpose and can make your life miserable. Over time, excessive inflammation also increases your risk of several life-threatening diseases.

The evidence implicating inflammation in diseases like heart disease, cancer, diabetes, and Alzheimer's has emerged only recently and comes as a surprise to many people. But the fact is that inflammation plays a significant role in all of the most common and serious degenerative diseases.

Conditions Characterized by Excessive Inflammation

- Heart disease
- Alzheimer's disease
- Cancer
- Obesity
- Diabetes
- Autoimmune diseases
- Asthma
- Allergies
- Arthritis
- Prostate disease

Why Excessive Inflammation Is So Common

If inflammation is a natural and necessary part of the body's defenses, what is causing this well-designed system to malfunction? Why are so many of us suffering from excessive inflammation? The answer is complex, but it boils down to this: we have lost our balance.

The body's inflammation response works through two complementary channels: one is pro-inflammatory, and the other anti-inflammatory. Our cells produce a variety of pro- and anti-inflammatory chemicals (called *prostaglandins*), using nutrients from the food we eat as the raw material. These prostaglandins are released into our tissues in response to the immune system's signals, promoting inflammation when there is danger and quelling inflammation when the danger has passed.

A key concept in this (oversimplified) portrayal is that *our bodies produce prostaglandins by using compounds from the foods we eat.* Specifically, it is the fatty acids in our foods that our bodies use to make prostaglandins. Certain types of fatty acids (primarily those from the omega-6 family) are converted into inflammatory prostaglandins, while other types (primarily from the omega-3 fam-

3

ily) are used to make anti-inflammatory prostaglandins. This is where we, as a modern society, have gotten into trouble.

To maintain a balance between its pro- and anti-inflammatory channels, the body relies on a balanced intake of omega-3 and omega-6 fatty acids. The problem is that those of us who live in modern industrial nations consume far too many omega-6 fatty acids and far too few omega-3 fatty acids. Paleontologists and anthropologists estimate that the diet of a Stone Age human contained roughly equal parts omega-3 and omega-6 fatty acids. Today, we consume about *twenty times as much omega-6 as we do omega-3*. As a result, our bodies tend to produce an overabundance of pro-inflammatory prostaglandins and a paucity of anti-inflammatory prostaglandins. The Inflammation-Free Diet helps to reestablish a natural balance and reverse this dangerous trend.

What Went Wrong with the Modern Diet

We frequently hear that the typical modern diet leaves much to be desired nutritionally. Most of us eat too many sweets, starches, empty calories, and highly processed foods. These dietary habits contribute to our problems with inflammation, for reasons we will explore in Chapter 2. But even more problematic—and harder to fix—is the fact that humans today consume more cereal grains (and the oils produced from them) than ever before in our history as a species. These grains and oils tend to be high in omega-6 fatty acids. At the same time, we eat fewer vegetables and legumes, which are natural sources of omega-3 fats.

Not only have *our* diets shifted toward the overconsumption of grains, but the diets of our livestock have followed the same trend. Cattle that would naturally graze on grasses and other plant matter now eat primarily grain-based feed. This means that the muscle tissue (meat), milk, and eggs of domesticated livestock are lower in omega-3 and higher in omega-6 fatty acids. And most recently, with the advent of aquaculture and farm-raised seafood, even the fish we eat have begun to eat a grain-based diet instead of a natural diet of algae and smaller fish.

We eat an overabundance of omega-6 fatty acids, and we consume animals that eat an overabundance of omega-6 fatty acids. The end result is a flood of pro-inflammatory prostaglandins cascading through our bodies, with a drought of anti-inflammatory prostaglandins. No wonder we are seeing an epidemic of inflammatory disease!

Who Is at Risk

Virtually anyone who eats a modern Western diet is at risk of excessive inflammation, for the reasons just given. But there are other factors that can increase the propensity toward inflammation and inflammation-related disease:

- **Smoking:** Smoking creates huge numbers of free radicals, which in turn produce inflammation in the tissues. Especially affected are the cells lining the bronchial passages and the small blood vessels that lead to the heart. Smokers usually have high levels of inflammatory chemicals in their blood and a dramatically increased risk of many inflammation-related diseases.
- **Excess weight:** Adults and children who are overweight also tend to have higher levels of inflammatory chemicals in their blood than those of normal weight. This is compounded by the fact that those who are overweight tend to be less active, which further contributes to inflammation.
- **Sedentary lifestyle:** Among its many benefits, exercise tends to balance the body's pro- and anti-inflammatory channels—provided, of course, that no injuries are sustained! Exercise also helps reduces inflammation by mitigating the effects of stress.
- **Stress:** Chronic stress—the garden-variety, too-many-demands-not-enough-time sort—dramatically alters our internal chemistry in ways that contribute to inflammation. Adrenaline and cortisol, the so-called stress hormones,

deplete our supply of DHEA, a hormone that is a natural anti-inflammatory agent.

- **Unprotected sun exposure:** The sun's ultraviolet rays create free radicals and inflammation when they strike unprotected skin. This inflammatory process in the skin is believed to be a primary factor in the development of lines, wrinkles, age spots, and skin cancer.
- **Hormone replacement therapy:** Studies have found that otherwise healthy women taking hormone replacement medications have significantly more inflammatory chemicals in their blood than women who do not use hormones. This may be a contributing factor in the increased risk of heart disease and cancer in women using hormone replacement.
- **Disease:** Degenerative diseases such as heart disease, Alzheimer's disease, cancer, diabetes, rheumatoid arthritis, lupus, and multiple sclerosis promote (and are promoted by) excessive inflammation in the body.

Determining Your Level of Systemic Inflammation

You may have symptoms, such as those listed in the box below, that make it crystal clear inflammation is a problem for you. Or perhaps one or more of the inflammation risk factors just discussed, such as smoking or being overweight, applies to you. Often, however, systemic inflammation does not produce any symptoms or warning signs.

Symptoms Suggesting Inflammatory Imbalance

- Allergies
- Joint pain or stiffness
- Asthma
- Skin disorders (eczema, psoriasis)
- Premature or excessive skin aging
- Prostatitis

Fortunately, there are medical tests that can measure the presence of inflammation long before a serious disease has developed. C-reactive protein (CRP) is a protein in the blood that indicates the presence and extent of inflammation in the body. If there is a lot of CRP in the blood, it means a significant amount of inflammation is happening somewhere in the body. This "marker" for inflammation can be measured with a relatively inexpensive ($30 to $50) blood test. Because CRP testing is easy, reliable, affordable, and widely available, it has become the standard and most widely used measure of systemic inflammation.

Fibrinogen, a compound that indicates the propensity of the blood to form clots, is sometimes used as a secondary indication of inflammation, especially in heart patients. As with CRP, higher levels of fibrinogen suggest increased inflammation. And most recently, researchers have discovered that elevated white blood cell counts indicate an increased risk of inflammation-related disease, particularly in women. A combination of these different tests can provide a physician with a nuanced picture of the patient's inflammatory processes. In general, however, a simple CRP test is entirely sufficient to screen for and track the presence of systemic inflammation.

Many physicians will include a CRP test in your annual blood workup if you ask them to. There are also labs (see box on page 8) that allow you to order blood tests directly, although health insurance policies often will not pay for tests that have not been ordered by a physician.

Who Should Be Tested?

Because diseases such as Alzheimer's disease, cancer, prostate disease, and heart disease all have inflammatory components, monitoring inflammation through CRP testing is a good investment in your health if you are forty or older. Annual CRP testing will tell you whether the steps you are taking to reduce and avoid inflammation are sufficient or whether you need to step up your defense with more aggressive measures. If CRP levels remain stubbornly high despite your efforts, you can make some adjustments in your

Ordering Your Own Blood Tests

The following laboratories work directly with consumers to arrange blood testing. Some labs offer consultations with a health professional to help you understand your results. It's a good idea to share and discuss your lab results with your own personal physician as well, especially if you have any concerns about your health or about your test results.

Life Extension Foundation
Fort Lauderdale, Florida
800-544-4440 or 954-766-8433
www.lef.org

LabSafe Direct Lab Services
Hollywood, Florida
888-333-5227
www.lab-safe.com

dietary targets, as discussed in Chapter 3, or increase your dosage of the anti-inflammatory nutrients discussed later in this chapter.

If you have a family or personal history of heart disease risk factors such as high blood pressure or high cholesterol, regular CRP testing is strongly recommended. CRP has emerged as one of the most accurate indicators of your risk of a future heart attack or stroke. Even if you are following the Inflammation-Free Diet, you want to be sure that you are keeping your CRP levels in a safe range.

If you have diabetes, monitoring your CRP levels and keeping them in safe ranges may help you avoid serious complications such as heart disease and nerve damage, which are driven by inflammation.

Understanding Your Test Results

The CRP test is not a test for any particular disease or condition. It will not tell you whether you have heart disease, cancer, or

Alzheimer's disease. A CRP test will tell you whether you have an excessive level of systemic inflammation. Your CRP levels also indicate your *risk* of developing various diseases, such as heart disease, in the future.

CRP is usually measured in milligrams per liter (mg/L). Anything less than 5.0 milligrams per liter is considered normal by most labs. Ideally, however, you want your CRP levels to be quite a bit lower. As you can see in Table 1.1, even slight elevations of CRP have been tied to an increased risk of heart attack, stroke, and other disease.

If you decide to have a CRP test done or already have results from a recent test, enter the results on the blank CRP Tracking Chart on page 10 (Figure 1.1). This information will help you determine which of the programs outlined in Chapter 3 is right for you. And if your levels are high, don't worry. The program described in this book is designed to bring high CRP levels down to safe ranges. You may want to retest your CRP level after following the Inflammation-Free Diet for several months to be sure

TABLE 1.1 CRP Levels and Disease Risks

Men

CRP	Risk of Future Heart Attack
0.55 mg/L or less	No increased risk; ideal
0.56–1.14 mg/L	Slightly more likely
1.15–2.10 mg/L	2½ times as likely
2.11 mg/L and higher	3 times as likely

Women

CRP	Risk of Future Heart Attack or Stroke
Less than 1.50 mg/L	No increased risk; ideal
1.50–3.79 mg/L	2½ times as likely
3.80–7.30 mg/L	3½ times as likely
7.31 mg/L and higher	5½ times as likely

Source: Life Extension Foundation (www.lef.org).

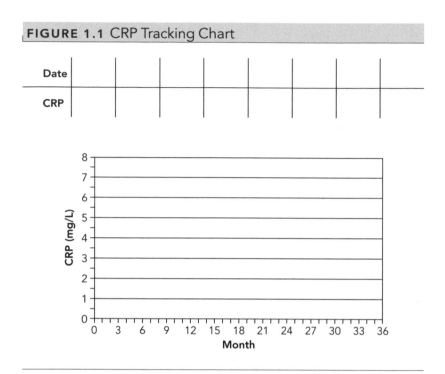

FIGURE 1.1 CRP Tracking Chart

Record your test results in the table at the top of the figure. You can also plot the values on the chart (as shown in Figure 1.2). Ideal values are 1.5 mg/L or less for women and .55 mg/L or less for men. Repeat the test annually once you reach your target value. Note: A recent injury or infection can temporarily elevate CRP levels. Wait two weeks before testing.

that you are progressing toward your goal. Once your levels are in the target zone, retesting every year or two is a good idea. Figure 1.2 on page 11 gives an example of how your chart might look.

Important note: Any infection or injury will cause a temporary rise in your CRP levels as the body's immune system responds to the crisis. If you experience an acute infection or injury, wait two weeks before scheduling a CRP test to screen for chronic, systemic inflammation to ensure an accurate result.

What You Can Do to Fight Inflammation

Whether or not you choose to have your CRP levels tested, you can begin reducing inflammation right away by following the

FIGURE 1.2 Sample CRP Tracking Chart

Date	1/15	4/20	6/12	3/5	3/2			
CRP	3.9	1.6	1.2	0.6	0.9			

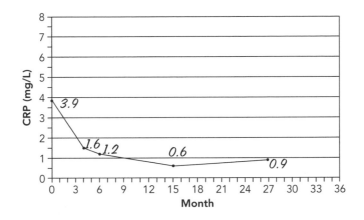

C-reactive protein (CRP) levels indicate the degree of systemic inflammation. Lower
levels translate to a reduced risk of inflammation-related conditions. Charting your
test results can help you track your progress over time.

Inflammation-Free Diet outlined in Chapter 3. Because the foods
we eat are the primary cause of inflammatory imbalance, making
changes to our diet is one of the most powerful things we can do
to reduce excessive inflammation. A recent study published in the
medical journal *Metabolism* (2004) showed that a diet that emphasizes antioxidant-rich vegetables, fruits, and whole grains while
reducing refined flours, sugar, and saturated and hydrogenated
fats, led to dramatic decreases in CRP levels (by 45 percent on
average) within just two weeks!

But you don't necessarily need to follow an extremely restrictive diet in order to combat inflammation. In fact, there are very
few foods that cannot be enjoyed on the Inflammation-Free Diet.
The trick is to balance your diet in a way that supports the natu-

ral equilibrium between the body's pro- and anti-inflammatory channels—moderating your consumption of inflammatory foods and offsetting them with anti-inflammatory foods.

Determining whether a particular food will have an inflammatory or anti-inflammatory effect—and how much of an effect it will have—is a complicated task due to the many factors that affect a food's inflammatory potential. In the next chapter, you'll learn about a tool called the IF Rating system, which makes this job much easier. And in Chapter 3, you'll learn how to use the IF Ratings to implement your personalized Inflammation-Free Diet.

Inflammation-Lowering Nutrients

To enhance the effectiveness of the Inflammation-Free Diet, consider supplementing your diet with one or more of the following anti-inflammatory nutrients and herbs. (See Table 1.2 on page 14 for specific dosage recommendations.)

Important note: If you take blood thinners such as Coumadin (warfarin) or have any sort of blood-clotting disorder, consult with your physician before adding fish oil or ginkgo to your diet. These substances can decrease blood coagulation and may affect your condition or the dosage of your medication.

- **Fish oil:** Oily fish such as salmon, tuna, herring, mackerel, and sardines are high in omega-3 fatty acids. Eating these fish helps to balance our consumption of omega-6 fatty acids in other foods. Fish oil can also be taken on a daily basis as a dietary supplement, which provides a concentrated source of these important omega-3 fatty acids. Unless you eat fish four or more times a week, a daily fish oil supplement is highly recommended. (Although it is a problem with certain types of fish, mercury contamination is not a concern with fish oil supplements.)
- **Aromatic spices:** Pungent spices like ginger, cayenne, and turmeric are widely used in herbal medicine as natural treatments for arthritis, joint pain, and other inflammatory

conditions. When taken in sufficient quantities, they can produce effects almost equivalent to over-the-counter drugs like aspirin or ibuprofen. You'll find these flavorful ingredients featured in several of the recipes included in Chapter 3. They can also be taken as nutritional supplements to boost the effects of an inflammation-reducing diet, especially if you have arthritis or other joint pain.

- **Anti-inflammatory plants:** Other inflammation-reducing herbs, such as stinging nettle and ginkgo biloba, are not as easily incorporated into the diet as food but can be beneficial when taken as nutritional supplements. You might find them included in herbal blends specifically designed to reduce inflammation, or you can take them individually. Nettle is especially recommended if you suffer from allergies or inflammation of the prostate. Ginkgo is known to reduce inflammation and increase circulation, especially in the brain.

- **Anti-inflammatory enzymes:** Bromelain is an anti-inflammatory enzyme that is isolated from fresh pineapple. (It is not found in canned or cooked pineapple because heat destroys the enzyme.) It is hard to eat enough fresh pineapple to take in a meaningful amount of bromelain, but you can take it as a dietary supplement. Bromelain is often recommended to people at risk of heart disease and to speed wound healing following surgery.

Benefits of Reducing Inflammation

The Inflammation-Free Diet will help to rebalance the pro- and anti-inflammatory channels in your body and reduce excessive inflammation. If you currently have symptoms related to inflammation, such as joint pain, hay fever, asthma, or skin allergies, you will most likely notice a substantial improvement in these symptoms within a few weeks.

The Inflammation-Free Diet will also help rejuvenate your skin, smoothing fine lines and wrinkles and improving your skin's

TABLE 1.2 Inflammation-Reducing Supplements

Nutrient/Herb	Dosage Recommended to Reduce Inflammation	Suggested Uses
Fish oil	2,000–3,000 mg/day	All-purpose; heart health
Ginger	1,000–2,000 mg/day	All-purpose; joint pain
Curcumin (turmeric)	1,000–2,000 mg/day	All-purpose; joint pain
Nettle leaf	1,000–2,000 mg/day	Allergies; prostate inflammation
Ginkgo biloba	100–250 mg/day	All-purpose; mental clarity
Bromelain	1,500–2,000 mg/day	Heart health; wound healing

texture and clarity. In addition to these immediate benefits, isn't it wonderful to know that by reducing inflammation, you are also lowering your chances of serious disease in the future?

- **Heart disease:** Reducing inflammation, particularly in the cells that line the blood vessels and heart, can reduce the likelihood of having a heart attack or stroke. It can also lower the chances of developing heart disease in the first place.
- **Alzheimer's disease:** Many neurologists now believe Alzheimer's disease to be *primarily* an inflammatory process. Those with less systemic inflammation have a lower risk of developing Alzheimer's disease. In those already afflicted, it is hoped that the progression of the disease can be slowed with anti–inflammatory therapies.
- **Cancer:** This dreaded disease, which is threatening to outpace heart disease as the number one killer of Americans, is associated with a variety of inflammatory processes in the blood and tissues. Anti–inflammatory therapies have been shown to reduce the incidence of cancer and may prove to be of value in the treatment of the disease as well.

What About Anti-Inflammatory Drugs?

Of course, there are drugs that can also help to reduce inflammation, such as nonsteroidal anti-inflammatory drugs (NSAIDs) like aspirin or ibuprofen. Millions of people take these drugs on a daily or near-daily basis to alleviate headaches, muscle pain, or mild to moderate joint pain from arthritis. In fact, the link between inflammation and heart disease, cancer, Alzheimer's, and other diseases was first revealed when researchers noticed that people who took NSAIDs on a regular basis were significantly less likely to suffer from these diseases.

There are even some drugs that are not designed to reduce inflammation but have anti-inflammatory effects. Certain cholesterol-reducing medications known as statin drugs have this interesting property. In fact, some researchers now suspect that the lifesaving benefits of cholesterol-reducing drugs may have at least as much to do with their ability to reduce inflammation as it does with their ability to reduce cholesterol.

The problem with using drugs like statins and NSAIDs to control systemic inflammation on an ongoing basis is that they can be expensive and can have serious side effects, especially with long-term use. NSAIDs can cause irritation of the gastric lining, internal bleeding, and anemia. Statin drugs can cause nausea, diarrhea, constipation, muscle aches, elevated liver enzymes, and memory loss.

There are safer, more natural ways to reduce inflammation and its damaging effects. Instead of artificially blocking the body's inflammatory processes with chemicals, the Inflammation-Free Diet can safely reduce the body's production of inflammatory compounds and increase its production of natural anti-inflammatory compounds.

The most important step in reducing unwanted inflammation is taking a closer look at the foods we eat every day and the ways they contribute to or fight inflammation. The next chapter introduces the IF Rating system, a simple and flexible method that allows you to reduce excessive inflammation while enjoying the foods you love.

CHAPTER 2

How the Foods You Eat Affect Inflammation

If you want to know how many calories are in a given food, or how much saturated fat, or how many grams of carbohydrates it contains, you can find these basic nutritional statistics on the nutrition facts label or look them up in any of the calorie, fat, and carbohydrate counters sold in the checkout aisle of your local supermarket. But if you want to know whether a particular food has inflammatory or anti-inflammatory effects in the body, you won't find this information on the label or in a standard nutrition counter.

To determine whether a certain food might promote or suppress inflammation and by how much, you have to weigh the effects of dozens of different factors. In fact, to get a really accurate answer, you need to know the precise composition of the food, down to the level of individual fatty-acid molecules. You have to consider the amount and type of fats, along with the quantities of various antioxidants, vitamins, and minerals. You also need to know the amount of sugar in the food and how fast that sugar is metabolized in the body. Finally, you have to take into account how the food was prepared, because any or all of these factors can be altered when a food is cooked or preserved.

Until now, there has been no practical way to gather, analyze, and combine all of this information—making it difficult to combat the effects of inflammation. Now, for the first time, there is a simple way to determine whether the foods you eat are contributing to chronic inflammation. The IF Rating assigns a single number that represents the total inflammatory or anti-inflammatory potential of a food. A positive number indicates anti-inflammatory tendencies, while a negative number signifies that the food has an inflammatory effect. The higher the number, the more significant the effect.

Foods with IF Ratings between 1 and 100 are considered to have mild anti-inflammatory effects. Ratings between 101 and 500 indicate increasingly potent anti-inflammatory actions. Foods that have ratings over 500 are strongly anti-inflammatory. On the other end of the scale, foods that have ratings between −1 and −100 are mildly inflammatory. Foods with ratings between −101 and −500 are increasingly inflammatory, and those with ratings of −500 and lower are considered highly inflammatory. A few foods have an IF Rating of 0, meaning they can be considered neutral, neither promoting nor combating inflammation.

Beginning on page 137, you'll find the complete IF Rating tables, which list thousands of foods and their IF Ratings. And in the next chapter, you'll see how easy it is to calculate the combined effects of meals and recipes and to create your own personalized Inflammation-Free Diet using the IF Rating system. But first, let's take a closer look at how the IF Ratings are determined.

How the IF Rating Is Calculated

The IF Rating integrates more than twenty different pro- and anti-inflammatory factors. The amounts of individual nutrients are considered, as well as the ratios between various nutrients. The formula also incorporates the glycemic index, which describes the impact a food has on blood sugar—whether it causes blood sugar to rise sharply or slowly.

Where does all this information come from? The U.S. Department of Agriculture (USDA) has conducted extensive nutritional analyses on thousands of raw, processed, and commercially prepared foods. This information makes up the National Nutritional Database for Standard Reference and is used as the basis for virtually all nutritional databases in this country. The most recent update of the database (SR17) was published in 2004 and provides much of the data used in the calculation of the IF Ratings.

The other primary source of information is the Glycemic Index Research Institute at Sydney University in Australia. Different foods affect blood sugar very differently, even when they contain the same amount of sugar or starch. You can't determine the glycemic index of a food simply by analyzing the food itself; you need human subjects.

To determine the glycemic index of a food, researchers give a precise quantity of the food to a number of test subjects. Then the subjects' blood sugar levels are recorded at regular intervals and compared with the same subjects' reaction to a control substance (such as pure glucose). The results from several tests of many individuals are averaged together to calculate the glycemic index of that food. The USDA does not conduct this type of research. Dr. Jennie Brand and her colleagues at the University of Sydney Human Nutrition Unit have been the global leaders of glycemic index research for a decade. The most extensive database of glycemic index values was published by Brand in 2002 and contains upwards of 1,500 foods. This database is the other primary source for the IF Rating analysis.

Once the raw data have been extracted from these sources, they are analyzed using the IF Rating formula. The effect that each nutrient or factor has on a food's IF Rating depends on three things: (1) how much of that factor is present in the food, (2) how much of that factor is required to have a positive or negative impact on inflammation, and (3) how strong that effect was found to be.

For example, large doses of vitamin E (about 560 milligrams) have been found to have a moderately anti-inflammatory effect.

But the modest amount of vitamin E that is found in an ounce of sunflower seeds (about 16 milligrams) adds only a few points to their IF Rating. Although the pro- or anti-inflammatory effects of the individual nutrients in a food may be relatively small, the IF Rating allows you to consider the cumulative effect of all of the factors—and whether those effects are strong or weak, positive or negative.

The IF Rating formula itself was developed using dozens of published studies that document the effects of different nutrients and dietary factors on inflammation. Should you want to delve into some of this research yourself, you'll find a list of references at the end of the book. Here, in summarized form, are the basic principles that influence the formula:

- **The amount of fat matters, but the type of fat matters even more.** Research has shown that diets that are higher in monounsaturated fats (such as olive oil) and lower in saturated fats (such as animal fats) tend to reduce inflammation and inflammation-related diseases. The so-called Mediterranean diet, which is associated with a significant decrease in heart disease, cancer, and other diseases, is a prime example of this type of diet.

  Back in the 1970s, when the adverse health effects of saturated fats were first documented, polyunsaturated fats—which are even more unsaturated than monounsaturated fats—were thought to be the most healthful choice. Well-meaning homemakers were exhorted to replace animal fats (like butter and lard) with corn oil and margarine. Now we know better.

  Although it may be made from polyunsaturated oils, margarine is created by artificially hydrogenating liquid oils to make them solid. This process rearranges the structure of the fat molecules, turning them into trans-fatty acids. What we didn't know back then but have since learned is that trans-fatty acids are even worse than saturated fats in terms of their inflammatory effects.

Even when they are not hydrogenated, many polyunsaturated oils contain primarily omega-6 fatty acids. As we saw in Chapter 1, our bodies work best when we consume a balance of omega-3 and omega-6 fats. When that balance tips too far toward the omega-6 family, we end up feeding the inflammatory pathways in our cells while we starve the anti-inflammatory pathways.

The IF Rating assigns positive or negative points based on the amounts of monounsaturated, saturated, and trans fats in a food. For polyunsaturated fats, the formula considers the ratio of omega-6 to omega-3 fats and subtracts points when that ratio gets too high.

- **Certain fatty acids are particularly active in creating or fighting inflammation.** Fatty acids are the individual building blocks that combine to form saturated and unsaturated fats. Of the dozens of fatty acids that are found in our food supply, four are of particular interest in terms of inflammation. Eicosapentaenoic acid (EPA), docosahexaenoic acid (DHA), and gamma-linolenic acid (GLA) promote the cellular production of anti-inflammatory chemicals. Arachidonic acid (ARA) does just the opposite, enhancing the production of inflammatory chemicals.

  EPA and DHA are found in large quantities in fish like salmon, tuna, and herring and in trace amounts in other foods. ARA is found primarily in eggs, dairy, and meats, particularly organ meats (liver, kidney, etc.). The richest sources of GLA are the seeds of the evening primrose and borage plants.

  In calculating the IF Rating, points are added for EPA, DHA, and GLA, and subtracted for ARA.

- **Antioxidants are also anti-inflammatory.** One of the ways that inflammation leads to disease is by creating huge numbers of free radicals, unstable molecules that damage cells. This sets up a vicious cycle, as the free radicals themselves trigger the production of more inflammatory chemicals. Antioxidants, which neutralize free radicals, play

21

a very important role in fighting and preventing systemic inflammation. Studies have shown that people with lower levels of certain antioxidants (especially vitamins C and E, selenium, and beta-carotene) have higher levels of inflammatory chemicals in their bodies. Further studies confirm that increasing the amount of these nutrients in the diet reduces inflammation and disease.

The amounts of various antioxidant nutrients contribute points to a food's IF Rating.

- **High homocysteine levels contribute to inflammation.** Much has been written in recent years about the dangers of homocysteine. High levels of this amino acid in the blood have been linked to an increased incidence of heart disease, Alzheimer's disease, arthritis, and many other conditions. It's no coincidence that the list of homocysteine-related diseases is almost identical to the list of inflammation-related conditions. Homocysteine is a highly inflammatory compound. Certain B vitamins, specifically B_6, B_{12}, and folic acid, are very effective in reducing homocysteine and in reducing inflammation.

  The IF Rating takes into account the amount of homocysteine-lowering vitamins a food contains.

- **Sugar feeds inflammation, too.** Sharp spikes in blood sugar can create inflammation in the body. (This is one of the reasons that people with diabetes need to be particularly concerned about excessive inflammation.) A food's IF Rating is affected by the food's effect on blood sugar, based on its glycemic index, the serving size, and other factors, such as the amount of fiber it contains. A high glycemic load has a negative impact on a food's IF Rating.

- **There's an anti-inflammatory vitamin that most people have never heard of.** Vitamin K hasn't received very much press. Up until recently, it was uncommon to see vitamin K included in a multivitamin formulation. But emerging research has demonstrated that this vitamin plays a critical role in maintaining bone health, preventing heart disease, and reducing inflammation.

Foods that contain a lot of vitamin K, such as kale and broccoli, get extra inflammation-fighting points in the IF Rating system.

- **Some foods contain anti-inflammatory phytochemicals.** Certain foods, such as turmeric, ginger, chili peppers, pineapple, garlic, and other related plants, have potent—almost druglike—anti-inflammatory actions. For millennia, these plants and spices have been used in traditional medicine to treat inflammatory conditions and as general health tonics. They can be used to great advantage in an inflammation-reducing diet.

The anti-inflammatory effects of these compounds are factored into their IF Ratings.

Table 2.1 summarizes how all of these nutrients and dietary factors affect a food's impact on inflammation and, therefore, the IF Rating.

TABLE 2.1 Inflammatory Factors in Foods

Factor	Description	Effect on Inflammation	Role in IF Rating
Saturated fats	Fats that are solid at room temperature; found primarily in animal fats (meat, eggs, and dairy) and in a few vegetable fats (coconut and palm kernel oils)	Diets that are high in saturated fats are correlated with increased inflammation.	Points subtracted

(continued)

TABLE 2.1 Inflammatory Factors in Foods, *continued*

Factor	Description	Effect on Inflammation	Role in IF Rating
Monounsaturated fats	Fats that are liquid at room temperature but solid at cold temperatures; chief dietary sources include olives, olive oil, canola, avocado	Diets high in monounsaturated fats are correlated with reduced inflammation.	Points added
Trans-fatty acids	Fats that have been chemically altered by heat or hydrogenation; chief sources are deep-fried foods, shortening, margarine, and packaged foods containing hydrogenated or partially hydrogenated oils	Disrupts cell function and fatty acid balance; strongly inflammatory	Points subtracted
Eicosapentaenoic acid (EPA)	A polyunsaturated fatty acid from the omega-3 family; chief dietary source is seafood	Promotes production of anti-inflammatory chemicals; strongly anti-inflammatory	Points added
Docosahexaenoic acid (DHA)	A polyunsaturated fatty acid from the omega-3 family; chief dietary source is seafood	Promotes production of anti-inflammatory chemicals; strongly anti-inflammatory	Points added

Factor	Description	Effect on Inflammation	Role in IF Rating
Arachidonic acid (ARA)	A polyunsaturated fatty acid from the omega-6 family; chief dietary sources are meat, dairy, and eggs	Promotes production of inflammatory chemicals; strongly inflammatory	Points subtracted
Omega-6/ omega-3 ratio	Two main families of polyunsaturated fatty acids; chief dietary sources are vegetable oils (those that remain liquid when cold), seeds, and nuts	A balanced intake of omega-6 and omega-3 fats is anti-inflammatory. Over-consumption of omega-6 fats in relation to omega-3 fats leads to inflammation.	Points subtracted when ratio exceeds 2:1
Vitamin C (ascorbic acid)	Water-soluble antioxidant; chief dietary sources are citrus and other tropical fruits, peppers, berries	Neutralizes free radicals; moderately anti-inflammatory	Points added
Vitamin E (alpha-tocopherol)	Fat-soluble antioxidant; chief dietary sources include nuts, oils, avocado, seafood	Neutralizes free radicals; moderately anti-inflammatory	Points added
Beta-carotene	Precursor to vitamin A, a fat-soluble antioxidant; chief dietary sources are sweet potato, carrots, leafy greens, squash, melon	Neutralizes free radicals; moderately anti-inflammatory	Points added

(continued)

TABLE 2.1 Inflammatory Factors in Foods, *continued*

Factor	Description	Effect on Inflammation	Role in IF Rating
Selenium	Antioxidant mineral; chief dietary sources include Brazil nuts, meats, seafood, grains	Neutralizes free radicals; moderately anti-inflammatory	Points added
Zinc	Antioxidant cofactor (helper nutrient); chief dietary sources include oysters, meats, legumes	Supports action of antioxidant nutrients; mildly anti-inflammatory	Points added
B vitamins (B_6, B_{12}, folic acid)	Water-soluble vitamins that help reduce homocysteine levels; chief dietary sources include grains and leafy greens	Reduces homocysteine; mild to moderately anti-inflammatory	Points added
Vitamin K (phylloquinone)	Fat-soluble vitamin that regulates blood coagulation, calcium balance, and heart function	Mildly anti-inflammatory	Points added
Glycemic load	Effect of a food on blood sugar levels	High glycemic load promotes inflammation.	Points subtracted
Anti-inflammatory phytochemicals	Compounds found in turmeric, ginger, garlic, onion, pineapple, and chili peppers	Strongly anti-inflammatory	Points added

What the IF Ratings Reveal

Now that you know a bit more about how the IF Ratings are calculated, let's take a look at what the ratings have to say about the foods we eat. Do they change our notions of which foods are good for us and which are not? Yes and no.

Some IF Ratings parallel conventional dietary wisdom. Most vegetables have positive ratings, while fried foods and sugary desserts earn negative ratings. No surprises there. At the same time, some foods we think of as healthful, such as fruits, dairy products, and whole grains, have negative ratings. This doesn't mean they need to be eliminated from your diet. But understanding why these foods rate the way they do can help you make choices that result in a more balanced and inflammation-reducing diet.

Although there are some general trends, which are outlined in this section, it is impossible to adequately summarize or predict how foods will affect inflammation. Similar foods can rate much differently based on small differences in their nutrient content or glycemic load. The same food can have different ratings depending on how it was prepared. With meats in particular, there are significant differences according to what part of the animal the meat comes from and even where the animals were raised. This is precisely why the IF Rating system was developed—to provide information about an important aspect of diet that is not available from any other source.

Trends and Surprises

Let's take a closer look at some of the trends—and some of the surprises—that you'll find as you begin to use the IF Ratings. In the process, I'll think you'll get a better understanding of how the rating system works and how you can use it to your best advantage.

Trend #1: Vegetables are mildly to moderately anti-inflammatory.
Vegetables get most of their IF Rating points from the antioxidants and other nutrients they contain. Most vegetables contain

only trace amounts of fat. In the IF Rating system, this means that most vegetables do not lose points for containing saturated or trans fats. By the same token, they don't earn many points for containing healthful fats, either. (Avocados, which are high in monounsaturated fat, are one exception to this rule.) Vegetables also tend to be low in carbohydrates and high in fiber, which results in a low glycemic load and a higher IF Rating. (Potatoes are an exception here.)

Because of their high IF Ratings and low carbohydrate and fat content, most vegetables can be eaten in unlimited quantities on the Inflammation-Free Diet. In Table 2.2 (page 35), you can see the vegetables with the highest and lowest rankings.

Surprise #1: Beans and legumes are slightly inflammatory. We think of dried beans as being healthful alternatives to meat and, indeed, they are an indispensable source of protein for strict vegetarians. For vegetarians and nonvegetarians alike, they are also great low-fat sources of fiber and vitamins and a staple in many favorite dishes. However, beans are also relatively high in starches and sugars, which elevate blood sugar, resulting in slightly negative IF Ratings. (Green beans and lentils are the exceptions.) Legumes are still a healthful choice, but their consumption should be balanced with anti-inflammatory foods. Anti-inflammatory foods like chili peppers and onions make the perfect complement to these somewhat bland foods—from an inflammatory as well as a culinary standpoint.

Trend #2: Lean cuts of pork and beef are good choices. Red meat is frequently portrayed as a dietary villain, chiefly because of its saturated-fat content. But in fact, beef frequently contains an equal or greater amount of heart-healthy monounsaturated fats as well. Beef is also a good source of folic acid, vitamin B_{12}, selenium, and zinc. The same is true of lean cuts of pork, such as the tenderloin. Lean cuts of pork and beef have positive IF Ratings and are fairly low in fat, making them good choices for an inflammation-reducing diet.

Surprise #2: Leaner is not always better. For many types of meat, the leaner cuts or portions rank higher in the IF Ratings, as you might expect. But in some cases, leaner is not better. For example, in the IF Rating tables, you'll find two listings for a serving of broiled T-bone steak, one that includes the fat typically found on this cut and one that assumes all visible fat has been trimmed away. The surprise is that the lean-only portion ranks lower than the portion containing more fat!

What is the explanation for this anomaly? The data reveal that when you trim the fat from a T-bone steak, you remove a disproportionate amount of anti-inflammatory omega-3 fatty acids, while the inflammatory omega-6 fatty acids are left behind in the meat. The net effect is a small but measurable decrease in the IF Rating. (Of course, a fattier cut of meat, even though it has a higher IF Rating, will use up more of the day's fat allowance.)

Because so many variables are involved, including the source of the meat, the cut, and the way it has been cooked, it is impossible to predict IF Ratings based on fat content or any other single factor. The IF Ratings are the only reliable way to know the inflammatory potential of a specific food. Table 2.2 (page 35) gives you an overview of the highest- and lowest-ranked types of meat. Table 4.2 (page 218) allows you to compare the IF Ratings for all the different meats, along with their fat content.

Trend #3: Organ meats are extremely inflammatory. Many people do not care for liver and other organ meats, no matter how nourishing they are purported to be. Unfortunately for those who relish them, the IF Rating reveals that organ meats are among the most inflammatory of foods. The problem is that these meats are extremely high in arachidonic acid, a fatty acid that fuels the inflammatory pathways in the body. As Table 2.2 indicates, organ meats are foods to limit or avoid.

Surprise #3: Meat from younger animals is more inflammatory than meat from mature livestock. I particularly enjoy lamb, so I was disappointed to discover that it is among the most inflammatory kinds of meat, along with veal. When I examined the individual inflammatory factors more closely, the reason became clear. As animals age, the composition of their tissue changes, and this turns out to have a significant impact on the inflammatory potential of the meat.

Comparing a similar cut, such as a sirloin, of veal and beef, we see that the veal is a bit leaner (9 grams of fat per serving for veal and 11 grams for beef). But if we investigate further, it turns out that the beef has more monounsaturated fat, less saturated fat, a greater concentration of selenium and other nutrients, and a more favorable ratio of omega-6 to omega-3 fats. These subtle but important differences translate into significantly lower IF Ratings for veal sirloin (−51) than for beef sirloin (+15).

I still enjoy lamb once in a while, but now that I am aware of its inflammatory impact, I have it less often, and I use the IF Ratings to choose the cuts that are the least inflammatory.

Trend #4: Low-fat dairy products are less inflammatory than higher-fat choices. In the IF Rating system, low-fat dairy products, including low-fat cottage cheese, cream cheese, milk, and yogurt, are less inflammatory than their whole-milk counterparts. As you'll see in the next chapter, the Inflammation-Free Diet is not a low-fat regimen per se. But most of the fat in dairy products is saturated, which has inflammatory effects.

If you are a cheese and dairy lover, however, there is no need to despair. There is plenty of room in the Inflammation-Free Diet for you to enjoy these foods, which can be a great source of calcium and protein, not to mention flavor! The inflammatory effects of most cheese and dairy products are mild to moderate and are a concern only when these foods are eaten in great quantities.

Surprise #4: Poultry and eggs are inflammatory. For a long time, we have been told that chicken and turkey are more healthful than beef and pork. How many times have you opted for "healthier" versions of chili, sausage, burgers, and other foods made with turkey or chicken instead of beef or pork?

But when you consult the IF Ratings, you will notice that eggs, chicken, and turkey all rank as mildly to moderately inflammatory—more inflammatory than many cuts of beef and pork. A high concentration of arachidonic acid is the primary reason for this, along with an unfavorable omega-6 to omega-3 ratio. Presumably, this is the result of a grain-based diet, which is high in omega-6 fatty acids. (Notice that goose and duck, which are more likely to eat a wild diet, are better choices.)

If you really enjoy chicken and turkey, there's no reason to stop eating them. The Inflammation-Free Diet is not about eliminating foods from your diet; it's about balancing your choices to promote equilibrium between the pro- and anti-inflammatory channels in the body. On the other hand, if you have been substituting chicken and turkey for pork and beef because you've been led to believe they are more healthful, you may want to reconsider in light of this new information.

Trend #5: Cold-water fish are anti-inflammatory all-stars. If you follow the health headlines, the trend in favor of cold-water fish will probably not come as much of a surprise. Fatty fish such as salmon, mackerel, tuna, herring, and sardines are known for being terrific sources of omega-3 fatty acids. In general, fatty cold-water fish are among the most anti-inflammatory foods available. But there is also a potential downside to eating large quantities of these fish. Changes in environmental conditions and fishing practices mean that many of the fish that reach our markets and tables are unacceptably high in mercury, a heavy-metal neurotoxin that can have devastating effects, particularly in pregnant women and young children. Fish that may contain high levels of mercury are noted with an asterisk (*) in the IF Rating charts. The Natural Resources Defense Council (NRDC) is a good source for more information about this issue. You can find the NRDC's website at www.nrdc.org.

Surprise #5: Farm-raised salmon does more harm than good. While wild-caught salmon is among the most anti-inflammatory

31

foods on the planet, farm-raised salmon is the most inflammatory fish you can eat! This is perhaps one of the biggest surprises to be found in the IF Ratings. It's also a great irony. Growing up near the Great Lakes, I only knew salmon as something that came in a can or on a bagel. Of course, few people had ever heard of an omega-3 fatty acid back then! But about fifteen years ago, salmon was discovered as the "heart-healthy steak." Since then, salmon has gone from a regional specialty to a staple menu item in every deli, café, and restaurant in America.

As salmon became more and more popular, the demand far outpaced the ability of salmon fishers to supply it, and aquaculture became a boom industry. Today, unless you live near the Pacific Northwest, most of the salmon you see in restaurants and grocery stores is raised on fish farms.

The omega-3 fatty acid content of farm-raised salmon is about the same as that of wild-caught salmon. The problem is that farm-raised salmon eat cereal grains that are high in omega-6 fatty acids, instead of the natural diet of algae and wild shrimp. As a result, the flesh of farm-raised salmon contains very high levels of inflammatory arachidonic acid. In fact, the inflammatory effects of the arachidonic acid in farm-raised salmon more than exceed the anti-inflammatory effects of the omega-3 fatty acid it contains. Unless the salmon you eat is wild, you are far better off eating a piece of lean beef.

How can you tell if the fish you are eating or buying is farm-raised? Don't be fooled by the color. Because farm-raised salmon tends to be pale, artificial food coloring is added to the feed or to the fish itself after slaughter to imitate the ruby color of wild salmon. Unless a menu or label specifies that it is wild-caught, you can assume it is farm-raised.

Trend #6: Spicy cuisines are anti-inflammatory. If you enjoy Indian, Asian, and Latin American foods, you are going to have a great time on the Inflammation-Free Diet! These exotic cuisines feature garlic, ginger, chili peppers, and curry, all of which are highly anti-inflammatory. And if you are not in the habit of enjoying these vibrant flavors, now is your chance to wake up your taste buds. Table 2.2 (page 35) lists the anti-inflammatory superstars of the spice cabinet and herb garden. Adding just a teaspoon of any of these ingredients can dramatically enhance the anti-inflammatory potential of any meal. Many of the recipes in Chapter 3 feature these flavorful inflammation fighters.

Surprise #6: Even whole grains are mildly to moderately inflammatory. You probably won't be surprised to learn that white bread and rolls have negative IF Ratings. These highly refined foods contribute little in the way of nutrients and trigger a quick rise in blood sugar, making them moderately inflammatory. But perhaps you will be somewhat surprised to find that whole grains such as brown rice and whole oats have slightly negative ratings. Although they offer more in the way of B vitamins, minerals, and fiber, whole grains are still mildly inflammatory due to their effect on blood sugar.

Grains are an important source of carbohydrates that our bodies need for fuel. They also satisfy the taste buds and appetite and make meals feel more satisfying. On the Inflammation-Free Diet, grains are chosen wisely and eaten in moderation in order to limit their inflammatory effects.

Trend #7: Nuts are mildly anti-inflammatory; seeds are mildly inflammatory. Although they are fairly high in fat, most nuts offer mild to moderate anti-inflammatory benefits, due to their monounsaturated fat content, very low glycemic impact, and balanced ratio of omega-6 and omega-3 fatty acids. (The chief exception is walnuts, which are high in omega-6 fatty acids.)

Most seeds, such as pumpkin, sunflower, and sesame, however, tend to be quite high in omega-6 fatty acids. The high ratio of omega-6 to omega-3 fatty acids makes most seeds slightly inflammatory. Seeds are still a great source of fiber, flavor, and some vitamins. Feel free to enjoy them in moderation.

Surprise #7: Many vegetable oils are inflammatory. Most people will not be surprised to see that butter, margarine, and shortening have inflammatory effects. Butter, of course, is high in saturated fats, and the others contain dangerous hydrogenated fats and trans-fatty acids. But many health-conscious people will be amazed to see that oils such as grape seed, sesame, walnut, and sunflower also rank low in the IF Rating system. Like many vegetable oils, these oils have a very high ratio of omega-6 to omega-3 fatty acids, which translates into negative IF Ratings.

In the context of the Inflammation-Free Diet, you can enjoy the unique flavor of walnut oil in a salad dressing or toasted sesame oil in a stir-fry. The rest of the time, choosing anti-inflammatory oils like olive oil and canola oil will help to keep your daily IF Rating totals on target.

Trend #8: Sugary, fatty, and junk foods are inflammatory. There are a few surprises in the IF Ratings, but the status of junk foods is not one of them. Sweets, fried foods, and junk foods lose points for high amounts of damaging fats and/or high sugar content. At the same time, they have little or nothing to offer in the way of nutrients that might offset these negatives. Fried foods, chips, candy, cakes, cookies, and ice cream are all moderately to highly inflammatory. You'll find that following the Inflammation-Free Diet, or any other healthful eating regimen, will require you to limit your indulgence in these pleasures to special occasions. If you do decide to indulge occasionally, the IF Rating system can help you balance your diet with extra anti-inflammatory foods.

Surprise #8: Fruits are mildly to moderately inflammatory. Fruits are a delectable and nutritious part of any diet and can be a great source of antioxidants and other nutrients. But most fruits also contain a fair amount of natural sugar, which can cause a moderate to sharp rise in blood sugar.

As with vegetables, fruits get most of their positive IF Rating points from the antioxidants, vitamins, and minerals they provide. However, they lose points due to their glycemic impact. Fruits with the highest glycemic impact are more inflammatory. Fruit juices, because they contain even more concentrated amounts of sugar and no fiber, are the most inflammatory of all. Two or three servings of fruit per day can be enjoyed on the Inflammation–Free Diet. Table 2.2 lists some of the most and least inflammatory fruits. Enjoy a variety of fruits, but try to emphasize those that are higher on the list and limit those that are lower.

The Highest- and Lowest-Ranked Foods

To give you a quick overview of your best and worst food choices, Table 2.2 lists the foods that rank highest and lowest in each category. At this point, some readers are bound to be thinking, "Great! I'll just memorize the twenty best foods and eat only those." But I don't recommend this—or any other—"super-food" approach, for several reasons.

No matter how healthful certain foods might be, you are better off eating a wide variety of foods than you are limiting your diet to a few super foods. In addition to being more enjoyable, a varied diet is the only way to get a rich and balanced blend of all the nutrients—those that are known along with those yet to be discovered—that nature provides for our nourishment.

TABLE 2.2 Highest- and Lowest-Ranked Foods

Type of Food	Best Choices	Limit/Avoid
Fruits	Acerola (West Indian) cherries	Mango
	Guava	Banana
	Strawberries	
	Cantaloupe	
	Lemon, lime	
	Rhubarb	
	Raspberries	
	Kumquat	
	Pink grapefruit	
	Mulberries	

(continued)

TABLE 2.2 Highest- and Lowest-Ranked Foods, *continued*

Type of Food	Best Choices	Limit/Avoid
Vegetables	Chili peppers	Corn
	Onions, including scallions and leeks	White potatoes
	Spinach	French fries
	Greens, including kale, collards, turnip and mustard greens	
	Sweet potatoes	
	Carrots	
	Garlic	
Legumes	Lentils	
Egg products	Liquid eggs	Duck eggs
	Egg whites	Goose eggs
Cheese	Cottage cheese	Excessive portion sizes (1 ounce of hard cheese is approximately the size of a pair of dice)
Dairy products	Cottage cheese	Fruited yogurt
	Nonfat cream cheese	Ice cream
	Plain yogurt	
Fish	Herring	Salmon (farmed)
	Oysters	
	Mackerel (not king)	
	Arctic char	
	Salmon (not farmed)	
	Bluefin tuna*	
	Halibut (Greenland)*	
	Bluefish*	

*High in mercury; eat only occasionally

Type of Food	Best Choices	Limit/Avoid
Fish, continued	Rainbow trout	
	Striped bass*	
	Whiting	
	Sardines	
	Sea bass*	
Poultry	Goose	Turkey (dark meat)
	Duck	Cornish game hens
		Chicken giblets
		Chicken liver
Meat	Pot roast	Veal loin
	Beef shank	Veal kidney
	Top blade cuts (beef)	Beef lung
	Eye of round (beef)	Beef kidney
	Flank steak	Beef heart
	Sirloin tip	Beef brain
	Prime rib	Pork chitterlings
	Skirt steak	Lamb rib chops
	Pork rib chops	
	Pork tenderloin	
Breads	Flour tortilla	Hot dog/hamburger buns
	Mixed-grain bread	English muffin
	Pumpernickel bread	Kaiser roll
	Rye bread	Bagel
	Whole wheat bread	French bread
		Vienna bread

*High in mercury; eat only occasionally

(continued)

TABLE 2.2 Highest- and Lowest-Ranked Foods, *continued*

Type of Food	Best Choices	Limit/Avoid
Cereal	All-Bran	Grape-Nuts
	Total	Crispix
	Bran flakes	Corn Chex
	Muesli (no sugar added)	Just Right
	Rolled oats	Rice Chex
		Cornflakes
		Rice Krispies
		Raisin bran
		Shredded wheat
Pasta and grains	Barley	White rice
	Whole wheat spaghetti	Millet
	Spaghetti	Corn pasta
	Macaroni	Cornmeal
	Kasha (buckwheat groats)	
	Rice noodles	
	Couscous	
Fats and oils	Safflower oil (high oleic)	Margarine
	Hazelnut oil	Wheat germ oil
	Olive oil	Sunflower oil (high linoleic)
	Canola oil	Poppy seed oil
	Avocado oil	Grape seed oil
	Almond oil	Safflower oil (high linoleic)
	Apricot kernel oil	Cottonseed oil
		Palm kernel oil
		Coconut oil

Type of Food	Best Choices	Limit/Avoid
Nuts and seeds	Brazil nuts	Excessive portion sizes (1 serving of nuts is 1 small handful)
	Macadamia nuts	
	Hazelnuts	
	Pecans	
	Almonds	
	Hickory nuts	
	Cashews	
	Flaxseed	
Herbs and spices	Garlic	
	Onion	
	Cayenne	
	Ginger	
	Turmeric	
	Chili peppers	
	Chili powder	
	Curry powder	
Sweeteners	Splenda	Honey
		Brown sugar
		White sugar
Crackers, cookies, and chips	Melba toast	Potato chips
	Saltines	Corn chips
	Tea biscuits	Pretzels
	Oyster crackers	
	Vanilla wafers	

(continued)

TABLE 2.2 Highest- and Lowest-Ranked Foods, *continued*

Type of Food	Best Choices	Limit/Avoid
Desserts	Ice milk	Limit consumption of desserts (even best choices)
	Pound cake	
	Angel food cake	
	Sponge cake	
	Vanilla pudding	
Candy	Miniature chocolate bar	Limit consumption of candy (even best choices)
	Fruit leather	
	Jelly beans	
Beverages	Carrot juice	Gatorade
	Tomato juice	Pineapple juice
	Black or green tea	Cranberry juice
	Club soda/seltzer	Lemonade
	Herbal tea	Cola
	Nonalcoholic wine	
	Spring water	

If your diet focuses on a small number of foods, you not only miss out on nutrients that are not in those particular foods, but you might also unwittingly overexpose yourself to harmful substances. Back in the early 1990s, for example, tuna enjoyed celebrity status as a super food. Those who were trying to cut carbohydrates and add lean protein to their diets were understandably attracted to the convenience and affordability of water-packed tuna. I remember coworkers who would eat a small can of tuna virtually every day for lunch. Many years later, we learned that canned tuna contains dangerous levels of mercury—so much that we are now advised to limit our consumption of canned tuna to a couple of servings a month. Obviously, if my health-conscious coworkers had eaten a more diverse diet, they would have reduced their exposure to this frightening health hazard.

Similarly, eating the same fruits and vegetables over and over again can lead to an increased consumption of certain pesticides and other agricultural chemicals. Even though organic foods are becoming popular, more affordable, and more available, few of us manage to eat a one hundred percent organic diet. Most of us still consume at least some produce that is treated with pesticides, fertilizers, or other chemicals. Ironically, some of the fruits and vegetables that rank highest in antioxidants and other nutrients, including strawberries and green peppers, also rank among the highest in terms of pesticide residues.

If we always choose the same "super" fruits and vegetables, we will increase our exposure to whatever chemicals are used on those particular crops. Although no chemicals are desirable, I would rather eat a small amount of many different chemicals than a large amount of one or two. Eating a diverse diet takes a bit more energy and imagination than relying on a few foods, but it is worth the small effort.

While the table of highest- and lowest-ranking foods gives you an overview of the anti-inflammatory superstars and worst offenders, the complete IF Rating tables allow you to build an inflammation-reducing diet using a wide variety of foods. In Chapter 4, you'll find the listings in two formats: organized A to Z for quick location of specific foods, and by category, which allows easy comparison of similar foods. In the next chapter, I'll discuss how you can easily use these ratings to create your own Inflammation-Free Diet.

Frequently Asked Questions About the Ratings

The IF Rating system is a new way of thinking about foods and their inflammatory effects. You may have some questions about the IF Ratings and how they can help fight the effects of inflammation. Here are answers to some of the most frequently asked questions about the IF Rating system.

How does the IF Rating system compare with other counters? In the diet and nutrition section of any bookstore, you will find calorie counters, carbohydrate counters, and fat counters, as well as books that rank foods by antioxidant content or glycemic index. All of these tools contain valuable information about the food we are eating. But none really gives you the whole picture.

The glycemic index, for example, measures a food's effect on blood sugar but has no way of balancing the glycemic impact of a food with its healthful benefits. Carrots have a much higher glycemic index (49) than celery (0). By that measure alone, celery appears to be a more healthful choice. But the glycemic index doesn't account for the nutritional value of the carrot, which far exceeds that of celery. Similarly, in a fat gram counter, green beans and jelly beans are equivalent. And if you consult only a carbohydrate counter, olive oil and butter rank the same. Any counter that focuses on a narrow range of factors is going to be limited in its usefulness. And cross-referencing a number of different counters is cumbersome.

The IF Rating integrates all of these individual factors—plus the inflammatory potential of a food—into one comprehensive rating system. Because it takes into account so many factors, the IF Rating offers a more balanced and useful way to compare different foods. In the IF Rating system, carrots (+60) rank higher than celery (+3), green beans (+15) rank higher than jelly beans (−80), and olive oil (+73) ranks higher than butter (−45).

How does the IF Rating compare with other inflammation indexes? There have been a few preliminary attempts to rank foods for their inflammatory impact. However, previous inflammation indexes have been limited to a few dozen foods and have focused on just one or two factors that relate to inflammation. The IF Rating considers every aspect of a food—from its fatty-acid composition to its antioxidant profile to its effect on homocysteine and blood sugar—to produce a comprehensive assessment of a food's inflammatory potential and overall nutritional value.

Also, the IF Rating listings include over 1,600 foods and can be used to calculate the combined effects of meals and recipes.

Are negative-IF foods bad for me? It's important to understand that foods with negative IF Ratings are not necessarily bad for you. In the next chapter, you'll see that a balanced diet includes many foods—such as fruits and whole grains—that have negative IF ratings. It is not necessary or desirable to avoid foods that have negative ratings. But at the same time, consuming too many inflammatory foods (or too few anti-inflammatory foods) defeats the body's ability to maintain a balance between its pro- and anti-inflammatory channels.

With the IF Ratings, you can easily calculate the cumulative effects of all the foods you eat on a given day. If your diet is tipping toward the inflammatory side of the equation, you can use the IF Ratings to adjust your choices and bring it back into balance.

For example, when I learned that lamb—one of my favorites— was one of the most inflammatory meats, I didn't stop eating it altogether. But I did make a few changes. First, I don't eat lamb quite as often as I used to. Second, when I do have lamb, I choose cuts and cooking methods that minimize the inflammatory potential. For example, I now choose loin chops (−31) over rib chops (−76). I also combine the lamb with vegetables and/or spices that have high IF Ratings, like garlic and spinach. This helps to balance the inflammatory impact of the lamb.

By the same token, if you enjoy egg salad, there is no reason not to include it in your diet. Still, you probably shouldn't eat it every day for lunch. And you might want to try a curried egg salad, such as the recipe in Chapter 3, which includes anti-inflammatory curry powder to offset the inflammatory effects of the eggs.

Or perhaps you love sunflower seeds. You don't have to give them up. But if today's IF Rating total is running in the negative because of the eggs and bacon you enjoyed for breakfast, choosing roasted almonds (+57) over roasted sunflower seeds (−41) to snack on before dinner can help balance the day's combined IF Rating. However, if the choice is between sunflower seeds and french fries (−213), sunflower seeds are obviously the winner!

Why do foods have different IF Ratings when they are cooked? In the IF Rating tables, you'll find separate listings for foods that are commonly eaten both raw and cooked, such as many vegetables. This is because cooking a food can affect its IF Rating in a number of ways, some positive and some negative. When foods are exposed to heat, they tend to shrink a bit due to water loss. They also get softer. So a cup of cooked broccoli often holds more broccoli (and nutrients) than a cup of raw broccoli. On the negative side, water-soluble vitamins get lost when foods are exposed to water. Cooking a food also can break down its starches and make them more easily digestible, which can increase the food's glycemic impact.

Meats also shrink when they are cooked due to loss of both water and fats. If you want to end up with a three-ounce serving of cooked meat, for example, you will need to begin with four to six ounces of raw meat. Fat loss can affect the IF Rating of cooked meats in various ways, depending on whether the fat that is lost is saturated or unsaturated and whether fat-soluble vitamins also are lost.

To make the IF Ratings as useful and as accurate as possible, the tables provide multiple listings for foods that are eaten both raw and cooked, such as vegetables, shellfish, and fish commonly eaten as sushi. And for foods like pasta, grains, and meats, the A-to-Z listings (Table 4.1) include both their uncooked and cooked measurements. You can look up the rating for a half cup of cooked rice, for example, or calculate the rating for a recipe that uses a cup of uncooked rice.

Why are there not more foods on the list? Accurately calculating the IF Rating of a food requires detailed information about the food's nutritional composition and its glycemic index. Unfortunately, for some foods, we don't have enough information to perform the necessary calculations. The Glycemic Index Research Institute in Sydney, Australia, has conducted testing on many packaged and commercial foods, along with ingredients and dishes that are native to Australia and Asia. However, many of these foods are not in the nutrient composition database compiled by the USDA. Conversely, there are thousands of foods in the USDA database that have not yet been tested for glycemic index.

The IF Rating tables in this book are as complete as we could make them, given the available data. If a particular food that you are looking for is not included in the IF Rating table, you can substitute a similar food from the table, or you can use the rating for another similar food as a rough estimate. Keep in mind, however, that similar foods do not always have similar IF Ratings. The closer you stick to the foods listed in the tables, the more accurate your combined IF Rating totals will be. As data become available for more foods, the IF Rating tables will be expanded to include them.

CHAPTER 3

Reducing Inflammation in Your Body

It's time to get started on your own Inflammation-Free Diet! This chapter outlines a flexible and easy-to-follow eating plan that will help you achieve your ideal weight, reduce pain and allergies, prevent disease, and slow the aging process. Here's how it works.

You'll have three target values for the foods you eat each day: total IF Rating, total fat grams, and total carbohydrate grams. (The IF Rating tables in Chapter 4 list all three factors.) All you have to do is keep your totals aligned with these target values. Hitting your target IF Rating will help protect you from excessive inflammation. Keeping your fat and carbohydrate numbers on target ensures that your diet remains balanced, including foods from all of the major food groups (vegetables, grains, fruits, protein foods, etc.) in the correct proportions.

Later in the chapter, you'll find worksheets for tallying up your daily totals, as well as some sample meal plans, recipes, and tips for planning your own meals and recipes. First, however, you'll need to determine your target values.

This chapter outlines three basic plans, each with different target values. If you have risk factors or symptoms associated with inflammation, you will benefit from the more aggressive Therapeutic plan. If your symptoms are fairly mild and you are interested in reducing your risk of disease and slowing the aging process, the Prevention/Maintenance program is for you. And if you need to lose weight or require fewer calories, a Reduced-Calorie option is provided. The following self-assessment will help determine which plan is best for you.

Inflammation Self-Assessment

Part 1: Health and Family History

1. Have you been diagnosed with any of the following conditions?
   - Osteoarthritis
   - Rheumatoid arthritis
   - Eczema or psoriasis
   - Asthma
   - Allergies
   - Heart disease
   - High blood pressure
   - High cholesterol
   - Alzheimer's disease
   - Diabetes
   - Cancer
2. Do you have a family history of heart disease?
3. Do you have a family history of cancer?
4. Do you currently smoke?
5. Have you smoked in the last ten years?

If you answered yes to any of the questions in Part 1, your health history suggests you are at increased risk for inflammation-related conditions. If you answered yes to several of the questions in Part 1, your risk may be substantial. The Therapeutic plan is recommended. If you answered no to all the questions in Part 1, the Prevention/Maintenance plan is recommended.

Part 2: Symptoms

Do you regularly or seasonally experience any of the following symptoms?

* Joint pain or stiffness
* Skin rashes
* Runny nose, postnasal drip
* Red, itchy eyes
* Wheezing
* Itchy throat
* Premature skin aging

Any of these symptoms suggests excessive inflammation. If your symptoms are severe, follow the Therapeutic plan but reevaluate your symptoms every six to eight weeks. Most inflammation-related symptoms will subside on the Inflammation-Free Diet. When your symptoms have improved, you may find that you can maintain these improvements on the Prevention/Maintenance plan. If your symptoms worsen on the Prevention/Maintenance plan, resume the Therapeutic plan.

Part 3: Calorie Requirements

1. Do you exercise irregularly or not at all?
2. Are you over 55?
3. Do you have a small frame?
4. Are you more than ten pounds above your ideal weight?

If you are more than ten pounds above your ideal weight, the Reduced-Calorie plan will help you reduce more quickly. When you have attained a healthy weight, you can continue on either

Which Plan Is Right for You?

Follow the Therapeutic plan if *any* of the following conditions apply:

- CRP levels higher than 2.0 milligrams per liter
- Personal or close family history of inflammation-related disease (see Self-Assessment, Part 1)
- Smoker
- Moderate to severe inflammatory symptoms (see Self-Assessment, Part 2)

Follow the Prevention/Maintenance plan if *all* of the following conditions apply:

- CRP levels (if known) lower than 2.0 milligrams per liter
- No personal or family history of inflammation-related disease (see Self-Assessment, Part 1)
- Mild or no symptoms (see Self-Assessment, Part 2)

Consider the Reduced-Calorie option if *any* of the following conditions apply:

- Overweight
- Small build
- Over 55
- Sedentary

the Prevention/Maintenance plan or the Therapeutic plan. If you are at a healthy weight but are over 55, have a small build, or a sedentary lifestyle, you may need to follow the Reduced-Calorie option in order to maintain your weight.

Once you have determined which program is right for you, you'll find the target values for each, along with recommended nutritional supplements, in Table 3.1 on page 51.

TABLE 3.1 Daily Target Values for the Inflammation-Free Diet

Diet Goals	Combined IF Rating	Total Fat	Total Carb	Recommended Supplements
Prevention/ Maintenance	50 or above	65 g	250 g	1. High-potency multivitamin and mineral 2. Calcium/ magnesium supplement 3. 1,000–2,000 mg fish oil 4. Inflammation-reducing supplements (optional)
Therapeutic	200 or above	65 g	250 g	1. High-potency multivitamin and mineral 2. Calcium/ magnesium supplement 3. 2,000–3,000 mg fish oil 4. Inflammation-reducing supplements (optional)
Reduced-Calorie	As shown for Prevention/ Maintenance or Therapeutic	55 g	200 g	As recommended for Prevention/ Maintenance or Therapeutic

Customizing Your Inflammation-Free Diet

The difference between the Prevention/Maintenance and Therapeutic plans is the target value for the total IF Rating. The Prevention/Maintenance plan is designed to help you maintain a balance between pro- and anti-inflammatory foods and prevent systemic inflammation. The higher target value associated with

51

the Therapeutic diet adjusts the balance to create a more anti-inflammatory diet, which will help reduce inflammation and bring the body back into balance.

Each of the plans suggests a minimum target for the total IF Rating. If you feel that you would benefit from a more intensive approach, you can adjust the IF Rating target upward. For example, if you are following the Therapeutic plan and feel you have gotten some relief but not as much as you had hoped, you can try raising your IF Rating target from 200 to 250 or 300 a day. Or perhaps you have experienced great results from the Therapeutic plan and have "graduated" to the Prevention/Maintenance plan. If you feel your symptoms creeping back with the lower IF Rating target, you can adjust that target upward to 100 or 150.

A high-potency multivitamin and mineral supplement, a calcium/magnesium supplement, and a daily dose of fish oil are highly recommended for everyone. To maximize the effectiveness of either plan, add one or more of the other anti-inflammatory supplements discussed in Chapter 1 (summarized in Table 1.2 on page 14).

Important note: If you take blood thinners such as Coumadin (warfarin) or have any sort of blood-clotting disorder, consult with your physician before adding fish oil or ginkgo to your diet. These substances can thin the blood (decrease blood coagulation) and may affect your condition or the dosage of your medication.

Adjusting Carbohydrate and Fat Intake

The Prevention/Maintenance and Therapeutic programs are designed to provide approximately 2,000 calories a day. This is the number of calories that average-sized, moderately active individuals require to maintain their weight—neither gaining nor losing. The Reduced-Calorie option, with lower allowances for fats and carbohydrates, results in a diet of approximately 1,600 calories per day. Only the fat and carbohydrate target values change for the Reduced-Calorie option. The target value for total IF Rating stays the same and depends on whether you are following the Prevention/Maintenance or Therapeutic program.

For all of the plans, the daily target values for fats and carbohydrates result in a diet that is approximately 50 percent carbohydrates, 30 percent fats, and 20 percent protein. Based on my experience, this is an ideal balance for good nutrition, weight management, and reducing excessive inflammation. If you prefer to follow a lower-carbohydrate or lower-fat diet, however, you can adjust your targets to achieve a different balance. Table 3.2 shows lower-carbohydrate (40 percent of daily calories) and lower-fat (20 percent of daily calories) options for the Inflammation-Free Diet plan. The total IF Rating remains the same.

I don't recommend reducing carbohydrates below 40 percent of daily calories. Very low carbohydrate diets have not been shown to be effective in reducing or maintaining weight over the long term. And the higher protein intake that results from a very low carbohydrate diet can increase the production of inflammatory compounds. I also don't recommend a diet that is lower than

TABLE 3.2 Options for Lower-Carbohydrate and Lower-Fat Plans

Options	Combined IF Rating	Total Fat	Total Carb
Lower carbohydrate (2,000 calories per day)	As recommended for Prevention/ Maintenance or Therapeutic	66 g	200 g
Lower fat (2,000 calories per day)	As recommended for Prevention/ Maintenance or Therapeutic	44 g	250–300 g
Lower carbohydrate (1,600 calories per day)	As recommended for Prevention/ Maintenance or Therapeutic	53 g	160 g
Lower fat (1,600 calories per day)	As recommended for Prevention/ Maintenance or Therapeutic	36 g	200–240 g

20 percent fat. Extremely low-fat diets can lead to fatty-acid deficiencies. Also, the extra carbohydrates or protein that are consumed when fat intake is reduced can contribute to inflammation.

Adjusting the Target Values for Children or Other Special Needs

Children, athletes, and pregnant and lactating women can all benefit from the Inflammation-Free Diet. While the IF Rating target values remain the same, the calorie needs for these special groups differ. Athletes and pregnant and lactating women will require more calories, while children may require fewer calories, depending on their size. For any of these special-needs diets, you can adjust the target values for fats and carbohydrates according to the number of calories required. Table 3.3 shows the fat and carbohydrate values for a variety of calorie requirements, using a 50/30/20 distribution of carbohydrates, fats, and protein. (Lower-carbohydrate and lower-fat regimens are not recommended for children or for pregnant or lactating women.)

TABLE 3.3 Adjusted Target Values for Different Calorie Needs

Calorie Requirement	Total Fat	Total Carb
800	26 g	100 g
1,000	33 g	125 g
1,200	40 g	150 g
1,400	47 g	175 g
1,600	53 g	200 g
1,800	60 g	225 g
2,000	67 g	250 g
2,200	73 g	275 g
2,400	80 g	300 g
2,600	87 g	325 g

Planning Your Meals

Now that you have your target values for the day's combined IF Rating, total fat, and total carbohydrate, you are ready to create your own inflammation-reducing meal plans. Of course, you can also skip right to the sample meal plans that are given later in this chapter. But learning how to plan your own meals will allow you to make the Inflammation-Free Diet fit your lifestyle and food preferences. The easiest way to plan meals is with a worksheet such as the one shown in Table 3.4. Write down each food and then enter its IF Rating and its fat and carbohydrate grams, using

Food	IF Rating	Fat (g)	Carb (g)
Total			
Goal			

TABLE 3.4 Meal-Planning Worksheet

the IF Rating tables. (The easiest way to quickly locate specific foods is to use the A-to-Z listing in Table 4.1 on page 137.)

You might begin by writing down everything you had to eat today or yesterday, or even what you plan to eat tomorrow. Once you have entered an entire day's meals and snacks on the worksheet, simply tally up each column and compare it with your target goals. How did you do? Is your combined IF Rating below the recommended target? Is your total fat or carbohydrate total too high?

If your totals are not lining up with your target values, take a look at the individual entries to see if you can locate obvious trouble spots. You may find that one or two foods are pulling down the day's total IF Rating or pushing your fat totals over the top. Using the IF Ratings listed by category on page 218 (Table 4.2), you can find similar foods with higher IF Ratings (or lower fat totals) to improve your meal plan. You can also use the table on page 35 (Table 2.2) to zero in on high-rated foods that can lift your combined IF Rating for the day.

On page 57 (Table 3.5), you'll see a sample worksheet that shows a meal plan for a 2,000-calorie diet. This plan features foods from each food group that are generally considered to be healthful, and the total fat and carbohydrate grams are close to the recommended values. Many dietitians might endorse this meal plan as being nearly ideal. Perhaps you've even followed diet plans that were much like this one. However, when we calculate the total IF Rating for the day, we see that this "healthful" meal plan is actually extremely inflammatory!

This example illustrates just how easy it is to accidentally fuel inflammation, even when you are trying to eat a healthful diet. Imagine the unintended effects of eating a highly inflammatory diet like this one, day after day. The IF Rating system allows you to bring your diet and your body back into balance and avoid the consequences of excessive inflammation.

On page 58 (Table 3.6), you can see how I adjusted the sample meal plan to bring the day's totals into line with the target values for a Prevention/Maintenance plan.

TABLE 3.5 Meal-Planning: A Typical Diet

Food	IF Rating	Fat (g)	Carb (g)
1 cup Special K	−34	0	22
½ cup skim milk	−14	0	6
1 banana	−118	1	28
1 cup low-fat fruit yogurt	−144	3	46
1 cup spinach leaves	80	0	1
2 tablespoons low-fat blue cheese dressing	−6	2	0
1 hard-boiled egg	−43	5	0
1 slice whole wheat bread	−72	1	13
1 cup tomato soup	−25	2	17
1 apple	−62	1	21
¼ cup pumpkin seeds	−26	13	5
6 ounces grilled salmon (farm-raised)	−360	22	0
1 cup steamed broccoli	110	0	10
1 cup brown rice	−206	2	44
2 teaspoons butter	−30	8	0
¾ cup low-fat vanilla ice cream	−153	6	30
Total	**−1,103**	**66**	**243**
Goal	**50+**	**65**	**250**

Tips for Planning Meals

Keep in mind that the target values for the Inflammation-Free Diet are guidelines, not absolutes. Although you should keep your daily intake aligned with these goals, you don't need to hit each target exactly in order to be successful. The target value for the IF Rating is the recommended minimum; aim for this value or higher each day. It's fine to be five or ten points over or under the target values for carbohydrate or fat grams.

TABLE 3.6 Meal-Planning: An Anti-Inflammatory Diet

Food	IF Rating	Fat (g)	Carb (g)
~~1 cup Special K~~	~~−34~~	~~0~~	~~22~~
1 cup bran flakes	12	1	31
½ cup skim milk	−14	0	6
1 banana	−118	1	28
~~1 cup low-fat fruit yogurt~~	~~−144~~	~~3~~	~~46~~
¾ cup low-fat cottage cheese	13	2	5
1 cup cantaloupe	21	0	11
1 cup spinach leaves	80	0	1
2 tablespoons low-fat blue cheese dressing	−6	2	0
1 hard-boiled egg	−43	5	0
½ cup diced chicken breast	−13	3	0
1 slice whole wheat bread	−72	1	13
1 cup tomato soup	−25	2	17
~~1 apple~~	~~−62~~	~~1~~	~~21~~
1 orange	−19	0	22
~~¼ cup roasted pumpkin seeds~~	~~−26~~	~~13~~	~~5~~
¼ cup cashews	26	13	9
~~6 ounces grilled salmon (farm-raised)~~	~~−360~~	~~22~~	~~0~~
6 ounces grilled rockfish	376	4	0
1 cup steamed broccoli	110	0	10
1 tablespoon olive oil	73	14	0
½ clove garlic	55	0	1
1 cup brown rice	−206	2	44
½ medium sweet potato	105	0	14
2 teaspoons butter	−30	8	0
¾ cup low-fat vanilla ice cream	−153	6	30
Total	**172**	**64**	**242**
Goal	**50+**	**65**	**250**

When you keep all three values (total IF Rating, fat, and carbohydrate) in the recommended zones, you will automatically end up with a diet that is both nutritious and well balanced. While the diet is designed to be fairly foolproof, you'll find that a little common sense will make following the program easier and enhance your results. Each day should include a variety of foods from all food groups. In particular, try to include five to seven servings of vegetables each day. That may seem like a lot, but remember that one serving is just a half cup of cooked vegetables or one cup of leafy greens. A good-sized salad can easily provide two or three servings of vegetables in a single sitting—and will make it easier to keep your IF Rating totals in the recommended range.

No foods are completely forbidden on the Inflammation-Free Diet. Foods with negative IF Ratings can be enjoyed in moderation as long as they are balanced by foods with positive IF Ratings. For best results, however, limit your consumption of foods that are extremely inflammatory (those with an IF Rating of −200 or lower per serving). Although it's possible to balance the day's total IF Ratings by including some very high IF foods, doing this on a regular basis will diminish the effectiveness of the program.

The High-Tech Option

If you are comfortable working with computers and have access to a simple spreadsheet program, you might find it convenient to plan your meals at your computer. The spreadsheet will do the math for you, automatically updating the totals when you add or change foods. You can print out your finished meal plans and place them in a binder. You can also save them on your computer for future use. (I find it much faster and easier to create a variation on an existing meal plan than to start all over from scratch.)

Evaluating and Revising Recipes

The IF Rating tables also allow you to calculate the IF Rating of a recipe that includes many different ingredients. This is done very much the way meal plans are calculated. In Table 3.7 below, you'll find a worksheet for calculating recipes. Usually, a recipe will make several servings. I find it easiest to tally the values for the entire recipe and then divide the total by the number of servings to arrive at the IF Rating for a single serving.

TABLE 3.7 Recipe Worksheet

Recipe Name:

Number of Servings:

Ingredient	IF Rating	Fat (g)	Carb (g)
Total			
Per Serving			

Tips for Calculating Recipes

The A-to-Z IF Ratings on page 137 (Table 4.1) include listings for individual servings as well as larger quantities that may be used in recipes—for example, a pound of meat or a half cup of oil. If the recipe calls for a quantity that is not listed, multiply or divide the listings as needed. Remember to adjust the fat and carbohydrate totals along with the IF Ratings.

Also, keep in mind that the volume and weight of a food can change dramatically when it is cooked. A half cup of uncooked rice will measure a cup after it is cooked, while a cup of spinach may be only a quarter of a cup after cooking. To help you make accurate calculations, the table lists many foods in both uncooked and cooked quantities.

Choose the listing that most closely resembles the finished product and not the raw ingredient. For example, if a recipe calls for a half cup of raw celery, which is then cooked into a stew, use the values for cooked celery in your calculations for the recipe. You may occasionally find that a particular food is not listed exactly the way you intend to use it. Use the closest possible match, and don't worry about it. Small discrepancies will not invalidate your results or undermine your success.

As with meals, you can improve a recipe's IF Rating by adding or substituting ingredients with higher IF Ratings. Adding ginger and garlic, where appropriate, can increase the anti-inflammatory impact of a dish. Or you might incorporate additional vegetables or substitute low-fat dairy products for whole-milk products to bring up the IF Rating of a recipe.

On page 62 (Table 3.8), you'll see a sample recipe worksheet that I used to calculate the IF Rating for a standard lasagna recipe, followed by a second worksheet that shows the adjustments I made to improve the IF Rating of the dish. The complete recipe for the improved version, Very Veggie Lasagna, appears later in this chapter.

As with the meal plans, I find it quickest to enter the numbers into a spreadsheet that tallies the columns for me and refigures the totals if I make any adjustments. Once I've calculated a recipe, I

TABLE 3.8 Recipe Worksheet: Standard Recipe

Recipe Name: Standard Lasagna

Number of Servings: 8

Ingredient	IF Rating	Fat (g)	Carb (g)
9 ounces lasagna noodles	−318	0	83
1 pound ground beef	−58	59	0
1 medium onion	236	0	10
2 cloves garlic	222	0	2
2 cans tomato puree	240	6	138
2 teaspoons fresh oregano	1	0	0
2 teaspoons fresh thyme	2	0	0
2 tablespoons fresh basil (or 2 teaspoons dried)	9	0	0
16 ounces ricotta cheese, whole milk	−140	64	15
1 egg	−43	5	0
12 ounces mozzarella cheese, part-skim	−138	68	13
½ cup grated Parmesan cheese	−31	14	2
Total	**−18**	**216**	**263**
Per Serving	**−2**	**27**	**33**

write the IF Rating (per serving), along with any adjustments I've made, directly onto the cookbook page or recipe card, so I don't have to figure it out again.

Meal Plans for the Inflammation-Free Diet

One of the great things about the Inflammation-Free Diet and the IF Rating system is that you aren't tethered to someone else's meal plans. As long as you are reaching the day's target values, the plan is flexible enough to use anywhere with anyone and with any kind of cuisine. But to get you started, here are three weeks' worth of sam-

TABLE 3.9 Recipe Worksheet: Revised Recipe

Recipe Name: Very Veggie Lasagna

Number of Servings: 8

Ingredient	IF Rating	Fat (g)	Carb (g)
9 ounces lasagna noodles	−318	0	83
1 tablespoon olive oil	73	14	0
1 medium onion	236	0	10
2 cloves garlic	222	0	2
2 cans tomato puree	240	6	138
1 cup carrot, grated	108	0	10
2 teaspoons fresh oregano (or ½ teaspoon dried)	1	0	0
2 teaspoons fresh thyme (or ½ teaspoon dried)	2	0	0
2 tablespoons fresh basil (or 2 teaspoons dried)	9	0	0
16 ounces ricotta cheese, part-skim	−28	40	24
10 ounces frozen spinach	640	1	11
1 egg	−43	5	0
12 ounces mozzarella cheese, part-skim	−138	68	13
½ cup grated Parmesan cheese	−31	14	2
Total	**973**	**148**	**293**
Per Serving	**122**	**18**	**37**

ple meal plans, with various target values. A Prevention/Maintenance plan starts on page 64 (Table 3.10). A Therapeutic meal plan begins on page 72 (Table 3.11), and a Reduced-Calorie (Therapeutic) plan begins on page 80 (Table 3.12). You can follow any of these meal plans just as they are or use them as a starting point for your own variations. Entries in **boldface** correspond to recipes that follow the meal plans. (An index to all of the recipes is on page 88.)

TABLE 3.10 Seven-Day Meal Plan: Prevention/Maintenance

	IF Rating	Fat (g)	Carb (g)
Daily Target Values	**50+**	**66**	**250**
Day 1			
Breakfast			
⅓ cup muesli, no sugar added	−41	4	14
1 cup nonfat yogurt	−4	0	17
½ cup fresh blueberries	−11	0	10
1 tablespoon honey (if desired)	−95	0	17
Breakfast total	**−151**	**4**	**58**
Lunch			
1 veggie burger	49	4	7
1 hamburger bun	−113	2	21
Lettuce and tomato	22	0	3
2 teaspoons reduced-fat mayonnaise	−8	2	0
1 serving **Avocado Salsa**	175	7	12
1 serving **Baked Tortilla Chips**	−54	5	17
1 large orange	−19	0	22
Lunch total	**52**	**20**	**82**
Dinner			
1½ servings **Fish with Spicy Tomato Sauce**	456	3	24
1 baked potato	−258	0	37
2 tablespoons sour cream	−18	6	2
Salad made with:			
1½ cups mixed greens	76	0	2
¼ cup garbanzo beans	−20	1	11
2 tablespoons salad dressing (olive oil and vinegar)	72	14	0
Dinner total	**308**	**24**	**76**

	IF Rating	Fat (g)	Carb (g)
Snacks			
½ cup red pepper strips	90	0	5
¼ cup oil-roasted cashews	23	14	9
½ cup reduced-fat vanilla ice cream	−102	4	20
Day 1 total	**220**	**66**	**250**
Day 2			
Breakfast			
1 plain bagel	−186	1	30
4 tablespoons reduced-fat cream cheese	−42	14	2
2 slices tomato	17	0	3
2 ounces smoked salmon	144	2	0
2 slices red onion	93	0	6
Breakfast total	**26**	**17**	**41**
Lunch			
1½ cups tomato soup	−36	3	25
1 serving **Garlic-Pumpernickel Croutons**	38	4	8
Sandwich made with:			
2 slices whole wheat bread	−144	2	26
2 ounces ham, extra lean	16	2	2
Lettuce	25	0	0
2 tablespoons reduced-fat mayonnaise	−24	10	2
2 plums	−50	0	18
Lunch total	**−175**	**17**	**81**

continued

TABLE 3.10 Seven-Day Meal Plan: Prevention/Maintenance, *continued*

	IF Rating	Fat (g)	Carb (g)
Dinner			
1 serving **Grilled Steak and Tomato Salad**	183	10	15
1½ servings **Brown Rice Pilaf with Almonds**	165	10	51
1½ servings **Tropical Fruit Salad**	35	0	30
Dinner total	**383**	**20**	**96**
Snacks			
½ cup raw cauliflower florets	15	0	2
¼ cup fat-free ranch dressing (dip for cauliflower)	0	0	0
½ cup chocolate pudding	−130	4	28
Day 2 total	**119**	**58**	**248**
Day 3			
Breakfast			
1 cup shredded wheat	−230	1	37
½ cup sliced strawberries	14	0	6
1 cup low-fat milk	−33	2	12
Breakfast total	**−249**	**3**	**55**
Lunch			
1 serving **Spinach-Dill Soup**	369	4	8
1 small whole wheat pita, toasted	−65	1	15
2 ounces Gouda cheese	−38	16	2
1 apple	−62	1	21
Lunch total	**204**	**22**	**46**

	IF Rating	Fat (g)	Carb (g)
Dinner			
1½ servings **Linguine with Clams and Broccoli**	267	6	108
Salad made with:			
1 yellow tomato, cut in wedges	21	1	6
2 teaspoons olive oil and 1 teaspoon balsamic vinegar	48	10	0
1 tablespoon roasted pine nuts	−10	5	1
1 teaspoon finely grated Parmesan cheese	−1	0	0
Dinner total	**325**	**22**	**115**
Snacks			
Trail mix made with:			
3 tablespoons raisins	−100	0	16
3 tablespoons peanuts	10	10	5
2 tablespoons chocolate chips	−76	7	12
Day 3 total	**114**	**64**	**249**
Day 4			
Breakfast			
1 cup raisin bran	−215	2	47
1 cup low-fat milk	−33	2	12
Breakfast total	**−248**	**4**	**59**
Lunch			
1½ servings **Spinach-Jalapeño Quesadillas**	66	13	59
¼ avocado, mashed	46	7	4

continued

TABLE 3.10 Seven-Day Meal Plan: Prevention/Maintenance, *continued*

	IF Rating	Fat (g)	Carb (g)
¼ cup salsa	52	0	4
1 large peach	−54	0	17
Lunch total	**110**	**20**	**84**
Dinner			
1 serving **Chicken with Apricots and Ginger**	335	14	20
1 cup couscous	−182	0	36
1½ servings **Asparagus Salad Vinaigrette**	261	2	11
Dinner total	**414**	**16**	**67**
Snacks			
⅓ cup roasted almonds	85	22	8
1 small oat bran muffin	−164	5	32
Day 4 total	**197**	**67**	**250**
Day 5			
Breakfast			
1 English muffin	−173	1	26
1 tablespoon reduced-fat cream cheese	−11	3	1
2 tablespoons fruit preserves	−136	0	26
¾ cup low-fat cottage cheese (1%)	13	2	5
1½ cups cantaloupe	31	0	16
Breakfast total	**−276**	**6**	**74**
Lunch			
Sandwich made with:			
2 pieces whole wheat bread	−144	2	26
1 serving **Curried Egg Salad**	161	13	4
Lettuce	22	0	1

	IF Rating	Fat (g)	Carb (g)
½ cup raw snow peas	26	0	4
½ cup baby carrots	93	0	7
2 tablespoons low-fat blue cheese dressing (dip for vegetables)	−6	2	0
1 pear	−74	1	25
Lunch total	**78**	**18**	**67**
Dinner			
1½ servings **Pulled Pork Tacos**	183	31	38
1 cup steamed broccoli	110	0	10
1 serving **Sweet and Spicy Carrot and Apple Salad**	36	4	22
Dinner total	**329**	**35**	**70**
Snacks			
12-ounce can spicy tomato juice (with Tabasco)	160	0	16
4 shortbread cookies	−105	8	20
Day 5 total	**186**	**67**	**247**
Day 6			
Breakfast			
Omelet made with 2 eggs, spinach, tomato, and feta cheese	−73	16	5
2 pieces whole wheat toast	−144	2	26
2 teaspoons butter	−30	8	0
½ pink grapefruit	1	0	9
Breakfast total	**−246**	**26**	**40**

continued

TABLE 3.10 Seven-Day Meal Plan: Prevention/Maintenance, *continued*

	IF Rating	Fat (g)	Carb (g)
Lunch			
1½ servings **Southwestern Chicken Salad**	87	16	46
1 cup mixed greens (top with chicken salad)	52	0	1
1 cup watermelon	−62	0	11
Lunch total	**77**	**16**	**58**
Dinner			
6 ounces red snapper, baked	250	2	0
1 cup brown rice	−206	2	44
1 serving **Curried Carrots and Chick-Peas**	235	6	47
1 serving **Spinach and Arugula Salad**	241	7	9
20 cherries	−32	0	20
Dinner total	**488**	**17**	**120**
Snacks			
1½ servings **Baked Tortilla Chips**	−81	8	26
¼ cup salsa	52	0	4
Day 6 total	**290**	**67**	**248**
Day 7			
Breakfast			
¾ cup low-fat cottage cheese (1%)	13	2	5
1 cup fresh pineapple	−37	1	19
1 piece mixed-grain toast	−33	1	12
1 teaspoon butter	−15	4	0
Breakfast total	**−72**	**8**	**36**

	IF Rating	Fat (g)	Carb (g)
Lunch			
1½ servings **Tomato-Cabbage Soup**	396	6	33
4 rye crisp crackers	−196	0	32
1 apple	−62	1	21
Lunch total	**138**	**7**	**86**
Dinner			
1½ servings **Very Veggie Lasagna**	180	27	56
Salad made with:			
1½ cups mixed greens	76	0	2
¼ cup garbanzo beans	−20	1	11
1 tablespoon scallion, 2 radishes	18	0	3
¼ cup cherry tomatoes	4	0	2
2 tablespoons low-fat French dressing	−4	4	8
1 serving **Sweet Potato Custard**	160	0	38
Dinner total	**414**	**32**	**120**
Snacks			
2 ounces cheddar cheese	−52	18	0
1 hard-boiled egg	−43	5	0
Day 7 total	**385**	**70**	**242**

TABLE 3.11 Seven-Day Meal Plan: Therapeutic

	IF Rating	Fat (g)	Carb (g)
Daily Target Values	**200+**	**66**	**250**
Day 1			
Breakfast			
1 cup shredded wheat	−230	1	37
½ cup fresh blueberries	−11	0	10
1 cup low-fat milk	−33	2	12
Breakfast total	**−274**	**3**	**59**
Lunch			
1½ servings **Fish Chowder**	114	9	30
1 serving **Sweet and Hot Pepper Crostini**	177	5	18
1 cup fresh pineapple chunks	−37	1	19
Lunch total	**254**	**15**	**67**
Dinner			
1½ servings **Southwestern Chicken Salad**	87	16	46
Salad made with:			
2 cups lettuce	104	0	2
2 tablespoons Italian dressing	−16	8	4
1 serving **Sweet Potato Custard**	160	0	38
Dinner total	**335**	**24**	**90**
Snacks			
½ cup baby carrots	93	0	7
¼ cup dry-roasted cashews	26	13	9
1 oatmeal cookie	−76	5	17
Day 1 total	**358**	**60**	**249**

	IF Rating	Fat (g)	Carb (g)
Day 2			
Breakfast			
¾ cup low-fat cottage cheese (1%)	13	2	5
2 kiwifruit	−28	0	26
1 small oat bran muffin	−164	5	32
Breakfast total	**−179**	**7**	**63**
Lunch			
1 serving **Seafood Salad**	378	6	8
1 cup lettuce (top with seafood salad)	52	0	1
1 can lentil soup	−68	4	37
4 saltines	−52	0	8
Lunch total	**310**	**10**	**54**
Dinner			
1½ servings **Very Veggie Lasagna**	180	27	56
1 serving **Citrus Watercress Salad**	116	4	12
1 oatmeal cookie	−76	5	17
Dinner total	**220**	**36**	**85**
Snacks			
1 serving **Roasted Eggplant Dip**	111	6	9
2 small whole wheat pitas, toasted	−130	2	30
2 large stalks celery with 1 ounce pimento cheese spread	−13	9	3
Day 2 total	**319**	**70**	**244**

continued

TABLE 3.11 Seven-Day Meal Plan: Therapeutic, *continued*	IF Rating	Fat (g)	Carb (g)
Day 3			
Breakfast			
Smoothie made with:			
1 cup soy milk	−9	5	4
½ cup frozen raspberries	5	1	8
2 tablespoons flaxseed	26	8	8
½ frozen banana	−59	1	14
1 piece mixed-grain toast	−33	1	12
1 teaspoon butter	−15	4	0
2 tablespoons fruit preserves	−136	0	26
Breakfast total	**−221**	**20**	**72**
Lunch			
Rollup made with:			
1 10″ flour tortilla	−69	5	36
1½ servings **Spinach Spread**	490	3	12
½ cup red pepper strips	90	0	5
1 apple	−62	1	21
Lunch total	**449**	**9**	**74**
Dinner			
6 ounces pork tenderloin, roasted	12	10	0
1 cup brown rice	−206	2	44
1 serving **Braised Cabbage with Ginger**	357	3	17
1 cup steamed carrots	224	0	12
Dinner total	**387**	**15**	**73**

	IF Rating	Fat (g)	Carb (g)
Snacks			
3 graham crackers	−111	3	15
2 tablespoons almond butter	82	19	7
Day 3 total	**586**	**66**	**241**
Day 4			
Breakfast			
¾ cup All-Bran, Extra Fiber	6	2	35
4 tablespoons raisins	−130	0	23
1 cup low-fat milk	−33	2	12
Breakfast total	**−157**	**4**	**70**
Lunch			
1 serving **Kale Soup with Rice and Lemon**	255	3	19
6 ounces grilled freshwater bass	334	8	0
1 cup seedless grapes	−113	0	29
Lunch total	**476**	**11**	**48**
Dinner			
1½ servings **Spaghetti with Spinach, Ricotta, and Basil**	336	11	77
Salad made with:			
¾ cup thinly sliced fennel bulb	8	0	5
1 tablespoon olive oil	73	14	0
1 tablespoon fresh lemon juice	3	0	1
2 figs	−54	0	10
Dinner total	**366**	**25**	**93**

continued

TABLE 3.11 Seven-Day Meal Plan: Therapeutic, *continued*	IF Rating	Fat (g)	Carb (g)
Snacks			
2 ounces Brie cheese	−32	16	0
4 rye crisps	−196	0	32
8 olives, mixed	48	8	0
Day 4 total	**505**	**64**	**243**
Day 5			
Breakfast			
Breakfast burrito made with:			
2 scrambled eggs with onion and green pepper	29	10	5
2 ounces cheddar cheese	−52	18	0
1 large flour tortilla	−69	6	36
¾ cup salsa	76	0	6
½ pink grapefruit	1	0	9
Breakfast total	**−15**	**34**	**56**
Lunch			
1 wedge iceberg lettuce with Russian dressing	24	2	19
1 cup tomato soup	−25	2	17
12 oyster crackers	−52	0	8
1 pear	−74	1	25
Lunch total	**−127**	**5**	**69**
Dinner			
1½ servings **Grilled Mahimahi with Mango Salsa**	484	11	42
1½ servings **Brown Rice Pilaf with Almonds**	165	10	51

	IF Rating	Fat (g)	Carb (g)
1 cup boiled green beans	30	0	10
Dinner totals	**679**	**21**	**103**

Snacks

	IF Rating	Fat (g)	Carb (g)
1½ servings **Raspberry-Orange Frozen Yogurt**	−12	3	39
Day 5 total	**525**	**63**	**267**

Day 6
Breakfast

	IF Rating	Fat (g)	Carb (g)
1 plain bagel	−186	1	30
4 tablespoons reduced-fat cream cheese	−42	14	2
2 slices tomato	17	0	3
2 ounces smoked salmon	144	2	0
1 slice red onion	93	0	4
Breakfast total	**26**	**17**	**39**

Lunch

	IF Rating	Fat (g)	Carb (g)
1 serving **Tomato-Cabbage Soup**	264	4	22
Sandwich made with:			
2 slices mixed-grain bread	−66	2	24
3 ounces white tuna canned in water	347	3	0
2 tablespoons reduced-fat mayonnaise	−24	10	2
2 tablespoons chopped onion	52	0	2
¼ cup chopped celery	5	0	1
4 black olives, chopped	16	4	0
1 cup fresh pineapple chunks	−37	1	19
Lunch total	**557**	**24**	**70**

continued

TABLE 3.11 Seven-Day Meal Plan: Therapeutic, *continued*	IF Rating	Fat (g)	Carb (g)
Dinner			
1 roasted chicken breast	−14	5	0
½ cup stuffing	−149	8	19
1½ servings **Roasted Vegetable Terrine**	412	6	48
Dinner total	**249**	**19**	**67**
Snacks			
1 apple	−62	1	21
1 cup low-fat fruit-flavored yogurt	−144	3	46
Day 6 total	**626**	**64**	**243**
Day 7			
Breakfast			
2 frozen waffles	−170	4	24
3 tablespoons maple syrup	−210	0	39
1 serving **Tropical Fruit Salad**	23	0	19
Breakfast Total	**−357**	**4**	**82**
Lunch			
1½ servings **Gazpacho**	222	0	18
1 serving **Garlic-Pumpernickel Croutons**	38	4	8
1½ cups carrot and cucumber sticks	100	0	12
1 small whole wheat pita, toasted	−65	1	15
1 serving **Spinach Spread** (dip for vegetables and pita)	327	2	8
Lunch total	**622**	**7**	**61**

	IF Rating	Fat (g)	Carb (g)
Dinner			
Grilled hamburger (6 ounces, 85% lean)	−14	26	0
1 hamburger bun	−113	2	21
Tomato and lettuce	22	0	3
Dill pickle	3	0	1
1½ servings **Rosemary Sweet Potato Salad**	433	15	37
1½ servings **Marinated Vegetables**	309	3	18
Dinner total	**640**	**46**	**80**
Snacks			
½ cup vanilla ice cream	−124	8	17
½ cup raspberries	5	1	8
Day 7 total	**786**	**66**	**248**

TABLE 3.12 Seven-Day Meal Plan: Reduced-Calorie (Therapeutic)

	IF Rating	Fat (g)	Carb (g)
Daily Target Values	200+	53	200
Day 1			
Breakfast			
1 small blueberry muffin	−179	4	32
¾ cup low-fat cottage cheese (1%)	13	2	5
1½ cups cantaloupe	30	0	16
Breakfast total	**−136**	**6**	**53**
Lunch			
1 serving **Asian Broccoli and Ginger Salad**	266	7	14
Tuna sashimi (4 pieces)	124	0	0
½ cup sushi rice	−145	0	18
30 grapes	−122	0	32
Lunch total	**123**	**7**	**64**
Dinner			
3 ounces roast pork tenderloin	6	5	0
1 serving **Sautéed Broccoli with Garlic**	206	4	8
1 serving **Baked Sweet Potato Fries**	231	1	27
1 oatmeal cookie	−76	5	17
Dinner total	**367**	**10**	**52**
Snacks			
1 cup raw snow peas	52	0	7
1 small toasted whole wheat pita	−65	1	15
1 ounce soft goat cheese with herbs (spread for pita)	−26	6	0

	IF Rating	Fat (g)	Carb (g)
¼ cup dry-roasted almonds	57	15	5
Day 1 total	**372**	**45**	**196**

Day 2
Breakfast

	IF Rating	Fat (g)	Carb (g)
1 cup Cheerios	−81	2	23
1 cup low-fat milk	−33	2	12
1 peach	−54	0	17
Breakfast total	**−168**	**4**	**52**

Lunch

	IF Rating	Fat (g)	Carb (g)
1 serving **Spinach-Jalapeño Quesadillas**	44	9	39
¼ avocado, mashed	46	7	4
¼ cup salsa	52	0	4
Lunch total	**142**	**16**	**47**

Dinner

	IF Rating	Fat (g)	Carb (g)
1 serving **Chicken with Apricots and Ginger**	335	14	20
¾ cup couscous	−137	0	27
1½ servings **Asparagus Salad Vinaigrette**	261	2	11
Dinner total	**459**	**16**	**58**

Snacks

	IF Rating	Fat (g)	Carb (g)
¼ cup dry-roasted pistachios	26	13	8
1 small oat bran muffin	−164	5	32
Day 2 total	**295**	**54**	**197**

continued

TABLE 3.12 Seven-Day Meal Plan: Reduced-Calorie (Therapeutic), *continued*

	IF Rating	Fat (g)	Carb (g)
Day 3			
Breakfast			
1 soft-boiled egg	−43	5	0
1 vegetarian breakfast patty	−6	3	4
1 piece whole wheat toast	−72	1	13
1 teaspoon butter	−15	4	0
2 tablespoons fruit preserves	−136	0	26
½ pink grapefruit	1	0	9
Breakfast total	**−271**	**13**	**52**
Lunch			
1 serving **Kale Soup with Rice and Lemon**	255	3	19
1 serving **Roasted Eggplant Dip**	111	6	9
1 small toasted whole wheat pita	−65	1	15
Lunch total	**301**	**10**	**43**
Dinner			
1 serving **Very Veggie Lasagna**	120	18	37
Salad made with:			
1½ cups lettuce	76	0	2
¼ cup garbanzo beans	−20	1	11
2 tablespoons low-fat French dressing	−4	4	8
1 tablespoon chopped scallion, 2 radishes	18	0	3
¼ cup cherry tomatoes	4	0	2
Dinner total	**194**	**23**	**63**

	IF Rating	Fat (g)	Carb (g)
Snacks			
1 serving **Tomato Crostini**	187	8	23
½ cup low-fat cottage cheese (1%)	9	1	3
½ cup fresh blueberries	−11	0	10
Day 3 total	**409**	**55**	**194**
Day 4			
Breakfast			
¾ cup All-Bran, Extra Fiber	6	2	35
3 tablespoons raisins	−87	0	15
1 cup low-fat milk	−33	2	12
Breakfast total	**−114**	**4**	**62**
Lunch			
Rollup made with:			
3 ounces sliced roasted turkey	33	3	3
1 large flour tortilla	−69	5	36
½ cup shredded lettuce	26	0	0
½ cup chopped tomato	18	0	4
¼ avocado, sliced	46	7	4
2 tablespoons sliced black olives	8	2	0
1 tablespoon reduced-fat mayonnaise	−12	5	1
½ cup cherries	−19	0	12
Lunch total	**31**	**22**	**60**

continued 83

TABLE 3.12 Seven-Day Meal Plan: Reduced-Calorie (Therapeutic), *continued*

	IF Rating	Fat (g)	Carb (g)
Dinner			
1 serving **Grilled Steak and Tomato Salad**	183	10	15
1 serving **Rosemary Sweet Potato Salad**	289	10	25
Dinner total	**472**	**20**	**40**
Snacks			
1 apple	−62	1	21
1 ounce string cheese (mozzarella)	−11	5	1
Day 4 total	**316**	**52**	**184**
Day 5			
Breakfast			
1 cup fruit-flavored yogurt	−144	3	46
½ cup muesli	−61	6	21
Breakfast total	**−205**	**9**	**67**
Lunch			
Salad made with:			
3 ounces sliced roasted chicken breast	−14	3	0
2 cups lettuce	104	0	1
½ cup cherry tomatoes	7	0	3
¼ cup sliced carrot	30	0	3
2 tablespoons low-fat French dressing	−4	4	8
2 tablespoons dry-roasted sunflower seeds	−21	7	4
1 pear	−74	1	25
Lunch total	**28**	**15**	**44**

	IF Rating	Fat (g)	Carb (g)
Dinner			
1 serving **Basil–Red Pepper Soup**	281	4	11
3 ounces grilled coho salmon	455	7	0
1½ cups steamed broccoli	165	0	15
1 ear corn on the cob	−111	1	22
2 teaspoons butter	−30	8	0
1 cup watermelon	−62	0	11
Dinner total	**698**	**20**	**59**
Snacks			
1 plain bagel	−186	1	30
2 tablespoons reduced-fat cream cheese	−21	7	1
Day 5 total	**314**	**52**	**201**
Day 6			
Breakfast			
1 cup Cheerios	−81	2	23
1 cup low-fat milk	−33	2	12
½ cup sliced strawberries	14	0	6
Breakfast total	**−100**	**4**	**41**
Lunch			
1½ cups tomato soup	−37	3	25
1 serving **Garlic-Pumpernickel Croutons**	38	4	8
3 rye crispbread crackers	−147	0	24
Lunch total	**−146**	**7**	**57**

continued

TABLE 3.12 Seven-Day Meal Plan:
Reduced-Calorie (Therapeutic), *continued*

	IF Rating	Fat (g)	Carb (g)
Dinner			
1 serving **Seafood Salad**	378	6	8
1 baked sweet potato	210	0	27
1 teaspoon butter	−15	4	0
1 serving **Swiss Chard au Gratin**	274	5	7
Salad made with:			
1½ cups lettuce	76	0	2
¼ cup garbanzo beans	−20	1	11
1 tablespoon chopped scallion, 2 radishes	18	0	3
¼ cup cherry tomatoes	4	0	2
2 tablespoons low-fat French dressing	−4	4	8
Dinner total	**921**	**20**	**68**
Snacks			
1 small oat bran muffin	−164	5	32
2 ounces Gouda cheese	−38	16	2
Day 6 total	**473**	**52**	**200**
Day 7			
Breakfast			
Breakfast burrito made with:			
2 scrambled eggs with onion and green pepper	29	10	5
1 ounce cheddar cheese	−26	9	0
1 large flour tortilla	−69	5	36
¾ cup salsa	76	0	6

	IF Rating	Fat (g)	Carb (g)
½ pink grapefruit	1	0	9
Breakfast total	**11**	**24**	**56**

Lunch

Salad made with:			
1 cup spinach	80	0	1
¼ cup sliced beets	−12	0	3
½ orange, sectioned	−10	0	11
¼ cup slivered almonds	51	14	5
2 tablespoons low-fat French dressing	−4	4	8
6 melba toasts	−78	0	12
Lunch total	**−27**	**18**	**40**

Dinner

1 serving **Salmon with Roasted Pepper and Onion Compote**	875	8	11
1 cup brown rice	−206	2	44
1 serving **Sautéed Broccoli with Garlic**	206	2	8
Dinner total	**875**	**12**	**63**

Snacks

1 piece angel food cake	−183	0	29
½ cup sliced peaches	−45	0	15
Day 7 total	**685**	**54**	**203**

Recipes for the Inflammation-Free Diet

Index to Recipes*

*Many recipes were developed by Tamara Holt and adapted by permission from Lynn Sonberg Book Associates.

Converting Recipes to Metric

Volume Measurements (for Liquid Ingredients)

1 teaspoon = 5 milliliters

1 tablespoon = 15 milliliters

1 fluid ounce = 30 milliliters

¼ cup = 2 fluid ounces = 60 milliliters

⅓ cup = 80 milliliters

1 cup = 8 fluid ounces = 240 milliliters

Weight Measurements

1 ounce = 28 grams

1 pound = 16 ounces = 450 grams

Common Ingredients

1 cup granulated sugar = 200 grams

1 cup powdered sugar = 100 grams

1 cup brown sugar, packed = 220 grams

1 cup cornmeal = 140 grams

1 cup flour = 120 grams

1 cup rice (uncooked) = 190 grams

1 cup macaroni (uncooked) = 140 grams

1 cup couscous (uncooked) = 180 grams

1 cup oats (uncooked) = 90 grams

1 teaspoon salt = 7 grams

1 tablespoon butter = 15 grams

Appetizers and Snacks

Avocado Salsa

Makes 4 servings

For a quick shortcut, combine a diced avocado with 1½ cups of prepared salsa. For fresh-made taste, garnish with freshly chopped cilantro and a squeeze of fresh lime juice.

1 ripe avocado, peeled and diced

2 tablespoons lime juice

1 large tomato, diced

½ yellow bell pepper, diced

½ cup diced red onion

1 jalapeño pepper, seeds and membranes removed, minced

1 clove garlic, minced

¼ cup (packed) cilantro leaves, chopped

½ teaspoon ground black pepper

Salt to taste

1. Place avocado and lime juice in large bowl, and toss gently to coat. (This will help to keep the avocado from browning.)
2. Add tomato, yellow pepper, onion, jalapeño, garlic, cilantro, and black pepper. Toss gently to combine.
3. Add salt to taste.

Nutritional information per serving: IF Rating: 175; Fat: 7 g; Carbohydrate: 12 g

Baked Tortilla Chips

Makes 4 servings

These easy, homemade tortilla chips have a higher IF Rating than store-bought tortilla chips, along with a fresh, hearty flavor that you just can't get in a bag.

1 tablespoon canola oil (or canola oil spray)

6 6-inch corn tortillas

Salt to taste

1. Preheat oven to 300 degrees. Brush or spray canola oil on both sides of each tortilla.
2. Using a sharp knife or kitchen shears, cut each tortilla into six wedges, and place on a jelly roll pan in a single layer. Sprinkle with salt.

3. Bake chips until golden brown and crisp. Baking time will vary depending on the thickness and moisture content of the tortillas. Test after 15 minutes by snapping a chip in two. If the chip does not break easily, return to oven, and check again after 5 minutes. Cool completely, and store in an airtight container.

Nutritional information per serving: IF Rating: −54; Fat: 5 g; Carbohydrate: 17 g

Garlic-Pumpernickel Croutons

Makes 8 servings

You can flavor these croutons in a variety of ways by adding fresh or dried herbs. Try oregano, parsley, basil, and/or rosemary.

4 slices pumpernickel bread, slightly stale
2 tablespoons olive oil
3 cloves garlic, minced
Salt and pepper to taste
2 tablespoons chopped fresh herbs (or 2 teaspoons dried)

1. Cut crusts from bread, and cut each slice into small cubes. If bread is very fresh, spread on a cookie sheet and dry for 5 minutes in 325-degree oven. Place bread cubes in large mixing bowl.
2. Heat oil in large skillet, and add garlic. Cook, stirring frequently, until garlic is golden but not brown, 2 to 3 minutes. Remove from heat, and cool briefly.
3. Pour seasoned oil over cubed bread, and toss to coat evenly. Add salt, pepper, and herbs.
4. Spread croutons in single layer on a baking sheet, and return to oven. Toast croutons until crisp and brown, stirring once. Baking time will vary according to moisture content of bread, 10 to 20 minutes. Cool completely, and store in airtight container.

Nutritional information per serving: IF Rating: 38; Fat: 4 g; Carbohydrate: 8 g

Ginger-Marinated Tuna Appetizer

Makes 4 servings

The tuna in this elegant appetizer is not cooked by heat, but by the acid in the marinade. Use only the freshest sushi-grade tuna, and do not marinate longer than 1 hour, as the fish will begin to lose its texture.

> 1 tablespoon soy sauce
> 3 tablespoons freshly squeezed lemon juice
> 1 tablespoon freshly grated gingerroot
> 2 tablespoons canola oil
> 1 pound fresh tuna, about 1 inch thick
> ¼ cup thinly sliced scallions

1. Combine soy sauce, lemon juice, and ginger in large bowl. Add oil in a thin stream while whisking briskly.
2. Add tuna to marinade, cover with plastic wrap, and refrigerate 40 minutes. Turn fish after 20 minutes. (Do not marinate longer than 1 hour.)
3. Slice fish thinly on the diagonal, and arrange on serving plates. Drizzle with marinade, and garnish with scallions.

Nutritional information per serving: IF Rating: 277; Fat: 7 g; Carbohydrate: 2 g

Marinated Vegetables

Makes 6 servings

Almost any vegetable can be used in this simple preparation. Choose any colorful combination of fresh seasonal vegetables.

> 2 large carrots, peeled and cut into small sticks
> ½ small cabbage, cut in 8 wedges

1 red or yellow bell pepper, seeded and cut into strips
5 Hungarian hot peppers (or other hot peppers)
1 small fennel bulb, with the stems and fronds removed, cut in
    wedges
¼ cup white wine vinegar or rice wine vinegar
4 cloves garlic, minced
2 tablespoons chopped fresh oregano (or 2 teaspoons dried)
1 teaspoon sugar
1 tablespoon extra-virgin olive oil

1. Using a steamer basket, steam carrots, cabbage, bell and
   Hungarian peppers, and fennel briefly over boiling water,
   until just tender and still vibrantly colored. Drain well.
2. Combine vinegar, garlic, oregano, and sugar in a large,
   shallow dish. Add oil to liquid in a thin stream while
   whisking briskly.
3. Add warm vegetables to marinade, and toss gently to coat.
   Cover with plastic wrap, and marinate at least 1 hour at
   room temperature or overnight in the refrigerator.

Nutritional information per serving: IF Rating: 206; Fat: 2 g; Carbohydrate:
12 g

Roasted Eggplant Dip

Makes 6 servings

If you find the raw garlic too sharp in flavor, try roasting the
unpeeled garlic cloves in a foil packet along with the eggplant.
With a sharp knife, cut off the tips of the roasted cloves, and
squeeze to extract the roasted garlic paste.

2 small eggplants
2 (or more) cloves garlic, roasted if desired
2 tablespoons olive oil
6 black olives, pitted
½ cup (packed) chopped fresh parsley

3 pieces sun-dried tomato

2 cups canned cannellini (white kidney) beans, drained

2 anchovy fillets (or 2 teaspoons anchovy paste)

2 tablespoons lemon juice

1 teaspoon salt, or to taste

1. Roast the eggplant (and garlic, if desired) in a 400-degree oven for 45 minutes, or until tender. Allow to cool briefly.

2. Peel eggplant and garlic, and place in bowl of food processor. Add olive oil, olives, parsley, sun-dried tomato, beans, anchovy fillets, lemon juice, and salt. Pulse mixture until smooth. Adjust seasoning to taste. Serve warm or cold.

Nutritional information per serving: IF Rating: 111; Fat: 6 g; Carbohydrate: 9 g

Spinach-Jalapeño Quesadillas

Makes 4 servings

Although these are most delicious when made and eaten fresh, you can also make them ahead and reheat them briefly on a paper towel in the microwave.

1 teaspoon canola oil

2 cloves garlic, minced

1 jalapeño pepper, seeds and membranes removed, minced

2 cups chopped fresh spinach (or 1 cup chopped frozen spinach, thawed and pressed to remove extra liquid)

4 10-inch flour tortillas

1½ ounces Monterey Jack cheese, shredded

1 medium tomato, thinly sliced (discard juice and seeds)

½ teaspoon ground black pepper

1. Heat oil in large skillet over medium heat. Add garlic, and cook 1 minute, stirring occasionally. Add jalapeño pepper,

and cook another 2 minutes. Add spinach, and cook until just wilted. Remove mixture, and wipe out pan.

2. Place one tortilla in skillet over medium heat. Sprinkle one-quarter of the cheese over half of the tortilla; top with one-quarter of the spinach mixture and one-quarter of the tomato slices. Sprinkle with pepper.

3. Fold the tortilla in half, and press down on filling. Heat until bottom is golden, about 2 minutes. Turn and cook on other side until bottom side is golden and cheese is melted.

4. Repeat with remaining tortillas. Cut in triangles to serve.

Nutritional information per serving: IF Rating: 44; Fat: 9 g; Carbohydrate: 39 g

Spinach Spread

Makes 6 servings

A microplane grater is the easiest way to grate lemon zest, hard cheeses, and fresh nutmeg. Originally designed as woodworking tools, inexpensive microplane graters are now sold in kitchen supply stores.

2 teaspoons canola oil

1 cup chopped onion

2 cloves garlic, minced

2 10-ounce packages frozen chopped spinach, thawed

½ cup water

1 cup low-fat (1%) cottage cheese

3 tablespoons fresh lemon juice

1 ounce Parmesan cheese, grated

½ teaspoon grated lemon zest

½ teaspoon pepper

⅛ teaspoon grated nutmeg

Salt to taste

1. Heat oil in a large skillet over medium heat. Add onion and garlic, and cook 6 to 7 minutes, stirring occasionally, until tender.
2. Add spinach and water, and cook until heated through.
3. Transfer mixture to a food processor, and add cottage cheese, lemon juice, Parmesan cheese, lemon zest, pepper, nutmeg, and salt. Puree until smooth.
4. Refrigerate at least 4 hours and up to 24 hours before serving.

Nutritional information per serving: IF Rating: 327; Fat: 2 g; Carbohydrate: 8 g

Sweet and Hot Pepper Crostini

Makes 4 servings

You can vary the heat of these open-faced sandwiches by substituting different types of sweet and hot peppers, according to taste and availability.

> 1 tablespoon olive oil
> 2 cloves garlic, minced
> 2 hot banana peppers (or Hungarian, jalapeño, etc.), seeded and diced
> 1 red bell pepper, seeded and diced
> 1 yellow bell pepper, seeded and diced
> 1 hot cherry pepper (or poblano, serrano, etc.), seeded and diced
> 1 tablespoon chopped fresh rosemary (or 1 teaspoon dried)
> Salt and black pepper to taste
> ¼ cup chopped fresh parsley
> 4 thick slices whole-grain bread, such as a country loaf or whole wheat baguette

1. Heat oil in large skillet over medium heat. Add garlic, and cook, stirring, just until golden.

2. Add peppers, and continue cooking, covered, until soft, about 10 to 15 minutes. Add rosemary, salt, and black pepper. Remove from heat, and add parsley.
3. Toast bread in toaster or under broiler until well browned. Top with pepper mixture.

Nutritional information per serving: IF Rating: 177; Fat: 5 g; Carbohydrate: 18 g

Tomato Crostini

Makes 4 servings

This simple preparation is a great way to make a meal of summer tomatoes and basil fresh from the garden or farmer's market, without heating up the kitchen.

2 tablespoons red wine vinegar
2 cloves garlic, minced
½ teaspoon ground pepper
1 tablespoon extra-virgin olive oil
4 medium tomatoes, diced (discard juice and seeds)
1 cup thinly sliced red onion
1 cup (packed) fresh basil leaves, chopped
Salt to taste
4 thick slices whole-grain bread, such as a country loaf or whole wheat baguette

1. Combine vinegar, garlic, and pepper in large bowl. Add oil in a thin stream while whisking briskly.
2. Add tomatoes, onion, basil, and salt.
3. Cover and marinate at room temperature for 1 to 2 hours. (Do not refrigerate.)
4. Toast or broil bread until well browned. Top with tomato mixture.

Nutritional information per serving: IF Rating: 187; Fat: 8 g; Carbohydrate: 23 g

Soups

Basil–Red Pepper Soup

Makes 4 servings

This dramatically colored soup makes a vibrant first course. Use yellow peppers for a golden variation.

>   5 large red bell peppers, seeded, cut in 1-inch pieces
>   3 cloves garlic, coarsely chopped
>   2½ cups water
>   ¼ cup (packed) fresh basil leaves, chopped
>   1 teaspoon red wine vinegar (or to taste)
>   1 tablespoon extra-virgin olive oil (optional)
>   Salt and black pepper to taste

1. Combine red peppers, garlic, and water in a medium saucepan. Bring to boil, and then reduce heat to low. Cover and simmer until tender, about 25 minutes.
2. Transfer red peppers and garlic to food processor, reserving cooking liquid. Process until smooth, adding cooking liquid as needed to reach desired consistency. Discard extra cooking liquid.
3. Return soup to pan, and heat to serving temperature. Stir in basil, vinegar, olive oil (if used), salt, and black pepper.

Nutritional information per serving: IF Rating: 281; Fat: 4 g; Carbohydrate: 11 g

Chicken Barley Soup

Makes 4 servings

You can substitute rice for barley in this home-style favorite.

>   6 cups water
>   4 chicken thighs with skins removed
>   3 cups thickly sliced carrots

1 cup diced onion

1 cup diced celery

½ cup barley

2 cloves garlic

1 bay leaf

½ cup (packed) fresh parsley leaves, chopped

2 teaspoons chopped fresh rosemary (or ½ teaspoon dried)

½ teaspoon ground pepper

Salt to taste

1. Combine water, chicken, carrots, onion, celery, barley, garlic, and bay leaf in large saucepan. Bring to a boil, and then reduce heat to low. Simmer, uncovered, until chicken is tender, about 40 minutes.
2. Remove chicken from pot. When cool enough to handle, pull chicken from bone by hand and tear into strips.
3. Return chicken to soup, and stir in parsley, rosemary, pepper, and salt.

Nutritional information per serving: IF Rating: 211; Fat: 5 g; Carbohydrate: 22 g

Fish Chowder

Makes 6 servings

You can use fresh or frozen fish in this mild chowder, which is a favorite with both kids and adults. If you are using leeks, be sure to clean them thoroughly of sand. Use only the white and light green portions.

1 tablespoon butter

1 tablespoon canola oil

2 leeks (or 1 medium onion), thinly sliced

3 medium potatoes, cubed

3 cups water

1 pound flounder or other mild fish fillets, in large cubes

1 cup whole milk or evaporated skim milk
½ cup fresh parsley, chopped
Salt and pepper to taste

1. Melt butter and oil in large saucepan or soup pot. Add leeks, and sauté until tender.
2. Add potatoes and water. Bring to a boil, and then reduce heat to low. Simmer until potatoes are almost tender, about 10 minutes.
3. Add fish, and simmer an additional 8 to 10 minutes until fish is opaque.
4. Stir in milk, and heat to serving temperature. Add parsley, salt, and pepper.

Nutritional information per serving: IF Rating: 76; Fat: 6 g; Carbohydrate: 20 g

Gazpacho

Makes 4 servings

This traditional Spanish soup balances cool summer vegetables with the heat of spicy peppers. It makes a refreshing summer appetizer.

2 pounds very ripe tomatoes, cut into chunks (about 5 cups)
1 large cucumber, peeled, seeded, and cubed
½ cup cubed green bell pepper
½ cup diced red onion
3 tablespoons chopped fresh cilantro
¼ to ½ jalapeño pepper, seeded and minced
1 clove garlic, minced
1 tablespoon red wine vinegar (or more to taste)
Salt to taste

1. Combine tomatoes, cucumber, green pepper, onion, cilantro, jalapeño, and garlic in food processor. Pulse until soup is smooth but still slightly chunky.

2. Add vinegar and salt. Serve in chilled cups or glasses, garnished with cilantro leaves.

Nutritional information per serving: IF Rating: 148; Fat: 0 g; Carbohydrate: 12 g

Kale Soup with Rice and Lemon

Makes 4 servings

If you find yourself at a loss as to what to do with kale, try this soup. The fresh lemon flavor is characteristic of classic Greek cuisine.

½ pound (8 ounces) fresh kale
2 cups chicken stock
2 cups water
2 teaspoons olive oil
1 cup chopped onion
½ cup brown rice
¼ cup lemon juice
1 teaspoon grated lemon zest
Salt to taste
½ teaspoon pepper

1. Coarsely chop kale, discarding thick stems.
2. Bring chicken stock and water to boil in medium saucepan. Set aside.
3. In large saucepan or soup pot, heat oil over medium heat, and add onion, cooking until translucent, 5 to 6 minutes.
4. Add broth, kale, rice, lemon juice, and zest to onions in soup pot. Bring to a boil, and then reduce heat to low. Cover and simmer 30 minutes, until rice is tender. Add salt and pepper.

Nutritional information per serving: IF Rating: 255; Fat: 3 g; Carbohydrate: 19 g

Spicy Curried Carrot Soup

Makes 6 servings

This soup has a complex flavor profile but is very simple to make, with ingredients you are likely to have on hand. Look for dried chili peppers in the fresh produce section of the supermarket.

    2 pounds carrots, peeled and cut in large slices
    5 cups chicken stock
    1 dried hot chili pepper
    1 tablespoon minced fresh gingerroot
    3 cloves garlic
    1 teaspoon curry powder
    1 teaspoon cumin
    ½ teaspoon black pepper
    ¼ cup chopped fresh cilantro

1. Combine carrots, chicken stock, chili pepper, ginger, garlic, curry powder, cumin, and black pepper in large saucepan or soup pot. Bring the mixture to a boil, and then reduce heat to low. Simmer, uncovered, until carrots are tender, about 30 minutes.
2. Transfer mixture to food processor or blender, 2 to 3 cups at a time. Puree until smooth.
3. Return to soup pot, and heat to serving temperature. Stir in cilantro immediately before serving.

Nutritional information per serving: IF Rating: 246; Fat: 1 g; Carbohydrate: 5 g

Spinach-Dill Soup

Makes 4 servings

This is a lighter and brighter-tasting variation of traditional cream-thickened spinach soups. It can be made ahead of time and reheated before serving.

1 tablespoon olive oil

3 cloves garlic, minced

1 pound fresh spinach

2 cups chicken stock

1 cup diced cooked potato

¼ cup chopped fresh dill

½ teaspoon salt

½ teaspoon pepper

1. Heat oil in large skillet over medium heat. Add garlic, and cook briefly, about 1 minute. Add spinach, and increase heat to high, tossing spinach until very soft, about 5 minutes.
2. Transfer spinach mixture to food processor or blender, and add chicken stock. Puree until very smooth.
3. Add potato, dill, salt, and pepper. Puree briefly, just until smooth. Add water if needed to achieve desired consistency.
4. If necessary, return soup to pot and heat to serving temperature.

Nutritional information per serving: IF Rating: 369; Fat: 4 g; Carbohydrate: 8 g

Tomato-Cabbage Soup

Makes 4 servings

This rich, warming soup has an Eastern European flavor. Try it as a hearty cold-weather lunch.

1 tablespoon olive oil

1 cup chopped onion

½ cup chopped carrot

½ cup chopped celery

3 cloves garlic, chopped

4 cups chopped green cabbage (½ large head)

1 28-ounce can plum tomatoes, chopped

2 cups chicken stock

3 tablespoons chopped fresh rosemary (or 2 teaspoons dried)

1 2″ × 1″ piece orange peel with the white pith removed
1 bay leaf
Salt and pepper to taste

1. Heat oil in large saucepan or soup pot over medium heat. Add onion, carrot, celery, and garlic. Cook until wilted, about 8 minutes.
2. Add cabbage, tomatoes (with juice), chicken stock, rosemary, orange peel, and bay leaf. Simmer 30 minutes.
3. Remove orange peel, and add salt and pepper. Let soup rest 5 minutes before serving.

Nutritional information per serving: IF Rating: 264; Fat: 4 g; Carbohydrate: 22 g

Vegetables and Side Dishes

Baked Sweet Potato Fries

Makes 4 servings

You may never go back to french fries once you've tried these!

4 sweet potatoes
1 teaspoon olive oil
⅛ teaspoon cayenne pepper
Salt to taste

1. Preheat oven to 450 degrees. Cut sweet potatoes (unpeeled) lengthwise into ½-inch slices, and cut each slice into sticks.
2. Combine oil and cayenne in large bowl, and add sweet potatoes. Toss to coat.
3. Place sweet potato slices in a single layer on baking sheet, and bake 15 minutes. Turn over with spatula, and continue baking until tender, another 15 minutes. Sprinkle with salt.

Nutritional information per serving: IF Rating: 231; Fat: 1 g; Carbohydrate: 27 g

Braised Cabbage with Ginger

Makes 6 servings

Fresh ginger adds zing to this versatile vegetable, making for an easy but interesting side dish.

1 large head green cabbage
1 tablespoon olive oil
1 large onion, sliced
3 tablespoons grated fresh gingerroot
1½ cups chicken stock

1. Remove outer leaves from cabbage, and cut head into 8 wedges. Leave core in place to hold wedges together.
2. Heat oil in large saucepan over medium heat. Add onion and ginger, and cook, stirring, for 1 minute. Stir in broth.
3. Arrange cabbage wedges in saucepan, standing them upright on the core end. Cover the pan, and cook over low to medium heat until cabbage is tender, about 20 minutes. Arrange cabbage on serving plate(s), spooning onion and ginger on top.

Nutritional information per serving: IF Rating: 357; Fat: 3 g; Carbohydrate: 17 g

Brown Rice Pilaf with Almonds

Makes 4 servings

Nutty brown rice is flavored with garlic, cumin, cinnamon, and orange for a fragrant and complex dish.

2 teaspoons canola oil
1 cup chopped onion
1 cup diced carrot
½ cup diced green or red bell pepper
1 clove garlic, minced
1 tablespoon cumin

1 cup brown rice

1½ cups chicken stock (or water)

½ cup orange juice

½ teaspoon cinnamon

½ teaspoon salt

½ cup (packed) fresh parsley leaves, chopped

4 teaspoons lemon juice

¼ cup slivered almonds, toasted

1. Heat oil in large, high-sided skillet or wide saucepan over medium heat. Add onion, carrot, bell pepper, garlic, and cumin, and cook, stirring frequently, 3 minutes. Add rice, and stir to coat with oil.
2. Stir in chicken stock or water, orange juice, cinnamon, and salt. Bring to a boil, then cover, reduce heat to low, and simmer until rice is tender, about 45 minutes.
3. Remove from heat, and let stand 5 minutes. Add parsley and lemon juice, and mix well. Sprinkle with almonds.

Nutritional information per serving: IF Rating: 110; Fat: 7 g; Carbohydrate: 34 g

Curried Carrots and Chick-Peas

Makes 4 servings

This delicious curry can be served as a side dish with lamb or another protein, or enjoyed as a vegetarian entree. Serve over rice or couscous to absorb the flavorful sauce.

2 tablespoons canola oil

½ cup chopped onion

3 cloves garlic, minced

1 tablespoon minced fresh gingerroot

1 tablespoon curry powder

½ teaspoon cumin

½ teaspoon cardamom

¼ teaspoon cinnamon

    2 cups sliced carrots or whole baby carrots

    1½ cups chicken stock

    2 cups peeled, cubed potatoes

    1 16-ounce can chick-peas, drained

    1 large tomato, diced

    ½ cup (packed) chopped fresh cilantro

    Salt and pepper to taste

1. Heat oil in large saucepan over medium heat. Add onion, and cook, stirring until tender.
2. Add garlic, ginger, curry powder, cumin, cardamom, and cinnamon, and continue cooking for 1 minute.
3. Add carrots, and cook 1 minute. Stir in stock, potatoes, chick-peas, tomato, and cilantro. Simmer gently, partly covered, about 35 minutes. Season with salt and pepper.

Nutritional information per serving: IF Rating: 235; Fat: 6 g; Carbohydrate: 47 g

Roasted Asparagus

Makes 4 servings

This recipe also works well on the grill. Use a sheet of heavy-duty foil instead of a baking sheet.

    1 pound asparagus, trimmed (about 28 medium spears)

    1 tablespoon olive oil

    ½ teaspoon salt

    ¼ teaspoon pepper

1. Preheat oven to 400 degrees. Drizzle asparagus with oil, and toss gently to coat. Spread in single layer on baking sheet, and season with salt and pepper.
2. Roast 10 minutes or until tender-crisp, turning once.

Nutritional information per serving: IF Rating: 118; Fat: 4 g; Carbohydrate: 5 g

Roasted Vegetable Terrine

Makes 6 servings

This dish requires a bit of time to prepare, but the delicious result is worth the effort. It makes a scene-stealing side dish or stands alone as a vegetarian entree. The peppers and tomatoes can be roasted ahead of time to save time. Roasting removes extra liquid and concentrates the flavors.

   1 28-ounce can plum tomatoes
   1 large eggplant (about 1½ pounds)
   Salt
   4 medium zucchini, thinly sliced lengthwise
   1 tablespoon olive oil
   6 red bell peppers
   ½ cup (packed) fresh parsley leaves, chopped
   1 teaspoon grated lemon zest
   3 cloves garlic, minced
   1 teaspoon black pepper
   ⅓ cup grated Parmesan cheese

1. Roast tomatoes by placing drained tomatoes on a lightly oiled baking sheet and roasting in a 350-degree oven for 90 minutes or until slightly blackened.
2. Slice eggplant in ½-inch slices, and sprinkle with salt. Place on paper towels and press with a weighted plate. (A large bag of sugar or flour or a large can of tomatoes makes a good weight.) After 20 minutes, rinse eggplant and squeeze dry.
3. Toss eggplant and zucchini slices with olive oil. Place on baking sheet, and broil until lightly browned, about 3 to 4 minutes per side.
4. Roast red peppers by placing on a foil-lined sheet under the broiler. Turn frequently until peppers are blackened on all sides. Remove from broiler, and crimp the foil closed around the peppers to capture the steam. When cool, peel and seed the peppers, and cut into strips.

5. Preheat oven to 350 degrees. Spray a loaf pan (8½″ × 5½″) with nonstick cooking spray. Combine parsley, lemon zest, garlic, black pepper, and Parmesan in small bowl.
6. Layer one-third of the peppers, half the eggplant, half the tomatoes, and half the zucchini, sprinkling each layer with Parmesan/herb mixture. Repeat and finish with remaining peppers.
7. Cover pan with foil, and bake 40 minutes. Remove foil, and bake an additional 25 minutes. Let rest 10 minutes before slicing.

Nutritional information per serving: IF Rating: 275; Fat: 4 g; Carbohydrate: 32 g

Sautéed Broccoli with Garlic

Makes 4 servings

If you've grown tired of steamed broccoli, try this simple but fla-vorful variation. A sprinkle of cracked red pepper at the end is another delicious touch.

4 cups broccoli florets
1 tablespoon olive oil
4 cloves garlic, slivered
Salt and black pepper to taste
¼ teaspoon cracked red pepper flakes (optional)

1. Using a steamer basket, steam broccoli over boiling water until just tender-crisp but still bright green. Run briefly under cool water to stop the cooking process, and drain.
2. Heat oil in large skillet over medium heat. Add garlic and cook, stirring constantly, 30 seconds. Add broccoli, and continue cooking until garlic is golden. Sprinkle with salt and pepper and with red pepper flakes, if desired.

Nutritional information per serving: IF Rating: 206; Fat: 4 g; Carbohydrate: 8 g

Swiss Chard au Gratin

Makes 4 servings

This dish is also delicious made with spinach.

    1 pound Swiss chard leaves, tough stems removed
    1½ ounces Gruyère cheese, grated
    1 tablespoon grated Parmesan cheese
    1 clove garlic, minced
    ½ teaspoon pepper

1. Spray 1-quart casserole with nonstick cooking spray, and preheat oven to 400 degrees.
2. Heat large skillet over high heat. Add damp chard, and cook, tossing gently, until wilted, 2 to 3 minutes.
3. Place half of chard in prepared casserole. Sprinkle with half the Gruyère, half the Parmesan, half the garlic, and half the pepper. Repeat.
4. Bake until cheeses are melted and bubbly, about 20 minutes.

Nutritional information per serving: IF Rating: 274; Fat: 5 g; Carbohydrate: 7 g

Pasta Dishes and Sauces

Herbed Two-Tomato Sauce

Makes 4 servings

Sun-dried tomatoes add depth and richness, balanced by the bright flavor of fresh herbs and a touch of orange zest.

    1 cup boiling water
    ⅓ cup chopped sun-dried tomatoes (1½ ounces)
    1 tablespoon olive oil
    1 cup chopped onion
    3 cloves garlic, minced
    1 28-ounce can chopped tomatoes

1½ teaspoons grated orange zest

1 bay leaf

⅓ cup (packed) fresh basil leaves, chopped

1 teaspoon chopped fresh thyme (or ½ teaspoon dried)

1. Pour boiling water over sun-dried tomatoes in small bowl, and let steep for 10 minutes.
2. Heat oil in large skillet over medium heat. Add onion, and cook until translucent, 4 to 5 minutes. Add garlic, and cook 1 additional minute.
3. Add sun-dried tomatoes along with water, canned tomatoes along with juice, orange zest, bay leaf, basil, and thyme. Bring mixture to a boil, and then reduce heat to low, simmering until thickened, about 15 minutes.

Nutritional information per serving: IF Rating: 227; Fat: 4 g; Carbohydrate: 14 g

Linguine with Clams and Broccoli

Makes 4 servings

If fresh clams are not available or time is at a premium, canned clams and frozen broccoli also work well.

2 dozen clams (or a 12-ounce can)

1 tablespoon olive oil

½ onion, chopped

⅓ cup finely chopped red bell pepper

2 cloves garlic, minced

⅓ cup dry white wine (optional)

12 ounces linguini

2 cups broccoli florets, lightly steamed (or frozen broccoli, thawed)

¼ cup (packed) fresh basil leaves, chopped

½ teaspoon cracked red pepper flakes

Salt and black pepper to taste

1. If using fresh clams, place in large pot with ½ cup water, and steam over high heat until clams have opened. (Discard

any unopened shells.) Carefully pour liquid into a bowl, avoiding any sand. Remove clams from shells, and chop. If using canned clams, drain and reserve liquid.

2. Heat oil in large skillet over medium heat. Add onion and bell pepper, and cook until onion is translucent, 4 to 5 minutes. Add garlic, and cook 1 additional minute. Add ½ cup of the clam liquid and wine (if desired), and simmer 3 minutes.

3. Cook pasta according to package directions, drain, and transfer to large serving dish. Add onion mixture, clams, broccoli, basil, and red pepper flakes to pasta, and toss to combine. Season with salt and black pepper.

Nutritional information per serving: IF Rating: 178; Fat: 4 g; Carbohydrate: 72 g

Pasta with Wilted Greens and Roasted Tomatoes

Makes 4 servings

Any of the nutrition-packed, bitter greens works well with this recipe. Try kale, Swiss chard, or dandelion, mustard, or beet greens.

    1 28-ounce can whole plum tomatoes
    8 ounces small pasta shells
    1 tablespoon olive oil
    2 cloves garlic, crushed
    1 pound greens, thick stalks removed and torn into 2-inch pieces
    1 tablespoon red wine vinegar
    1 teaspoon pepper

1. Preheat oven to 350 degrees. Drain tomatoes, cut into quarters, and place on lightly oiled baking sheet. Roast 90 minutes, turning once, until very soft and slightly blackened.

2. Cook pasta according to package directions. Drain, reserving one-fourth of the cooking liquid.

113

3. Heat oil in large skillet over medium heat. Add garlic, and cook until golden, 1 to 2 minutes. Add greens, increase heat to high, and cook, tossing constantly, until just wilted, 4 to 5 minutes. Add pasta, reserved cooking liquid, tomatoes, vinegar, and pepper. Toss gently to combine, and serve immediately.

Nutritional information per serving: IF Rating: 125; Fat: 4 g; Carbohydrate: 46 g

Spaghetti with Spinach, Ricotta, and Basil

Makes 4 servings

This dish gets its rich, creamy texture from protein-rich ricotta cheese instead of heavy cream. For the best flavor, use a high-quality Parmesan cheese, and grate it just before using.

    2 10-ounce packages frozen chopped spinach
    1 cup part-skim ricotta cheese
    ½ cup (packed) fresh basil leaves, chopped
    ¼ cup grated Parmesan cheese
    1½ teaspoons pepper
    12 ounces spaghetti

1. Cook spinach according to package directions. Drain well, pressing slightly to remove extra liquid.
2. Place spinach, ricotta, basil, Parmesan, and pepper in bowl of food processor, and puree until smooth.
3. Cook pasta according to package directions, and drain, reserving ½ cup of cooking liquid. Combine pasta, spinach mixture, and reserved cooking liquid in large bowl, and toss well.

Nutritional information per serving: IF Rating: 224; Fat: 7 g; Carbohydrate: 51 g

Very Veggie Lasagna

Makes 8 servings

This ever-popular casserole can be made ahead and refrigerated for up to 3 days (or frozen) before baking.

9 ounces lasagna noodles (about 9)
1 tablespoon olive oil
1 medium onion, diced
2 cloves garlic, minced
2 cans tomato puree
1 cup grated carrot
1 teaspoon fresh oregano (or ½ teaspoon dried)
1 teaspoon fresh thyme (or ½ teaspoon dried)
16 ounces low-fat ricotta cheese
1 egg
½ cup grated Parmesan cheese
12 ounces part-skim mozzarella cheese, shredded
1 10-ounce package frozen spinach, thawed and pressed to
      remove liquid

1. Preheat oven to 375 degrees. Boil noodles according to package directions (or use noodles that can be used without precooking).
2. Heat oil in skillet over medium heat. Add onion and garlic, and cook until golden. Add tomato puree, carrot, oregano, and thyme, and simmer 10 minutes.
3. Mix ricotta, egg, and ⅓ cup of the Parmesan cheese in a large bowl.
4. Spread 1 cup of tomato sauce in the bottom of a 9″ × 13″ × 3″ lasagna pan. Place a single layer of noodles over sauce. Spread with half the ricotta mixture and one-third of the mozzarella.
5. Mix spinach into remaining ricotta cheese mixture. Build another layer, using 1½ cups sauce, 3 noodles, all of the spinach/ricotta mixture, and half of the remaining mozzarella.

6. Finish with a final layer of noodles, sauce, and the remaining mozzarella and Parmesan cheese. Bake, covered with foil, until bubbly, 50 to 60 minutes. Remove foil, and continue baking 5 minutes until cheese is melted. Let stand 10 to 15 minutes before serving.

Nutritional information per serving: IF Rating: 120; Fat: 17 g; Carbohydrate: 37 g

Entrees

Chicken with Apricots and Ginger

Makes 4 servings

Dried fruits and spices are the classic components of Moroccan cuisine. This dish pairs well with rice or couscous.

8 chicken thighs, skins removed
1 teaspoon pepper
½ teaspoon salt
1 tablespoon canola oil
1½ cups chopped onion (1 large)
1 tablespoon grated fresh gingerroot
2 cloves garlic, minced
2" × 1" piece of orange peel with the white pith removed
2 teaspoons cardamom
1 teaspoon turmeric
¼ teaspoon ground cloves
1 cup chicken stock
6 ounces dried apricots, sliced in ¼-inch strips (1 cup)

1. Preheat oven to 350 degrees. Season chicken with pepper and salt.
2. Heat oil over medium heat in large, ovenproof pot or Dutch oven. Add onion, and cook until translucent. Add ginger, garlic, orange peel, cardamom, turmeric, and cloves,

and continue cooking 1 minute. Add stock and apricots. Remove from heat.

3. Nestle chicken pieces in apricot mixture. Cover pot with foil and then with lid to create a tight seal. Bake until chicken is tender, about 90 minutes. Remove orange peel before serving.

Nutritional information per serving: IF Rating: 335; Fat: 14 g; Carbohydrate: 20 g

Fish with Spicy Tomato Sauce

Makes 4 servings

This low-fat yet flavorful entree also works with halibut or other mild, firm-fleshed fish.

2 teaspoons olive oil
1 cup chopped onion
2 cloves garlic, minced
¾ cup dry white wine (or nonalcoholic wine)
1 28-ounce can plum tomatoes, coarsely chopped
1 cup water
1 teaspoon grated orange zest
⅓ to ½ teaspoon hot red pepper flakes
1 sprig fresh rosemary
4 cod fillets (about 6 ounces each)

1. Heat oil over medium–high heat in large skillet. Add onion, and cook, stirring, until tender, 4 to 5 minutes. Add garlic, and cook 1 additional minute. Add wine, and continue cooking, stirring until liquid has evaporated.
2. Add tomatoes and their juice, water, orange zest, pepper flakes, and rosemary sprig. Simmer until thickened, about 15 minutes.
3. Nestle fish fillets in tomato mixture. Cover loosely, and cook on stovetop until fish is just cooked through. Serve

fillets topped with sauce. (Remove rosemary before serving.)

Nutritional information per serving: IF Rating: 304; Fat: 2 g; Carbohydrate: 16 g

Grilled Mahimahi with Mango Salsa

Makes 4 servings

Mango salsa makes a luscious accompaniment to a simple grilled or broiled fish. If fresh mangoes are not available, you can use mangoes from a jar, although there is some loss of nutrients and flavor.

    4 mahimahi steaks (about 6 ounces each)
    ½ cup plus 3 tablespoons fresh lime juice
    1 tablespoon olive oil
    2 mangoes, peeled, seeded, and diced (2 cups)
    2 cups diced tomatoes
    ½ cup diced red onion
    ⅓ cup (packed) chopped fresh cilantro
    1 tablespoon grated fresh gingerroot
    ½ teaspoon pepper
    ¼ teaspoon grated lime zest
    Salt to taste

1. Place fish in shallow dish. Place ½ cup lime juice in a small bowl, and add oil in thin stream, whisking briskly. Pour over fish, cover with plastic wrap, and refrigerate 20 minutes.
2. Combine mangoes, tomatoes, onion, cilantro, remaining lime juice, ginger, pepper, lime zest, and salt in medium bowl. Set aside for 10 minutes to allow flavors to mingle.
3. Grill or broil mahimahi until just cooked through. Serve with salsa.

Nutritional information per serving: IF Rating: 323; Fat: 7 g; Carbohydrate: 28 g

Grilled Steak and Tomato Salad

Makes 4 servings

Marinating the steak adds flavor and also tenderizes. But because most of the marinade is discarded, the ingredients are not included in the calculation of the IF Rating.

For the marinade:
- 1 clove garlic
- ¼ teaspoon hot sauce (Tabasco)
- 2 chopped shallots
- 1 teaspoon ground thyme
- ½ cup red wine vinegar
- 2 tablespoons Worcestershire sauce

For the salad:
- 12 ounces lean flank steak, trimmed
- 12 plum tomatoes, roasted
- 1 cup sliced red onion
- 1 red bell pepper, seeded and cut into thin strips
- 1 orange, peeled and sectioned
- 2 tablespoons chopped fresh rosemary
- 1 tablespoon orange juice
- 2 teaspoons olive oil
- 1 clove garlic, minced
- ½ teaspoon black pepper
- Salt to taste
- 3 cups arugula leaves

1. Prepare the marinade by combining garlic, hot sauce, shallots, thyme, vinegar, and Worcestershire sauce in a large ziplock freezer bag. Place steak in bag, and remove the air to maximize the amount of marinade touching the steak. Refrigerate 12 to 24 hours.
2. Heat oven to 350 degrees. Spread tomatoes on lightly oiled baking sheet, and roast in oven 90 minutes, turning after 45 minutes, until very soft and slightly blackened.

3. Remove the steak from the bag, and grill about 6 minutes per side or to preferred doneness. (If you prefer, you can broil the steak in your oven.)
4. Let steak sit 5 minutes, and then slice diagonally (across the grain) in thin slices.
5. Combine tomatoes, onion, red pepper, orange, rosemary, orange juice, olive oil, garlic, black pepper, and salt in a large bowl. Add arugula, and toss gently. Serve with sliced steak.

Nutritional information per serving: IF Rating: 183; Fat: 10 g; Carbohydrate: 15 g

Mango and Fennel Salad with Shrimp and Peanuts

Makes 4 servings

The salty crunch of peanuts and the slippery sweetness of mango add both flavor and texture.

24 large shrimp, peeled and deveined
2 mangoes, peeled, seeded, and thinly sliced
2 small fennel bulbs, thinly sliced
¼ cup (packed) chopped fresh cilantro
¼ cup fresh lime juice
2 tablespoons seasoned rice vinegar
½ teaspoon cayenne pepper
Salt to taste
⅓ cup chopped roasted peanuts

1. Boil shrimp until just cooked through, 3 to 4 minutes. Rinse shrimp with cold water to stop the cooking process, drain, and pat dry with paper towels.
2. Combine mangoes, fennel, cilantro, lime juice, vinegar, cayenne, and salt in a large bowl. Mix gently but thoroughly.
3. Divide salad onto serving plates. Arrange shrimp on top, and sprinkle with peanuts.

Nutritional information per serving: IF Rating: 64; Fat: 7 g; Carbohydrate: 25 g

Pulled Pork Tacos

Makes 4 servings

Long, slow cooking makes the meat melt-in-your-mouth tender. For an easy make-ahead meal, use your slow cooker.

1 pound pork shoulder roast
1 medium onion, chopped
2 tablespoons chili powder
1 tablespoon oregano
1 teaspoon cumin
8 corn taco shells
2 cups shredded lettuce
½ cup salsa
1 4-ounce can green chilies or jalapeños, chopped

1. Place pork, onion, chili powder, oregano, and cumin in large saucepan or Dutch oven. Add enough water to cover pork. Cover and bring to a boil over high heat. Reduce heat to medium low, and simmer 3 hours or until meat pulls apart easily with fork. (This step also can be done in a Crock-Pot or other slow cooker at low heat for 8 hours. Reduce water by half.)
2. Transfer meat to baking pan (reserving cooking liquid), and bake 20 minutes at 450 degrees until surface is brown and crisp.
3. While meat is baking, skim any fat from cooking liquid, and bring to a boil over high heat. Boil 20 minutes or until mixture reduces to about 1 cup.
4. Shred meat with two forks. Add meat to reduced cooking liquid. Cover and simmer 10 minutes, or until meat absorbs most of the liquid.

5. To assemble tacos, fill each taco shell with ¼ cup meat, ¼ cup lettuce, 2 tablespoons salsa, and 1 teaspoon chopped green chilies.

Nutritional information per serving: IF Rating: 122; Fat: 21 g; Carbohydrate: 25 g

Salmon with Roasted Pepper and Onion Compote

Makes 4 servings

Farm-raised salmon is very high in inflammatory compounds. Whenever possible, choose wild-caught salmon. This recipe was calculated using wild-caught coho salmon.

> 4 bell peppers, a mixture of red, green, yellow, and/or orange varieties
> 2 cups very thinly sliced red onion
> 3 cloves garlic, minced
> 2 tablespoons chopped fresh thyme (or 1 teaspoon dried)
> 4 salmon fillets (5 ounces each)
> ½ cup dry white wine (or nonalcoholic wine)
> 3 tablespoons fresh lemon juice
> ½ teaspoon black pepper

1. Place whole peppers on foil-lined baking sheet, and roast under broiler, 2 to 3 inches from heat. Turn frequently, and continue roasting until skins of peppers are blackened. Close foil around peppers to seal in steam, and allow peppers to cool 20 minutes or more. Peel, core, and seed peppers with a sharp knife, and slice into strips.
2. Preheat oven to 450 degrees. Combine onion, roasted peppers, garlic, and thyme in a 13″ × 9″ baking dish. Arrange salmon filets on top of vegetables, then add wine, lemon juice, and black pepper. Cover with foil.
3. Bake until fish is just cooked through, 18 to 20 minutes. Allow to rest 5 minutes before serving.

Nutritional information per serving: IF Rating: 875; Fat: 8 g; Carbohydrate: 11 g

Seafood Salad

Makes 6 servings

Shrimp, scallops, and mussels in a piquant Italian marinade . . . a seafood lover's feast.

    4 red bell peppers
    8 ounces medium shrimp, cooked, peeled, and deveined
    8 ounces bay scallops, steamed until barely cooked through
    ¾ cup sliced pitted green olives
    3 tablespoons fresh lemon juice
    4 teaspoons extra-virgin olive oil
    ½ cup (packed) fresh parsley leaves, chopped
    1 tablespoon dried marjoram
    2 garlic cloves, lightly crushed with the side of a knife
    18 mussels, well scrubbed and debearded

1. Place whole peppers on foil-lined baking sheet, and roast under broiler, 2 to 3 inches from heat. Turn frequently, and continue roasting until skins of peppers are blackened. Close foil around peppers to seal in steam, and allow peppers to cool 20 minutes or more. Peel, core, and seed peppers with a sharp knife, and slice into strips.
2. Combine shrimp, scallops, red peppers, olives, lemon juice, oil, parsley, marjoram, and garlic in large bowl.
3. Place mussels in large skillet, cover, and heat until they open. Discard any unopened shells. Remove meat from remaining shells, and toss with seafood mixture.
4. Refrigerate 2 hours or more before serving to allow flavors to blend. Bring salad to room temperature before serving.

Nutritional information per serving: IF Rating: 378; Fat: 6 g; Carbohydrate: 8 g

Southwestern Chicken Salad

Makes 4 servings

This alternative to traditional chicken salad explodes with flavor and color. You can make this salad spicier by adding extra jalapeños.

 2 cups diced cooked chicken breast
 2 cups cooked brown rice (about 1 cup uncooked)
 ½ ripe avocado, peeled, pitted, and diced
 2 cups diced tomato
 ½ red bell pepper, seeded and diced
 ½ cup diced onion
 ¼ cup (packed) fresh cilantro leaves, chopped
 1 jalapeño pepper, seeds and membranes removed, minced
 1 teaspoon cumin
 2 tablespoons fresh lime juice
 Hot sauce (Tabasco), to taste
 1 tablespoon canola oil

1. Combine chicken, rice, avocado, tomato, red pepper, onion, cilantro, and jalapeño in a large bowl.
2. Heat cumin in small saucepan over low heat until fragrant, about 1 minute. Transfer to small bowl, and add lime juice and hot sauce. Add oil in a thin stream, whisking briskly. Pour over chicken mixture, and toss.

Nutritional information per serving: IF Rating: 58; Fat: 11 g; Carbohydrate: 31 g

Salads

Asian Broccoli and Ginger Salad

Makes 4 servings

This salad will have the brightest color and flavor if the broccoli is blanched (cooked until just tender-crisp but still bright green).

Immediately after blanching, plunge the broccoli into cold water to assure that it does not get mushy.

    4 cups broccoli florets
    12 almonds, coarsely chopped
    1 tablespoon canola oil
    1 tablespoon soy sauce
    2 tablespoons lemon juice
    2 tablespoons seasoned rice wine vinegar
    2 teaspoons grated fresh gingerroot
    1 teaspoon grated lemon zest
    1 teaspoon pepper
    ½ clove garlic, minced
    3 scallions, thinly sliced

1. Using steamer basket, steam broccoli over boiling water until just tender, 5 to 7 minutes. Run broccoli under cool water to stop cooking, and drain.
2. Heat medium skillet over medium heat. Add almonds and ½ teaspoon of oil to hot pan. Cook, stirring frequently, 3 to 4 minutes, until nuts are just toasted. Add 2 teaspoons soy sauce, and stir until coated. Remove from heat and cool.
3. Whisk together lemon juice, vinegar, ginger, lemon zest, pepper, 1 teaspoon soy sauce, and garlic in medium bowl. Add 2½ teaspoons oil in a thin stream, whisking briskly.
4. Add broccoli and scallions to dressing, and toss to coat. Sprinkle with toasted nuts.

Nutritional information per serving: IF Rating: 266; Fat: 7 g; Carbohydrate: 14 g

Asparagus Salad Vinaigrette

Makes 4 servings

Although easy to make, this salad is elegant enough to serve to company.

24 asparagus spears, trimmed
3 tablespoons balsamic vinegar
1 clove garlic, minced
¼ teaspoon black pepper
1 teaspoon extra-virgin olive oil
1 red bell pepper, seeded and sliced thin
¼ cup thinly sliced red onion

1. Using a steamer basket, steam asparagus until just tender, about 5 minutes. Transfer to serving plate.
2. Combine vinegar, garlic, and black pepper in small bowl. Add oil in a thin stream, whisking briskly. Add red pepper and onion, and toss to coat.
3. Pour dressing over asparagus. Let stand 30 minutes before serving.

Nutritional information per serving: IF Rating: 174; Fat: 1 g; Carbohydrate: 7 g

Citrus Watercress Salad

Makes 4 servings

This salad pairs the peppery and slightly bitter flavor of watercress with sharp citrus. If watercress is not available, arugula and endive make good substitutes.

1 large orange, peeled and sectioned
1 grapefruit, peeled and sectioned
1 lime, peeled and sectioned
1 tablespoon extra-virgin olive oil
2 cloves garlic, minced
¼ teaspoon pepper
Salt to taste
4 cups watercress

1. Combine one-fourth of orange and one-fourth of grapefruit with lime, oil, garlic, pepper, and salt. Mix well, mashing fruit slightly with fork.

2. Add remaining fruit and watercress to bowl, tossing gently to combine.

Nutritional information per serving: IF Rating: 116; Fat: 4 g; Carbohydrate: 12 g

Curried Egg Salad

Makes 4 servings

This salad makes a good sandwich filling, or spread it on crackers or cucumber rounds for a savory appetizer or snack.

6 eggs
5 tablespoons reduced-fat mayonnaise
½ teaspoon dry or prepared mustard
2 teaspoons curry powder
¼ cup chopped black olives
¼ cup diced celery
¼ cup diced onion

1. To hard–boil eggs, place in a saucepan, and cover with cool water. Bring to a boil over medium heat, reduce heat to low, and simmer 5 minutes. Remove from heat, and cover, allowing to rest until water is lukewarm. Drain and refrigerate until needed.
2. Peel eggs (discarding two yolks), and place in large bowl. Mash eggs with back of a fork.
3. In small bowl, mix mayonnaise, mustard, and curry powder. Add to eggs, along with olives, celery, and onion. Mix thoroughly.

Nutritional information per serving: IF Rating: 161; Fat: 13 g; Carbohydrate: 4 g

Rosemary Sweet Potato Salad

Makes 4 servings

Try serving this colorful salad at your next picnic or barbeque for a welcome change from standard potato salad.

1½ pounds sweet potatoes
2 tablespoons raisins or currants
½ cup hot water
1 red bell pepper, seeded and thinly sliced
½ cup thinly sliced red onion
¼ cup chopped fresh parsley
1 teaspoon lemon zest
2 tablespoons lemon juice
2 teaspoons chopped fresh rosemary (or ½ teaspoon dried)
2 tablespoons canola oil
¼ cup sliced almonds

1. Pierce sweet potatoes with a fork, and bake at 400 degrees until soft, about 45 minutes. When cool enough to handle, peel and cube.
2. Soak raisins or currants in hot water 10 minutes, and drain well.
3. Combine sweet potatoes, red pepper, onion, parsley, lemon zest, and raisins or currants in large bowl.
4. Combine lemon juice and rosemary in small bowl. Add oil in a thin stream, whisking briskly. Pour over potato mixture, and toss gently to coat.
5. Toast almonds in dry skillet over medium heat until just toasted, about 5 minutes. Sprinkle over salad.

Nutritional information per serving: IF Rating: 289; Fat: 10 g; Carbohydrate: 25 g

Spinach and Arugula Salad with Raspberry Vinaigrette

Makes 4 servings

You can use spinach, arugula, or a combination in this salad.

    4 cups (packed) spinach and arugula
    2 strips bacon, chopped
    ¼ cup balsamic vinegar
    ¼ teaspoon pepper
    Salt to taste
    4 teaspoons extra-virgin olive oil
    1 cup fresh raspberries
    ½ cup thinly sliced red onion

1. Rinse greens thoroughly, and remove tough stems. Dry on paper towels, or use a salad spinner.
2. Cook bacon over medium heat until crisp, 8 to 10 minutes. Drain on paper towels.
3. Whisk together vinegar, pepper, and salt in small bowl. Add oil in a thin stream, whisking briskly. Add raspberries, crushing gently with a fork.
4. Divide greens onto serving plates. Drizzle with dressing, and top with onion and bacon.

Nutritional information per serving: IF Rating: 241; Fat: 7 g; Carbohydrate: 9 g

Sweet and Spicy Carrot and Apple Salad

Makes 4 servings

The toasty flavor of cumin and a dash of hot sauce give a decidedly different twist to this Waldorf-type salad.

    1 teaspoon cumin
    1 tablespoon fresh lime juice
    ¼ teaspoon salt

3 dashes Tabasco or other hot sauce
1 tablespoon canola oil
2 cups grated carrots
2 green apples, cored and grated
3 tablespoons chopped fresh cilantro
¼ cup raisins

1. Heat cumin in small skillet over low heat just until fragrant, about 1 minute. Remove from heat.
2. Whisk together cumin, lime juice, salt, and hot sauce in small bowl. Add oil to liquid in a thin stream, whisking briskly.
3. Combine carrots, apples, cilantro, and raisins in large bowl. Add dressing, and toss to coat.

Nutritional information per serving: IF Rating: 36; Fat: 4 g; Carbohydrate: 22 g

Desserts

Chilled Melon Soup

Makes 4 servings

This "soup" makes a quick and refreshing summer dessert. It's a great way to use a melon that is slightly underripe or lacking in flavor.

6 cups cubed cantaloupe
½ cup (packed) fresh mint leaves, chopped
2 tablespoons freshly squeezed lime juice
½ to 1 tablespoon honey (if needed to sweeten)

1. Place all ingredients in blender or food processor, and blend until smooth. Adjust flavor by adding honey to sweeten or additional lime juice to intensify the flavor.
2. Serve immediately in chilled cups, garnished with fresh mint leaves.

Nutritional information per serving: IF Rating: 25; Fat: 0 g; Carbohydrate: 5 g

Raspberry-Orange Frozen Yogurt

Makes 4 servings

This creamy frozen dessert is easy to make, even if you don't have a commercial ice cream maker. If you do have one, follow steps 1 and 2, and then follow the instructions for your ice cream maker.

> 1 cup orange juice
> ¼ cup Splenda (sucralose) or sugar
> 1 envelope plain gelatin
> 1 12-ounce package frozen raspberries, thawed
> 1⅓ cups plain nonfat yogurt
> 2 teaspoons grated orange zest

1. Combine orange juice, Splenda or sugar, and gelatin in small saucepan. Heat over very low heat, stirring, until sweetener and gelatin have dissolved. Cool to room temperature.
2. Add raspberries, yogurt, and orange zest to gelatin mixture. Whisk well to combine.
3. Transfer mixture to shallow metal baking pan, and freeze 2 hours, then whisk again. Freeze until solid, 3 to 4 hours. Before serving, transfer mixture to food processor. Process until very smooth, about 1 minute.

Nutritional information per serving (using Splenda): IF Rating: −8; Fat: 2 g; Carbohydrate: 26 g

Spicy Poached Fruit

Makes 4 servings

This unusual combination of winter fruits with hot pepper and ginger makes a good winter dessert or topping for ice cream or

131

cake. You can use other dried fruits, such as cherries or cranberries, in place of apricots.

1 cup orange juice
¼ cup lemon juice
½ cup water
1 cinnamon stick
5 cloves
2 ¼-inch slices peeled fresh gingerroot
1 dried hot red pepper
2 pears, peeled, cored, and cubed
1 tart apple, peeled, cored, and cubed
6 ounces (1 cup) chopped dried apricots or other dried fruits

1. Combine orange and lemon juices, water, cinnamon, cloves, ginger, and pepper in medium saucepan. Bring to a boil, and reduce heat to low. Simmer 10 minutes.
2. Add pears, apple, and dried fruits to saucepan. Simmer until fruit is tender, about 15 minutes.
3. Remove fruit from liquid. Strain liquid and return it to clean pan. Boil liquid until it is reduced to a syrupy consistency, 6 to 8 minutes. Pour over fruit.

Nutritional information per serving: IF Rating: 9; Fat: 1 g; Carbohydrate: 10 g

Sweet Potato Custard

Makes 4 servings

Leftover sweet potatoes? Use them to make this creamy comfort food, a lighter version of the heavy custard found in southern-style sweet potato pie. To fill a pie shell, double the recipe.

4 medium sweet potatoes
2 tablespoons light brown sugar
¼ cup orange juice

4 teaspoons lemon juice
¾ cup plain low-fat yogurt
Freshly grated nutmeg (optional)

1. Pierce skins of sweet potatoes with a fork, and bake at 400 degrees until soft, about 45 minutes. (Or use leftover cooked sweet potatoes.)
2. Remove pulp from skin, and combine pulp with sugar and orange and lemon juices in medium bowl. Beat with electric mixer or whisk until sugar is dissolved and potatoes are light. Fold in yogurt.
3. Transfer mixture to individual serving cups, and refrigerate until cold. Garnish with freshly grated nutmeg, if desired.

Nutritional information per serving: IF Rating: 160; Fat: 0 g; Carbohydrate: 38 g

Tropical Fruit Salad

Makes 4 servings

This refreshing salad is an antioxidant powerhouse, containing large amounts of vitamin A as well as anti–inflammatory ginger.

1 cup cubed cantaloupe
1 papaya, peeled, seeded, and cubed
2 kiwifruit, peeled and sliced
1 cup fresh pineapple chunks
1 lime, peeled and sectioned
½ teaspoon grated fresh gingerroot
1 tablespoon chopped fresh mint leaves

1. Combine all ingredients, and toss gently. Serve immediately.

Nutritional information per serving: IF Rating: 23; Fat: 0 g; Carbohydrate: 19 g

CHAPTER 4

The IF Rating Tables

How to Use the Tables

This chapter includes the complete IF Rating tables, which list the IF Ratings, along with fat and carbohydrate grams, for over 1,600 foods. The A-to-Z table, which begins on page 137, allows you to quickly locate individual foods by name and quantity. You'll find this table helpful when evaluating meals and recipes. (Worksheets for calculating your meal plans and recipes, along with target values for the Inflammation-Free Diet, appear in Chapter 3.)

The second table, which begins on page 218, organizes the listings by category and rates food in standardized serving sizes. Consult this listing to compare the values for similar foods, such as various cuts of meat or types of breakfast cereal. The IF Ratings by Category table allows you to select the most anti-inflammatory foods for your meal plans and to find alternatives for inflammatory foods that you wish to avoid or limit. To see an overview of the best (and worst) foods in each category, see Table 2.2 on page 35.

Key to IF Rating Tables

Abbreviations Used in IF Rating Tables
tsp. = teaspoon
tbsp. = tablespoon
oz. = ounce
lb. = pound

Serving Size Equivalents
1 piece of sashimi = 1 ounce
1 medium slice processed cheese or meat = 1 ounce
1-ounce serving of cheese = size of a pair of dice
1-ounce serving of nuts = 1 small handful
3-ounce serving of meat = size of a deck of cards
½ cup vegetables or grains = size of an ice cream scoop

Units of Measure and Conversions
1 tablespoon = 3 teaspoons = 15 milliliters
1 ounce (fluid) = 2 tablespoons = 30 milliliters
8 ounces (fluid) = 1 cup = 240 milliliters
12 ounces (fluid) = soda can or bottle = 360 milliliters
16 ounces = 1 pound = 2.2 kilograms

Cooking Methods
baked/roasted = cooked slowly in dry, indirect heat
boiled/poached = cooked quickly in boiling water
braised/simmered/stewed = cooked slowly in liquid
broiled/grilled = cooked quickly over/under direct heat source
fried = cooked quickly in hot oil
steamed = cooked over (but not in) boiling water

TABLE 4.1 IF Ratings: A to Z

Food	Amount	IF Rating	Fat (g)	Carb (g)
Abalone, raw	1 oz.	20	0	2
Cherries, acerola	10 cherries	340	0	4
Cherries, acerola	1 cup, pitted	680	0	8
Alfalfa sprouts	½ cup	4	0	1
All-Bran, Extra Fiber	1 serving (½ cup)	4	1	23
All-Bran Bran Buds	1 serving (⅓ cup)	50	1	24
Allspice, ground	1 tsp.	0	0	1
Almond butter	2 tbsp.	82	19	7
Almond oil	1 tbsp.	62	14	0
Almond oil	½ cup	496	108	0
Almonds, dry-roasted	¼ cup	57	15	5
Almonds, dry-roasted	4 oz.	227	60	22
Almonds, oil-roasted	¼ cup	56	16	5
Almonds, oil-roasted	4 oz.	225	63	20
Almonds, raw	¼ cup	54	14	6
Almonds, raw	4 oz.	216	57	22
Almonds, raw, blanched	¼ cup	54	14	6
Almonds, raw, blanched	1 cup, slivered	205	55	21
Almonds, raw, blanched	4 oz.	217	57	23
Ama-ebi (raw shrimp)	1 large	13	0	0
American cheese, pasteurized	1 oz.	−23	9	0
Anago (saltwater eel)	1 oz.	15	4	0
Anchovy, canned in oil	1 fillet	42	0	0
Anchovies, canned in oil	1 oz.	297	3	0

TABLE 4.1 IF Ratings: A to Z, *continued*

Food	Amount	IF Rating	Fat (g)	Carb (g)
Anchovies, canned in oil	2-oz. can	594	6	0
Angel food cake	1 piece	−183	0	29
Aniseed	1 tsp.	2	0	7
Apple	1 cup, sliced	−45	0	14
Apple	1 medium	−62	1	21
Apple, dried	1 ring	−10	0	4
Apple, dried	1 cup	−137	0	56
Apple juice, canned or bottled	8 oz.	−72	0	29
Apple juice, from concentrate	8 oz.	−84	0	28
Apricot, canned (light syrup)	2 halves	−60	0	13
Apricot, dried	2 halves	−8	0	4
Apricot, dried	1 cup	−148	0	74
Apricot, fresh	1 fruit	−7	0	4
Apricot, fresh	1 cup, sliced	−34	1	18
Apricot kernel oil	1 tbsp.	33	13	0
Apricot kernel oil	½ cup	268	109	0
Arctic char (farmed)	3 oz.	622	10	0
Artichoke, boiled	1 artichoke	25	0	13
Artichoke, Jerusalem, raw	½ cup, sliced	5	0	15
Artichoke hearts	½ cup	17	0	9
Artichoke hearts, frozen	10-oz. package	25	0	13
Arugula, raw	1 cup (loosely packed)	16	0	0
Arugula, raw	1 lb.	240	0	0
Asparagus, boiled	6 spears	55	0	4

Food	Amount	IF Rating	Fat (g)	Carb (g)
Asparagus, canned	6 spears	53	0	3
Asparagus, frozen	6 spears	87	0	4
Aubergine, cooked	½ cup, cubed	2	0	4
Avocado, raw	½ cup, mashed	105	17	10
Avocado, raw	1 fruit	184	29	17
Avocado oil	1 tbsp.	66	14	0
Avocado oil	½ cup	527	109	0
Awabi (raw abalone)	1 oz.	20	0	2
Bacon, Canadian-style,† grilled	2 slices	17	4	1
Bacon, Canadian-style,† grilled	6 oz. (uncooked weight)	50	12	3
Bacon,† pan-fried	2 strips	−8	7	0
Bacon,† pan-fried	1 lb. (uncooked weight)	−138	121	0
Bacon, vegetarian	2 strips	−12	6	2
Bagel, plain	1 bagel	−186	1	30
Baked beans	½ cup	−65	0	27
Baked beans	16-oz. can	−227	2	95
Baked beans, with pork	½ cup	−52	1	24
Baked beans, with pork	16-oz. can	−185	4	83
Baking powder, double-acting	1 tsp.	0	0	1
Baking soda	1 tsp.	0	0	0

*High in mercury; eat only occasionally.

**Very high in mercury; avoid eating.

†May contain nitrates and nitrites; eat only occasionally.

‡Associated with health risks and/or adverse reactions.

TABLE 4.1 IF Ratings: A to Z, *continued*

Food	Amount	IF Rating	Fat (g)	Carb (g)
Bamboo shoots, canned	½ cup, sliced	1	0	1
Banana	1 medium	−118	1	28
Banana	1 cup, sliced	−150	1	35
Banana	1 cup, mashed	−225	1	53
Banana bread	1 slice	−151	6	33
Banana pepper, hot, pickled	1 pepper	66	0	1
Banana pepper, raw	1 pepper	65	0	2
Barley, pearled	1 cup, cooked	−78	1	44
Barley, pearled	½ cup, uncooked	−78	1	44
Basil, dried	1 tsp.	8	0	1
Basil, fresh	2 tbsp.	9	0	0
Bass, freshwater, baked or grilled	3 oz.	167	4	0
Bass, sea,* baked or grilled	3 oz.	331	2	0
Bass, striped,* baked or grilled	3 oz.	421	3	0
Bay leaf, dried	1 tsp.	0	0	0
Bean sprouts	½ cup	8	0	3
Beef bouillon, dehydrated	1 cube	1	0	1
Beef breakfast strips,† grilled	2 strips	23	12	0
Beef brisket, braised	3 oz.	17	27	0
Beef brisket, braised	1 lb. (uncooked weight)	72	114	0
Beef brisket, braised, lean portions only	3 oz.	10	11	0
Beef broth/bouillon, canned	8 oz.	2	1	0

Food	Amount	IF Rating	Fat (g)	Carb (g)
Beef broth/bouillon, canned	8 oz.	2	1	0
Beef heart, simmered or braised	3 oz.	−155	4	0
Beef heart, simmered or braised	1 lb. (uncooked weight)	−775	20	1
Beef jerky†	1 oz.	11	1	1
Beef kidney, simmered or braised	3 oz.	−131	4	0
Beef kidney, simmered or braised	1 lb. (uncooked weight)	−653	20	0
Beef liver, braised	3 oz.	−6	4	3
Beef liver, braised	1 lb. (uncooked weight)	−29	21	15
Beef liver, pan-fried	3 oz.	−12	4	4
Beef liver, pan-fried	1 lb. (uncooked weight)	−60	20	22
Beef lungs, braised	3 oz.	−130	3	0
Beef lungs, braised	1 lb. (uncooked weight)	−650	16	0
Beef shanks, simmered	3 oz.	27	12	0
Beef shanks, simmered	1 lb. (uncooked weight)	40	18	0

*High in mercury; eat only occasionally.

**Very high in mercury; avoid eating.

†May contain nitrates and nitrites; eat only occasionally.

‡Associated with health risks and/or adverse reactions.

TABLE 4.1 IF Ratings: A to Z, *continued*

Food	Amount	IF Rating	Fat (g)	Carb (g)
Beef shanks, simmered, lean portions only	3 oz.	30	5	0
Beet greens, raw	1 cup, chopped	68	0	2
Beets, canned	½ cup, sliced	−23	0	6
Belgian endive	1 cup	8	0	4
Bibb lettuce	1 cup, shredded	22	0	1
Bison, roasted	3 oz.	−20	2	0
Bison, roasted	1 lb. (uncooked weight)	−60	6	0
Black bean soup	1 cup	−79	2	20
Black bean soup	16-oz. can	−143	4	36
Black beans, boiled	1 cup	−22	0	40
Black pepper, ground	1 tsp.	1	0	1
Black-eyed peas, boiled	1 cup	−24	0	36
Blue cheese	1 oz.	−22	8	1
Blue cheese	1 cup, crumbled	−105	39	3
Blue cheese dressing	2 tbsp.	−32	16	2
Blue cheese dressing, low-fat	2 tbsp.	−6	2	0
Blueberries, fresh	1 cup	−22	0	20
Blueberries, fresh	1 pint	−63	1	58
Blueberries, frozen	1 cup	−21	1	19
Bluefin tuna,* baked or grilled	3 oz.	591	5	0
Bluefin tuna,* raw	1 oz.	154	1	0
Bluefish,* baked or grilled	3 oz.	439	5	0
Boar, roasted	3 oz.	−70	4	0

Food	Amount	IF Rating	Fat (g)	Carb (g)
Boar, roasted	1 lb. (uncooked weight)	−210	11	0
Bok choy, raw	1 cup, shredded	67	0	2
Bologna, beef†	1 oz.	9	8	1
Bologna, low-fat†	1 oz.	8	6	1
Bologna, pork†	1 oz.	8	5	0
Bologna, turkey†	1 oz.	−15	4	1
Bonito (raw skipjack tuna)	1 oz.	38	0	0
Borage, raw	1 cup, chopped	16	1	3
Boston lettuce	1 cup, shredded	43	0	1
Bottom round (beef), braised	3 oz.	17	10	0
Bottom round (beef), braised	1 lb. (uncooked weight)	54	31	0
Bottom round (beef), braised, lean portions only	3 oz.	5	7	0
Bottom round (beef), roasted	3 oz.	19	10	0
Bottom round (beef), roasted	1 lb. (uncooked weight)	61	32	0
Bottom round (beef), roasted, lean portions only	3 oz.	3	6	0
Brain (beef), simmered or braised	3 oz.	−357	9	0

*High in mercury; eat only occasionally.

**Very high in mercury; avoid eating.

†May contain nitrates and nitrites; eat only occasionally.

‡Associated with health risks and/or adverse reactions.

TABLE 4.1 IF Ratings: A to Z, *continued*

Food	Amount	IF Rating	Fat (g)	Carb (g)
Bran flakes	1 serving (¾ cup)	9	1	23
Bratwurst†	1 sausage	−51	25	2
Braunschweiger†	1 oz.	28	8	1
Brazil nuts, raw	¼ cup	175	19	3
Brazil nuts, raw	4 oz.	698	75	14
Bread, French	1 slice	−261	2	33
Bread, gluten-free	1 slice	−133	6	19
Bread, mixed-grain	1 slice	−33	1	12
Bread, pumpernickel	1 slice	−42	1	15
Bread, rye	1 slice	−63	1	15
Bread, sourdough	1 slice	−261	2	33
Bread, Vienna	1 slice	−261	2	33
Bread, white	1 slice	−77	1	13
Bread, whole wheat	1 slice	−72	1	13
Breakfast patty, vegetarian	1 patty	−6	3	4
Brick cheese	1 oz.	−21	8	1
Brick cheese	1 cup, shredded	−83	34	3
Brick cheese	1 cup, melted	−165	66	6
Brie	1 oz.	−16	8	0
Brie	1 cup, melted	−141	66	1
Broad beans, boiled	1 cup	−148	0	34
Broccoli, boiled	½ cup	73	0	4
Broccoli, frozen	½ cup	55	0	5
Broccoli, raw	1 spear	17	0	2
Broccoli, raw	½ cup, diced	25	0	2

Food	Amount	IF Rating	Fat (g)	Carb (g)
Brown rice, cooked	½ cup	−103	1	22
Brown rice, uncooked	½ cup	−206	2	44
Brown sugar	½ cup, packed	−746	0	110
Brussels sprouts, boiled	½ cup	61	0	6
Brussels sprouts, frozen	½ cup	83	0	8
Burger, vegetarian	1 patty	49	4	7
Burger crumbles, vegetarian	3 oz.	−6	9	5
Butter	1 pat (1 tsp.)	−15	4	0
Butter	1 tbsp.	−45	12	0
Butter	1 stick (¼ lb.)	−358	92	0
Butter	1 cup	−716	183	0
Butter, whipped	1 tbsp.	−25	8	0
Butter beans, boiled or canned	1 cup	−38	0	40
Butter flavoring, powdered	1 tsp.	0	0	1
Butter oil	1 tbsp.	−42	13	0
Butterhead lettuce	1 cup, shredded	43	0	1
Cabbage, green, boiled	½ cup, shredded	18	0	3
Cabbage, green, raw	1 cup, shredded	26	0	4
Cabbage, green, raw	1 small head	260	0	40
Cabbage, napa, boiled	½ cup, shredded	14	0	1

*High in mercury; eat only occasionally.

**Very high in mercury; avoid eating.

†May contain nitrates and nitrites; eat only occasionally.

‡Associated with health risks and/or adverse reactions.

TABLE 4.1 IF Ratings: A to Z, *continued*

Food	Amount	IF Rating	Fat (g)	Carb (g)
Cabbage, red, boiled	½ cup, shredded	17	0	5
Cabbage, red, raw	1 cup, shredded	36	0	5
Cabbage, red, raw	1 small head	270	0	37
Cabbage, savoy, boiled	½ cup, shredded	13	0	4
Cabbage, savoy, raw	1 cup, shredded	40	0	4
Cake, angel food	1 piece	−183	0	29
Cake, chocolate, with chocolate frosting	1 piece	−115	11	35
Cake, yellow, with vanilla frosting	1 piece	−163	9	38
Camembert	1 oz.	−14	7	0
Canola oil	1 tbsp.	72	14	0
Canola oil	½ cup	580	109	0
Cantaloupe	1 cup	21	0	11
Capers	1 tbsp.	1	0	0
Caraway seed	1 tbsp.	6	1	3
Cardamom, ground	1 tsp.	1	0	1
Caribou, roasted	3 oz.	−99	4	0
Caribou, roasted	1 lb. (uncooked weight)	−297	11	0
Carp, baked or grilled	3 oz.	41	6	0
Carrot juice	8 oz.	396	0	22
Carrots, canned	½ cup, sliced	72	0	4
Carrots, frozen	½ cup, sliced	112	0	6

Food	Amount	IF Rating	Fat (g)	Carb (g)
Carrots, raw	½ cup, grated	54	0	5
Carrots, raw	½ cup, sliced	60	0	6
Carrots, raw	1 large carrot	71	0	7
Carrots, raw	8 baby carrots	93	0	7
Cashews, dry-roasted	¼ cup	26	13	9
Cashews, dry-roasted	4 oz.	105	53	37
Cashews, oil-roasted	¼ cup	23	14	9
Cashews, oil-roasted	4 oz.	91	54	34
Catfish (farmed), baked or grilled	3 oz.	59	7	0
Catfish (wild), baked or grilled	3 oz.	46	2	0
Cauliflower, boiled	½ cup	19	0	3
Cauliflower, raw	½ cup	15	0	2
Caviar, black and red	1 tbsp.	421	3	1
Cayenne, ground	1 tsp.	509	0	1
Celery, boiled	1 cup, diced	34	0	6
Celery, raw	1 medium stalk	3	0	1
Celery, raw	½ cup, diced	10	0	2
Celery seed	1 tbsp.	10	2	3
Chamomile tea	8 oz.	1	0	0
Chard, raw	1 cup, chopped	94	0	1
Cheddar cheese	1 oz.	−26	9	0

*High in mercury; eat only occasionally.

**Very high in mercury; avoid eating.

†May contain nitrates and nitrites; eat only occasionally.

‡Associated with health risks and/or adverse reactions.

TABLE 4.1 IF Ratings: A to Z, *continued*

Food	Amount	IF Rating	Fat (g)	Carb (g)
Cheddar cheese	1 cup, shredded	−103	37	1
Cheddar cheese	1 cup, melted	−224	82	3
Cheddar cheese, low-fat	1 oz.	−1	3	1
Cheddar cheese, low-fat	1 cup, shredded	−2	8	2
Cheddar cheese, low-fat	1 cup, melted	−4	14	4
Cheerios	1 serving (1 cup)	−81	2	23
Cheese dog†	1 sausage	16	12	1
Cheese food, spreadable cold pack	2 tbsp.	−16	7	2
Cherries, sweet	10 cherries	−16	0	10
Cherries	1 cup, unpitted	−29	0	19
Cherries	1 cup, pitted	−38	1	24
Cherry pepper, hot, pickled	1 pepper	33	0	1
Cherry tomatoes	1 cup	15	0	6
Chervil, dried	1 tsp.	1	0	0
Chicken bouillon, dehydrated	1 cube	0	1	1
Chicken breast, fried, meat only	1 breast	−50	8	1
Chicken breast, roasted, meat only	3 oz.	−14	3	0
Chicken breast, roasted, meat only	1 cup, diced	−26	5	0
Chicken breast, roasted, with skin	1 breast	−14	5	0
Chicken breast, roasted, with skin	3 oz.	−23	7	0

Food	Amount	IF Rating	Fat (g)	Carb (g)
Chicken breast, stewed, meat only	1 cup, diced	−23	4	0
Chicken breast, stewed, with skin	3 oz.	−21	6	0
Chicken broth	8 oz.	2	1	1
Chicken drumstick, battered and fried, with skin	1 drumstick	−50	11	6
Chicken drumstick, roasted, with skin	1 drumstick	−35	6	0
Chicken drumstick, stewed, with skin	1 drumstick	−35	6	0
Chicken giblets, simmered	1 cup, diced	−159	8	1
Chicken liver pâté	1 oz.	18	8	0
Chicken livers	3 oz.	−258	6	1
Chicken spread, canned	2 oz.	5	10	2
Chicken stock	8 oz.	2	1	1
Chicken thigh, battered and fried, with skin	1 thigh	−46	9	5
Chicken thigh, fried, meat only	1 thigh	−56	6	1
Chicken thigh, roasted, meat only	1 cup, diced	−136	14	0
Chicken thigh, roasted, with skin	1 thigh	−53	10	0
Chicken thigh, simmered, meat only	1 thigh	−40	5	0
Chicken thigh, stewed, with skin	1 thigh	−55	10	0

*High in mercury; eat only occasionally.

**Very high in mercury; avoid eating.

†May contain nitrates and nitrites; eat only occasionally.

‡Associated with health risks and/or adverse reactions.

TABLE 4.1 IF Ratings: A to Z, *continued*

Food	Amount	IF Rating	Fat (g)	Carb (g)
Chicken thigh, stewed, meat only	1 cup, diced	−117	13	0
Chicken wing, fried	1 wing	−24	2	0
Chick-peas, boiled	½ cup	−39	2	22
Chili pepper, dried	1 pepper	252	0	0
Chili pepper, red, canned	½ cup, chopped	488	0	3
Chili pepper, red, raw	1 pepper	286	0	4
Chili powder	1 tbsp.	230	0	4
Chinese cabbage, boiled	½ cup, shredded	11	0	1
Chinese cabbage, raw	1 cup, shredded	67	0	2
Chitterlings (pork), simmered	3 oz.	−124	17	0
Chives, dried	1 tbsp.	1	0	0
Chives, fresh	2 tbsp.	24	0	0
Chocolate bar (milk chocolate)	1 miniature bar	−19	2	4
Chocolate bar (milk chocolate)	1 bar	−156	13	26
Chocolate cake with chocolate frosting	1 piece	−115	11	35
Chocolate chips	1 cup	−598	52	99
Chocolate kisses	10 kisses	−166	14	28
Chocolate milk	1 cup	−116	8	26
Chocolate milk, low-fat	1 cup	−80	3	26
Chocolate milk powder	2 tbsp. (to make 1 cup)	−101	1	19
Chorizo†	1 sausage	−19	23	1

Food	Amount	IF Rating	Fat (g)	Carb (g)
Chum, baked or grilled	3 oz.	331	4	0
Chum, canned	3 oz.	447	5	0
Cider vinegar	1 tbsp.	0	0	0
Cilantro, dried	1 tbsp.	12	0	1
Cilantro, fresh	¼ cup	7	0	0
Cinnamon, ground	1 tsp.	1	0	2
Cisco, smoked	3 oz.	447	10	0
Clam, raw	1 medium	11	0	0
Clam, raw	1 large	20	0	1
Clams, canned	1 cup, drained	338	3	8
Clams, steamed	3 oz. (9 small)	190	2	4
Cloves, ground	1 tsp.	1	0	1
Club soda	12 oz.	1	0	0
Coca-Cola Classic	12 oz.	−215	0	41
Cocoa butter oil	1 tbsp.	−39	14	0
Cocoa butter oil	½ cup	−314	109	0
Cocoa Krispies	1 serving (¾ cup)	−149	1	27
Coconut oil	1 tbsp.	−112	14	0
Coconut oil	½ cup	−899	109	0
Cod, Atlantic, baked or grilled	3 oz.	71	1	0
Cod, Atlantic, dried and salted	3 oz.	222	2	0

*High in mercury; eat only occasionally.

**Very high in mercury; avoid eating.

†May contain nitrates and nitrites; eat only occasionally.

‡Associated with health risks and/or adverse reactions.

TABLE 4.1 IF Ratings: A to Z, *continued*

Food	Amount	IF Rating	Fat (g)	Carb (g)
Cod, Pacific, baked or grilled	3 oz.	129	1	0
Cod liver oil	1 tbsp.	1,028	14	0
Coffee, brewed	8 oz.	0	0	1
Coffee, brewed, decaf	8 oz.	0	0	0
Coffee, instant	8 oz.	0	0	1
Coffee, instant, decaf	8 oz.	0	0	1
Coffee, instant, with chicory	8 oz.	0	0	1
Coffee substitute (grain-based)	8 oz.	1	0	2
Coho (farmed), baked or grilled	3 oz.	455	7	0
Coho (wild), poached	3 oz.	451	6	0
Colby cheese	1 oz.	−23	9	1
Colby cheese	1 cup, shredded	−92	36	3
Colby cheese	1 cup, melted	−184	72	6
Colby cheese, low-fat	1 oz.	−1	3	1
Colby cheese, low-fat	1 cup, shredded	−2	8	2
Colby cheese, low-fat	1 cup, melted	−4	14	4
Collard greens, boiled	½ cup, chopped	205	0	5
Collard greens, raw	1 cup, chopped	83	0	2
Coriander seed	1 tbsp.	8	1	3
Corn, frozen	½ cup	−62	1	17
Corn, on cob, boiled	1 ear	−111	1	22
Corn, white, canned	½ cup, drained	−72	1	15

Food	Amount	IF Rating	Fat (g)	Carb (g)
Corn, yellow, canned	½ cup, drained	−108	1	32
Corn Chex	1 serving (1 cup)	−151	0	26
Corn chips	1 oz.	−116	9	16
Corn chips	8-oz. bag	−928	75	129
Cornflakes	1 serving (1 cup)	−182	0	24
Corn oil	1 tbsp.	−49	14	0
Corn oil	½ cup	−395	109	0
Corn pasta, cooked	½ cup	−124	1	20
Corn syrup	1 tbsp.	−98	0	14
Corn syrup	¼ cup	−396	0	58
Corn tortilla	6″ tortilla	−48	1	11
Corned beef, canned	3 oz.	41	13	0
Corned beef brisket	3 oz.	42	11	0
Corned beef brisket	1 lb.	228	61	2
Cornish game hen, roasted	3 oz.	−115	3	0
Cornish game hen, roasted	1 bird	−298	9	0
Cornmeal, yellow	½ cup	−279	2	47
Cottage cheese, 1% fat	½ cup	9	1	3
Cottage cheese, 1% fat	16 oz.	36	5	12
Cottage cheese, 2% fat	½ cup	7	2	4
Cottage cheese, 2% fat	16 oz.	28	8	16

*High in mercury; eat only occasionally.

**Very high in mercury; avoid eating.

†May contain nitrates and nitrites; eat only occasionally.

‡Associated with health risks and/or adverse reactions.

TABLE 4.1 IF Ratings: A to Z, *continued*

Food	Amount	IF Rating	Fat (g)	Carb (g)
Cottage cheese, creamed	½ cup	−4	5	3
Cottage cheese, creamed	16 oz.	−16	20	12
Cottage cheese, nonfat	½ cup	14	0	2
Cottage cheese, nonfat	16 oz.	56	0	8
Cottonseed oil	1 tbsp.	−92	14	0
Cottonseed oil	½ cup	−735	109	0
Courgette, boiled	½ cup, sliced	19	0	4
Courgette, raw	1 cup, chopped	22	0	4
Courgette, raw	1 medium	33	0	6
Couscous, cooked	½ cup	−91	0	18
Crab, Alaska king, steamed or boiled	3 oz.	60	1	0
Crab, Alaska king, steamed or boiled	1 leg	121	1	0
Crab, blue, canned	3 oz.	127	1	0
Crab, blue, canned	1 cup	204	2	0
Crab, blue, steamed or boiled	3 oz.	171	1	0
Crab, blue, steamed or boiled	1 cup	276	2	0
Crab, imitation	3 oz.	238	1	9
Crab, imitation	1 cup	357	2	13
Crab, queen or snow, steamed or boiled	3 oz.	205	1	0
Crab, queen or snow, steamed or boiled	1 cup	307	2	0
Cranberry juice cocktail	8 oz.	−150	0	36
Crayfish (farmed), steamed or boiled	3 oz.	47	1	0

Food	Amount	IF Rating	Fat (g)	Carb (g)
Crayfish (wild), steamed or boiled	3 oz.	55	1	0
Cream, half-and-half	1 tbsp.	−5	2	1
Cream, half-and-half	1 oz.	−10	3	1
Cream, half-and-half	1 cup	−40	14	5
Cream, heavy (whipping)	1 tbsp.	−18	6	0
Cream, heavy (whipping)	1 oz.	−35	11	1
Cream, heavy (whipping)	1 cup	−280	88	8
Cream, light (table)	1 tbsp.	−15	5	0
Cream, light (table)	1 oz.	−30	9	1
Cream, light (table)	1 cup	−240	75	7
Cream cheese	2 tbsp.	−31	10	1
Cream cheese	1 small package (3 oz.)	−95	30	2
Cream cheese	8-oz. brick	−253	79	6
Cream cheese, nonfat	2 tbsp.	2	0	1
Cream cheese, nonfat	1 small package (3 oz.)	7	1	5
Cream cheese, nonfat	8-oz. brick	19	3	13
Cream cheese, reduced-fat	2 tbsp.	−21	7	1
Cream cheese, reduced-fat	1 small package (3 oz.)	−63	20	3
Cream cheese, reduced-fat	8-oz. brick	−167	53	7
Cream of tartar	½ tsp.	0	0	1

*High in mercury; eat only occasionally.

**Very high in mercury; avoid eating.

†May contain nitrates and nitrites; eat only occasionally.

‡Associated with health risks and/or adverse reactions.

TABLE 4.1 IF Ratings: A to Z, *continued*

Food	Amount	IF Rating	Fat (g)	Carb (g)
Cream of Wheat, instant	1 serving (¾ cup)	−122	0	24
Cream of Wheat, regular	1 serving (¾ cup)	−135	0	20
Crispix	1 serving (1 cup)	−149	0	25
Croissant	1 croissant	−179	12	26
Cube steak, braised	3 oz.	18	8	0
Cube steak, braised	1 lb. (uncooked weight)	57	24	0
Cube steak, braised, lean portions only	3 oz.	11	7	0
Cube steak, roasted, lean portions only	3 oz.	12	6	0
Cucumber, raw	1 large	24	0	12
Cucumber, raw	½ cup, sliced	4	0	2
Cumin seed	1 tbsp.	9	1	3
Cumin, ground	1 tsp.	4	0	1
Curry powder	1 tbsp.	378	1	4
Cuttlefish, steamed	3 oz.	146	1	1
Dandelion greens, boiled	½ cup, chopped	92	0	3
Dandelion greens, raw	½ cup, chopped	76	0	5
Date, dried	1 fruit	−26	0	6
Dates, dried	½ cup, chopped	−291	0	67
Deer, roasted	3 oz.	1	3	0

Food	Amount	IF Rating	Fat (g)	Carb (g)
Deer, roasted	1 lb. (uncooked weight)	3	9	0
Delmonico steak, broiled or grilled, lean portions only	3 oz.	3	8	0
Diet Coke‡	12 oz.	0	0	0
Dill, dried	1 tsp.	0	0	1
Dill, fresh	¼ cup	2	0	0
Dill seed	1 tsp.	2	0	1
Doughnut, plain, cake	1 doughnut	−171	10	23
Duck, roasted, meat only	3 oz.	14	10	0
Duck, roasted, meat only	½ bird	35	24	0
Duck, roasted, with skin	3 oz.	26	24	0
Duck, roasted, with skin	½ bird	115	108	0
Ebi (shrimp)	1 large	6	0	0
Edam cheese	1 oz.	−18	8	0
Edamame (soybeans), boiled	½ cup, shelled	−7	8	8
Eel, baked or grilled	1 oz.	15	4	0
Eel, baked or grilled	3 oz.	44	13	0
Egg	1 large	−43	5	0
Egg, dried	1 tbsp.	−14	2	0
Egg, duck	1 egg	−163	10	1
Egg, goose	1 egg	−290	19	2

*High in mercury; eat only occasionally.

**Very high in mercury; avoid eating.

†May contain nitrates and nitrites; eat only occasionally.

‡Associated with health risks and/or adverse reactions.

TABLE 4.1 IF Ratings: A to Z, *continued*

Food	Amount	IF Rating	Fat (g)	Carb (g)
Egg, hard-boiled	1 cup, chopped	−124	14	2
Egg, quail	1 egg	−6	1	0
Egg, turkey	1 egg	−62	9	1
Egg substitute, frozen	¼ cup (equiv. to 1 egg)	−7	7	2
Egg substitute, liquid	¼ cup (equiv. to 1 egg)	14	2	0
Egg white	1 large	5	0	0
Egg white	1 cup (8 egg whites)	36	0	3
Egg white, dried	1 tbsp.	17	0	1
Egg yolk	1 large	−48	5	1
Egg yolk, dried	1 tbsp.	−16	2	0
Eggplant, cooked	½ cup, cubed	2	0	4
Endive, raw	1 cup, chopped	52	0	2
English mufffin	1 muffin	−173	1	26
Equal	1 packet	0	0	0
Espresso	1 shot (1 oz.)	0	0	0
Eye of round (beef), roasted	3 oz.	21	8	0
Eye of round (beef), roasted	1 lb. (uncooked weight)	66	26	0
Eye of round (beef), roasted, lean portions only	3 oz.	23	3	0
Fava beans, boiled	1 cup	−148	0	34
Fennel bulb, raw	1 cup, sliced	10	0	6
Fennel bulb, raw	1 small bulb	20	0	12
Fennel seed	1 tbsp.	6	1	3

Food	Amount	IF Rating	Fat (g)	Carb (g)
Feta cheese	1 oz.	−20	6	1
Feta cheese	1 cup, crumbled	−108	32	6
Fig, dried	1 fruit	−27	0	5
Filberts, blanched	¼ cup	118	17	5
Filberts, blanched	4 oz.	473	69	19
Filberts, dry-roasted	¼ cup	107	18	5
Filberts, dry-roasted	4 oz.	427	71	20
Filberts, raw	1 cup, ground	285	46	13
Filet mignon, broiled or grilled	3 oz.	10	15	0
Filet mignon, broiled or grilled	1 lb. (uncooked weight)	32	47	0
Filet mignon, broiled or grilled, lean portions only	3 oz.	13	7	0
Filet mignon, roasted	3 oz.	−8	20	0
Filet mignon, roasted	1 lb. (uncooked weight)	−21	54	0
Filet mignon, roasted, lean portions only	3 oz.	−17	10	0
Fish sticks, frozen	1 stick	0	3	7
Fish stock	1 cup	64	2	0
Flank steak, braised	3 oz.	23	14	0

*High in mercury; eat only occasionally.

**Very high in mercury; avoid eating.

†May contain nitrates and nitrites; eat only occasionally.

‡Associated with health risks and/or adverse reactions.

TABLE 4.1 IF Ratings: A to Z, *continued*

Food	Amount	IF Rating	Fat (g)	Carb (g)
Flank steak, braised	1 lb. (uncooked weight)	73	45	0
Flank steak, broiled or grilled	3 oz.	−8	8	0
Flank steak, broiled or grilled	1 lb. (uncooked weight)	−41	42	0
Flaxseed	2 tbsp.	26	8	8
Flounder, baked or grilled	3 oz.	204	1	0
Flounder, raw	1 oz.	25	0	0
Flour tortilla	6" tortilla	−30	2	16
Flour tortilla	10" tortilla	−69	5	36
Fontina cheese	1 oz.	−21	8	0
Fontina cheese	1 cup, shredded	−83	34	2
Fontina cheese	1 cup, melted	−178	72	4
Frankfurter, turkey†	1 sausage	−8	8	1
Frankfurter, vegetarian	1 sausage	−8	7	2
French bread	1 slice	−261	2	33
French dressing	2 tbsp.	−54	20	0
French dressing, low-fat	2 tbsp.	−4	4	8
French fries, fast-food	1 small order	−213	16	34
French fries, fast-food	1 medium order	−336	25	53
French fries, frozen	10 fries	−86	4	16
Froot Loops	1 serving (1 cup)	−128	1	26
Frosted Flakes (Kellogg's)	1 serving (¾ cup)	−123	0	28

Food	Amount	IF Rating	Fat (g)	Carb (g)
Fruit cocktail, canned (water pack)	1 cup	−85	0	20
Fruit leather roll	1 small	−61	0	12
Fruit leather snack	1 oz.	−136	0	24
Garbanzo beans, boiled	½ cup	−39	2	22
Garlic, raw	1 clove	111	0	1
Garlic powder	1 tsp.	440	0	2
Gatorade sport drink	8 oz.	−119	0	15
Gelatin, dry, unflavored	1 envelope	1	0	0
Ginger, ground	1 tsp.	501	0	1
Gingerroot, fresh	1 tbsp.	390	0	1
Goat cheese, hard	1 oz.	−45	10	1
Goat cheese, semisoft	1 oz.	−39	8	1
Goat cheese, soft	1 oz.	−26	6	0
Goat meat, roasted	3 oz.	−42	3	0
Goat meat, roasted	1 lb. (uncooked weight)	−126	8	0
Goose, roasted, meat only	3 oz.	20	11	0
Goose, roasted, meat only	½ bird	136	77	0
Goose, roasted, with skin	3 oz.	38	19	0
Goose, roasted, with skin	½ bird	348	170	0
Goose liver pâté	1 oz. (2 tbsp.)	−16	11	1
Gouda cheese	1 oz.	−19	8	1

*High in mercury; eat only occasionally.

**Very high in mercury; avoid eating.

†May contain nitrates and nitrites; eat only occasionally.

‡Associated with health risks and/or adverse reactions.

TABLE 4.1 IF Ratings: A to Z, *continued*

Food	Amount	IF Rating	Fat (g)	Carb (g)
Graham cracker	1 cracker	−37	1	5
Graham cracker crumbs	1 cup	−445	8	65
Grapefruit, pink	1 cup sections	2	0	19
Grapefruit, pink	½ fruit	1	0	9
Grapefruit, white	½ fruit	−1	0	10
Grapefruit, white	1 cup sections	−2	0	19
Grapefruit juice, from concentrate	8 oz.	−76	0	24
Grape-Nuts	1 serving (⅓ cup)	−219	1	35
Grape-Nuts Flakes	1 serving (¾ cup)	−144	1	24
Grapes, red or green, seedless	15 grapes	−57	0	15
Grapes, red or green, seedless	1 cup	−113	0	29
Grapes, red or green, with seeds	15 grapes	−61	0	16
Grapes, red or green, with seeds	1 cup	−108	0	28
Grape seed oil	1 tbsp.	−84	14	0
Grape seed oil	½ cup	−674	109	0
Green beans, boiled	½ cup	15	0	5
Green beans, canned	½ cup	12	0	3
Green beans, frozen	½ cup	9	0	5
Green beans, raw	½ cup	15	0	4
Green onion, raw	2 tbsp., chopped	33	0	1
Green onion, raw	1 large	68	0	2

Food	Amount	IF Rating	Fat (g)	Carb (g)
Green pepper, boiled	½ cup, chopped	27	0	5
Green pepper, raw	1 medium	50	0	6
Green pepper, raw	1 cup, chopped	63	0	7
Ground beef, 70% lean, baked	3 oz.	6	13	0
Ground beef, 70% lean, baked	1 lb. (uncooked weight)	27	56	0
Ground beef, 75% lean, baked	3 oz.	−5	14	0
Ground beef, 75% lean, baked	1 lb. (uncooked weight)	−23	60	0
Ground beef, 75% lean, broiled or grilled	3 oz.	−3	16	0
Ground beef, 75% lean, broiled or grilled	1 lb. (uncooked weight)	−13	68	0
Ground beef, 80% lean, baked	3 oz.	−14	14	0
Ground beef, 80% lean, baked	1 lb. (uncooked weight)	−58	59	0
Ground beef, 80% lean, broiled or grilled	3 oz.	−5	15	0
Ground beef, 80% lean, broiled or grilled	1 lb. (uncooked weight)	−23	65	0

*High in mercury; eat only occasionally.

**Very high in mercury; avoid eating.

†May contain nitrates and nitrites; eat only occasionally.

‡Associated with health risks and/or adverse reactions.

TABLE 4.1 IF Ratings: A to Z, *continued*

Food	Amount	IF Rating	Fat (g)	Carb (g)
Ground beef, 80% lean, pan-fried	3 oz.	−30	16	0
Ground beef, 80% lean, pan-fried	1 lb. (uncooked weight)	−130	69	0
Ground beef, 85% lean, baked	3 oz.	−7	12	0
Ground beef, 85% lean, baked	1 lb. (uncooked weight)	−30	52	0
Ground beef, 85% lean, broiled or grilled	3 oz.	−7	13	0
Ground beef, 85% lean, broiled or grilled	1 lb. (uncooked weight)	−29	56	0
Ground beef, 90% lean, baked	3 oz.	−6	9	0
Ground beef, 90% lean, baked	1 lb. (uncooked weight)	−28	40	0
Ground beef, 90% lean, broiled or grilled	3 oz.	−7	10	0
Ground beef, 90% lean, broiled or grilled	1 lb. (uncooked weight)	−31	43	0
Ground beef, 90% lean, pan-fried	3 oz.	−17	15	0
Ground beef, 90% lean, pan-fried	1 lb. (uncooked weight)	−74	64	0
Ground beef, 95% lean, baked	3 oz.	−4	5	0

Food	Amount	IF Rating	Fat (g)	Carb (g)
Ground beef, 95% lean, baked	1 lb. (uncooked weight)	−15	23	0
Ground beef, 95% lean, broiled or grilled	3 oz.	−7	6	0
Ground beef, 95% lean, broiled or grilled	1 lb. (uncooked weight)	−28	26	0
Ground beef, 95% lean, pan-fried	3 oz.	−9	14	0
Ground beef, 95% lean, pan-fried	1 lb. (uncooked weight)	−40	58	0
Ground lamb, broiled or grilled	3 oz.	−24	17	0
Ground lamb, broiled or grilled	1 lb. (uncooked weight)	−87	62	0
Ground pork, cooked	3 oz.	−31	17	0
Ground pork, cooked	1 lb. (uncooked weight)	−116	65	0
Ground turkey	1 lb. (uncooked weight)	−240	43	0
Ground turkey, cooked	3 oz.	−60	11	0
Ground veal, broiled or grilled	3 oz.	−57	6	0

*High in mercury; eat only occasionally.

**Very high in mercury; avoid eating.

†May contain nitrates and nitrites; eat only occasionally.

‡Associated with health risks and/or adverse reactions.

TABLE 4.1 IF Ratings: A to Z, *continued*

Food	Amount	IF Rating	Fat (g)	Carb (g)
Ground veal, broiled or grilled	1 lb. (uncooked weight)	−199	23	0
Grouper,** baked or grilled	3 oz.	83	1	0
Gruyère cheese	1 oz.	−17	9	0
Gruyère cheese	1 cup, shredded	−68	35	0
Guava	1 fruit	35	1	8
Haddock, baked or grilled	3 oz.	100	1	0
Haddock, smoked	3 oz.	103	1	0
Halibut, Atlantic,* baked or grilled	3 oz.	78	3	0
Halibut, Greenland,* baked or grilled	3 oz.	493	15	0
Halibut, Pacific,* baked or grilled	3 oz.	78	3	0
Halibut, raw	1 oz.	19	1	0
Ham, canned,† extra lean	3 oz.	26	4	0
Ham, canned,† extra lean	1 lb.	91	15	2
Ham, canned,† regular	3 oz.	45	13	0
Ham, canned,† regular	1 lb.	159	45	1
Ham, roasted	3 oz.	28	8	0
Ham, roasted	1 cup, cubed	46	13	0
Ham, roasted	1 lb.	98	27	0
Ham, roasted, extra lean	3 oz.	28	5	1
Ham, roasted, extra lean	1 cup, cubed	45	8	2
Ham, roasted, extra lean	1 lb.	97	16	4
Ham and cheese loaf†	1 oz.	11	5	1

Food	Amount	IF Rating	Fat (g)	Carb (g)
Ham luncheon meat†	1 oz.	0	2	1
Ham luncheon meat,† extra lean	1 oz.	8	1	1
Hamaguri (raw clam)	1 large	20	0	1
Hamaguri (raw clam)	1 medium	11	0	0
Hamburger bun	1 roll	−113	2	21
Hard salami†	1 oz.	16	8	1
Hawara (raw mackerel)	1 oz.	177	2	0
Hazelnut oil	1 tbsp.	85	14	0
Hazelnut oil	½ cup	679	109	0
Hazelnuts, blanched	¼ cup	118	17	5
Hazelnuts, blanched	4 oz.	473	69	19
Hazelnuts, dry-roasted	¼ cup	107	18	5
Hazelnuts, dry-roasted	4 oz.	427	71	20
Hazelnuts, raw	1 cup, ground	285	46	13
Palm hearts, canned	1 piece	5	0	2
Herbal tea	8 oz.	1	0	0
Herring, Atlantic, baked or grilled	3 oz.	790	10	0
Herring, Atlantic, kippered	1 oz.	289	4	0
Hickory nuts, raw	¼ cup	28	18	5
Hirame (raw flounder)	1 oz.	25	0	0
Honey	½ cup	−763	0	140
Honey	1 tbsp.	−95	0	17

*High in mercury; eat only occasionally.

**Very high in mercury; avoid eating.

†May contain nitrates and nitrites; eat only occasionally.

‡Associated with health risks and/or adverse reactions.

TABLE 4.1 IF Ratings: A to Z, *continued*

Food	Amount	IF Rating	Fat (g)	Carb (g)
Horseradish, prepared	1 tsp.	1	0	1
Hot chili pepper, dried	1 pepper	252	0	0
Hot dog,† turkey	1 sausage	−8	8	1
Hot dog bun	1 roll	−113	2	21
Hot sauce (Tabasco)	1 tsp.	370	0	0
Hotate-gai (raw scallop)	1 scallop	16	0	0
Hungarian pepper, raw	1 pepper	63	0	2
Ice cream, chocolate	½ cup	−127	7	19
Ice cream, chocolate, premium	½ cup	−91	13	15
Ice cream, vanilla	½ cup	−124	8	17
Ice cream, vanilla, light	½ cup	−102	4	20
Ice cream, vanilla, premium	½ cup	−165	17	24
Iced tea, from powdered mix, sugar-free‡	8 oz.	0	0	0
Ice milk, vanilla	½ cup	−80	3	15
Iceberg lettuce	1 cup, shredded	13	0	2
Ika (raw squid)	1 oz.	72	0	1
Ikura (roe)	1 tbsp.	139	1	0
Italian dressing	2 tbsp.	−16	48	4
Italian dressing, low-fat	2 tbsp.	−14	6	2
Italian sausage†	1 sausage	23	18	3
Jack mackerel, baked or grilled	3 oz.	686	9	0
Jack mackerel, canned	3 oz.	465	5	0
Jalapeño pepper, canned	1 pepper	56	0	1
Jalapeño pepper, raw	1 pepper	55	0	1

Food	Amount	IF Rating	Fat (g)	Carb (g)
Jam, various fruit	1 tbsp.	−67	0	14
Jello, sugar-free‡	½ cup	6	0	1
Jelly beans	10 small	−80	0	10
Jelly beans	10 large	−204	0	26
Jerusalem artichoke, raw	½ cup, sliced	5	0	15
Just Right	1 serving (1 cup)	−172	2	45
Kaiser roll	1 roll	−185	2	30
Kajiki** (raw swordfish)	1 oz.	78	1	0
Kale, boiled	½ cup, chopped	232	0	4
Kale, boiled	1 lb. (uncooked weight)	1,276	0	22
Kamaboko (imitation crab)	1 oz.	79	0	3
Karei (raw sole)	1 oz.	25	0	0
Kasha (buckwheat)	½ cup	−73	1	17
Katsuo (raw skipjack tuna)	1 oz.	38	0	0
Kelp, raw	2 tbsp.	5	0	1
Kidney beans, light, boiled	½ cup	−6	0	20
Kidney beans, dark, boiled	½ cup	−4	0	20
Kielbasa†	4" section	30	23	2
King mackerel,** baked or grilled	3 oz.	214	2	0
Kiwi	1 fruit	−14	0	13
Knackwurst†	1 sausage	21	20	2

*High in mercury; eat only occasionally.

**Very high in mercury; avoid eating.

†May contain nitrates and nitrites; eat only occasionally.

‡Associated with health risks and/or adverse reactions.

TABLE 4.1 IF Ratings: A to Z, *continued*

Food	Amount	IF Rating	Fat (g)	Carb (g)
Kohlrabi, boiled, sliced	½ cup	23	0	6
Kumquat, with peel	1 fruit	4	0	3
Lamb chop (Australian), broiled or grilled	3 oz.	−19	12	0
Lamb chop (Australian), broiled or grilled	1 lb. (uncooked weight)	−38	23	0
Lamb chop (Australian), broiled or grilled, lean portions only	3 oz.	−9	7	0
Lamb chop (domestic), broiled or grilled	3 oz.	−31	20	0
Lamb chop (domestic), broiled or grilled	1 lb. (uncooked weight)	−61	39	0
Lamb chop (domestic), broiled or grilled, lean portions only	3 oz.	−5	8	0
Lamb chop (New Zealand), broiled or grilled	3 oz.	−31	20	0
Lamb chop (New Zealand), broiled or grilled	1 lb. (uncooked weight)	−61	40	0
Lamb chop (New Zealand), broiled or grilled, lean portions only	3 oz.	−19	7	0
Lamb leg (Australian), broiled or grilled	3 oz.	−13	10	0
Lamb leg (Australian), broiled or grilled	1 lb. (uncooked weight)	−20	15	0
Lamb leg (Australian), broiled or grilled, lean portions only	3 oz.	−7	7	0

Food	Amount	IF Rating	Fat (g)	Carb (g)
Lamb leg (Australian), roasted	3 oz.	−17	13	0
Lamb leg (Australian), roasted	1 lb. (uncooked weight)	−26	19	0
Lamb leg (Australian), roasted, lean portions only	3 oz.	−4	7	0
Lamb leg (domestic), roasted	3 oz.	−17	14	0
Lamb leg (domestic), roasted	1 lb. (uncooked weight)	−26	22	0
Lamb leg (domestic), roasted, lean portions only	3 oz.	4	7	0
Lamb leg (New Zealand), roasted	3 oz.	−13	13	0
Lamb leg (New Zealand), roasted	1 lb. (uncooked weight)	−20	20	0
Lamb leg (New Zealand), roasted, lean portions only	3 oz.	−15	6	0
Lamb loin (Australian), broiled or grilled	3 oz.	−16	10	0
Lamb loin (Australian), broiled or grilled	1 lb. (uncooked weight)	−48	31	0
Lamb loin (Australian), broiled or grilled, lean portions only	3 oz.	−11	7	0

*High in mercury; eat only occasionally.

**Very high in mercury; avoid eating.

†May contain nitrates and nitrites; eat only occasionally.

‡Associated with health risks and/or adverse reactions.

TABLE 4.1 IF Ratings: A to Z, *continued*

Food	Amount	IF Rating	Fat (g)	Carb (g)
Lamb loin (domestic), roasted	3 oz.	−43	20	0
Lamb loin (domestic), roasted	1 lb. (uncooked weight)	−129	60	0
Lamb loin (domestic), roasted, lean portions only	3 oz.	−30	8	0
Lamb rib (Australian), roasted	3 oz.	−26	17	0
Lamb rib (Australian), roasted	1 lb. (uncooked weight)	−52	35	0
Lamb rib (Australian), roasted, lean portions only	3 oz.	−14	10	0
Lamb rib (domestic), broiled or grilled	3 oz.	−76	23	0
Lamb rib (domestic), broiled or grilled	1 lb. (uncooked weight)	−152	45	0
Lamb rib (domestic), broiled or grilled, lean portions only	3 oz.	−57	11	0
Lamb rib (domestic), roasted	3 oz.	−50	23	0
Lamb rib (domestic), roasted	1 lb. (uncooked weight)	−100	47	0
Lamb rib (domestic), roasted, lean portions only	3 oz.	−38	11	0
Lamb rib (New Zealand), roasted	3 oz.	−38	22	0
Lamb rib (New Zealand), roasted	1 lb. (uncooked weight)	−76	44	0

Food	Amount	IF Rating	Fat (g)	Carb (g)
Lamb rib (New Zealand), roasted, lean portions only	3 oz.	−20	9	0
Lamb shank (Australian), roasted	3 oz.	−16	12	0
Lamb shank (Australian), roasted	1 lb. (uncooked weight)	−24	18	0
Lamb shank (Australian), roasted, lean portions only	3 oz.	−3	6	0
Lamb shank (domestic), roasted	3 oz.	−2	11	0
Lamb shank (domestic), roasted	1 lb. (uncooked weight)	−3	18	0
Lamb shank (domestic), roasted, lean portions only	3 oz.	16	6	0
Lamb shoulder (Australian), roasted	3 oz.	−33	18	0
Lamb shoulder (Australian), roasted	1 lb. (uncooked weight)	−99	55	0
Lamb shoulder (Australian), roasted, lean portions only	3 oz.	−18	11	0
Lamb shoulder (domestic), braised	3 oz.	−54	21	0
Lamb shoulder (domestic), braised	1 lb. (uncooked weight)	−162	62	0
Lamb shoulder (domestic), braised, lean portions only	3 oz.	−38	14	0

*High in mercury; eat only occasionally.

**Very high in mercury; avoid eating.

†May contain nitrates and nitrites; eat only occasionally.

‡Associated with health risks and/or adverse reactions.

TABLE 4.1 IF Ratings: A to Z, *continued*

Food	Amount	IF Rating	Fat (g)	Carb (g)
Lamb shoulder (domestic), broiled or grilled	3 oz.	−39	16	0
Lamb shoulder (domestic), broiled or grilled	1 lb. (uncooked weight)	−117	49	0
Lamb shoulder (domestic), broiled or grilled, lean portions only	3 oz.	−32	9	0
Lamb shoulder (domestic), roasted	3 oz.	−43	17	0
Lamb shoulder (domestic), roasted	1 lb. (uncooked weight)	−129	51	0
Lamb shoulder (domestic), roasted, lean portions only	3 oz.	−27	9	0
Lamb shoulder (New Zealand), braised	3 oz.	−34	22	0
Lamb shoulder (New Zealand), braised	1 lb. (uncooked weight)	−102	67	0
Lamb shoulder (New Zealand), braised, lean portions only	3 oz.	−23	13	0
Lard	1 tbsp.	−3	13	0
Lard	½ cup	−23	103	0
Lasagna noodles	16-oz. package	−560	0	147
Lebanon bologna†	1 oz.	13	3	0
Leek, boiled	½ cup, chopped	134	0	4
Lemon, without peel	1 fruit	21	0	8
Lemonade, from frozen concentrate	8 oz.	−166	0	26

Food	Amount	IF Rating	Fat (g)	Carb (g)
Lemonade, from powdered mix, sugar-free‡	8 oz.	3	0	1
Lemongrass, fresh	2 tbsp.	2	0	3
Lemon juice	1 tbsp.	3	0	1
Lemon-lime soda, sugar-free‡	12 oz.	0	0	0
Lemon peel (zest), fresh	1 tbsp.	4	0	1
Lentils, boiled	½ cup	6	0	20
Lentil soup	1 cup	−37	2	20
Lentil soup	16-oz. can	−68	4	37
Lettuce, Bibb	1 cup, shredded	22	0	1
Lettuce, Boston	1 cup, shredded	43	0	1
Lettuce, butterhead	1 cup, shredded	43	0	1
Lettuce, iceberg	1 cup, shredded	13	0	2
Lettuce, leaf	1 cup, shredded	52	0	1
Lettuce, romaine	1 cup, shredded	61	0	2
Life cereal	1 serving (¾ cup)	−52	1	25
Lima beans, baby, boiled	½ cup	−28	0	17
Lima beans, large, boiled	½ cup	−19	0	20
Limburger cheese	1 oz.	−14	8	0

*High in mercury; eat only occasionally.

**Very high in mercury; avoid eating.

†May contain nitrates and nitrites; eat only occasionally.

‡Associated with health risks and/or adverse reactions.

TABLE 4.1 IF Ratings: A to Z, *continued*

Food	Amount	IF Rating	Fat (g)	Carb (g)
Limburger cheese	8-oz. package	−113	62	1
Lime, without peel	1 fruit	10	0	7
Lime juice	1 tbsp.	3	0	2
Linseed	2 tbsp.	26	8	8
Liverwurst†	1 oz.	23	8	1
Lobster, Maine,* steamed or boiled	3 oz.	80	1	1
Lobster, Maine,* steamed or boiled	1 cup	120	1	2
London broil, braised	3 oz.	12	10	0
London broil, braised	1 lb. (uncooked weight)	36	30	0
London broil, braised, lean portions only	3 oz.	11	5	0
London broil, broiled or grilled	3 oz.	15	8	0
London broil, broiled or grilled	1 lb.	59	31	0
London broil, broiled or grilled, lean portions only	3 oz.	12	4	0
Lox, smoked	1 oz.	72	1	0
Macadamia nuts, dry-roasted	¼ cup	137	22	4
Macadamia nuts, dry-roasted	4 oz.	546	86	15
Macadamia nuts, raw	¼ cup	133	21	4
Macadamia nuts, raw	4 oz.	533	86	16
Macaroni elbows, cooked	½ cup	−76	0	20

Food	Amount	IF Rating	Fat (g)	Carb (g)
Macaroni elbows, uncooked	8 oz.	−684	0	180
Macaroni shells, cooked	½ cup	−55	0	16
Macaroni shells, uncooked	8 oz.	−495	0	144
Mace, ground	1 tsp.	0	1	1
Mackerel, Atlantic, baked or grilled	3 oz.	512	15	0
Mackerel, jack, canned	3 oz.	465	5	0
Mackerel, king,** baked or grilled	3 oz.	214	2	0
Mackerel, king,* raw	1 oz.	268	4	0
Mackerel, Pacific, baked or grilled	3 oz.	686	9	0
Mackerel, Pacific, raw	1 oz.	177	2	0
Mahimahi, baked or grilled	3 oz.	91	1	0
Mango	1 fruit	−106	1	35
Maple syrup (100% pure)	½ cup	−550	0	106
Maple syrup (100% pure)	1 tbsp.	−70	0	13
Margarine, corn	1 tbsp.	−25	11	0
Margarine, corn	1 stick (¼ lb.)	−200	92	1
Margarine, corn and soy, 80% fat	1 tbsp.	−14	11	0
Margarine, corn and soy, 80% fat	1 stick (¼ lb.)	−115	88	2
Margarine, liquid (soybean oil)	1 tbsp.	−44	11	0
Margarine, soy	1 tbsp.	−19	11	0

*High in mercury; eat only occasionally.

**Very high in mercury; avoid eating.

†May contain nitrates and nitrites; eat only occasionally.

‡Associated with health risks and/or adverse reactions.

TABLE 4.1 IF Ratings: A to Z, *continued*

Food	Amount	IF Rating	Fat (g)	Carb (g)
Margarine, soy	1 stick (¼ lb.)	−155	91	1
Margarine, soy and cottonseed	1 tbsp.	3	11	0
Margarine, soy and cottonseed	1 stick (¼ lb.)	21	91	1
Margarine, sunflower	1 tbsp.	−52	11	0
Margarine, sunflower	1 stick (¼ lb.)	−420	91	1
Margarine, tub, 40% fat	1 tbsp.	−3	6	0
Margarine, tub, 60% fat	1 tbsp.	16	9	0
Margarine, tub, 70% fat	1 tbsp.	−5	10	0
Margarine, tub, nonfat	1 tbsp.	−3	0	1
Margarine-butter blend	1 tbsp.	−26	11	0
Margarine-butter blend	1 stick (¼ lb.)	−210	91	1
Marjoram, dried	1 tsp.	2	0	0
Marmalade, orange	1 tbsp.	−62	0	13
Mars almond bar	1 bar	−190	12	31
Masu* (raw trout)	1 oz.	6	1	0
Mayonnaise	1 tbsp.	−33	12	0
Mayonnaise	½ cup	−267	93	0
Mayonnaise, imitation	1 tbsp.	−1	0	1
Mayonnaise, imitation	½ cup	−9	1	13
Mayonnaise, reduced-fat	1 tbsp.	−12	5	1
Mayonnaise, reduced-fat	½ cup	−96	265	66
Mayonnaise, tofu	1 tbsp.	−10	5	1
Mayonnaise, tofu	½ cup	−78	38	5
Melba toast	1 toast	−13	0	2
Milk, chocolate	1 cup	−116	8	26

Food	Amount	IF Rating	Fat (g)	Carb (g)
Milk, chocolate, low-fat	1 cup	−80	3	26
Milk, low-fat (1%)	1 cup	−33	2	12
Milk, nonfat dry powder	¼ cup	−35	0	16
Milk, nonfat (skim)	1 cup	−28	0	12
Milk, reduced-fat (2%)	1 cup	−41	5	11
Milk, sweetened condensed	½ cup	−525	14	83
Milk, sweetened condensed	14-oz. can	−1,837	47	291
Milk, whole	1 cup	−45	8	11
Milk chocolate	1 miniature bar	−19	2	4
Milk chocolate	1 bar	−156	13	26
Millet, cooked	½ cup	−135	1	21
Mint, dried	1 tsp.	1	0	0
Mint, fresh	2 tbsp.	3	0	1
Miracle Whip	1 tbsp.	−26	11	1
Miracle Whip	½ cup	−206	86	4
Miracle Whip, light	1 tbsp.	−8	3	3
Miracle Whip, light	½ cup	−66	22	28
Monterey Jack cheese	1 oz.	−22	9	0
Monterey Jack cheese	1 cup, shredded	−86	34	1
Moose, roasted	3 oz.	−53	1	0
Moose, roasted	1 lb. (uncooked weight)	−159	2	0

*High in mercury; eat only occasionally.

**Very high in mercury; avoid eating.

†May contain nitrates and nitrites; eat only occasionally.

‡Associated with health risks and/or adverse reactions.

TABLE 4.1 IF Ratings: A to Z, *continued*

Food	Amount	IF Rating	Fat (g)	Carb (g)
Mozzarella, part-skim	1 oz.	−11	5	1
Mozzarella, part-skim	1 cup, shredded	−46	23	4
Mozzarella, part-skim	16-oz. package	−184	91	17
Mozzarella, whole-milk	1 cup, shredded	−41	25	2
Mozzarella, whole-milk, shredded	1 oz.	−10	6	1
Mozzarella, whole-milk, shredded	16-oz. package	−164	100	10
Muenster cheese	1 oz.	−22	8	0
Muenster cheese	1 cup, shredded	−88	34	1
Muesli, no sugar added	1 serving (⅓ cup)	−41	4	14
Muffin, blueberry	1 small	−179	4	32
Muffin, oat bran	1 small	−164	5	32
Mulberries	10 berries	0	0	0
Mullet, baked or grilled	3 oz.	86	4	0
Multi-Bran Chex	1 serving (1 cup)	−118	1	41
Mung bean sprouts	½ cup	8	0	3
Mung beans, boiled	½ cup	−9	0	19
Mushrooms, cremini	1 mushroom	4	0	1
Mushrooms, enoki	1 mushroom	1	0	0
Mushrooms, oyster	1 mushroom	4	0	1
Mushrooms, straw, canned	½ cup	17	1	4
Mushrooms, white	½ cup, sliced	4	0	1
Mushrooms, white, canned	½ cup, sliced	5	0	4

Food	Amount	IF Rating	Fat (g)	Carb (g)
Mussel, blue, raw	1 medium	33	0	1
Mussel, blue, raw	1 large	45	0	1
Mussel, blue, steamed	3 oz. (8 medium)	293	4	6
Mustard, prepared	1 tsp.	3	0	0
Mustard greens, boiled	½ cup, chopped	117	0	1
Mustard seed	1 tbsp.	37	3	4
Napa cabbage, boiled	½ cup, shredded	14	0	1
Navy beans, canned	½ cup	−51	1	27
Neufchâtel cheese	2 tbsp.	−21	7	1
Neufchâtel cheese	1 small package (3 oz.)	−63	20	3
Neufchâtel cheese	8-oz. brick	−168	53	7
New York strip, broiled or grilled	3 oz.	6	17	0
New York strip, broiled or grilled	1 lb. (uncooked weight)	18	51	0
New York strip, broiled or grilled, lean portions only	3 oz.	5	8	0
Nonalcoholic wine	4 oz.	0	0	0
Northern pike, baked or grilled	3 oz.	46	1	0
Nutmeg, ground	1 tsp.	−5	1	1

*High in mercury; eat only occasionally.

**Very high in mercury; avoid eating.

†May contain nitrates and nitrites; eat only occasionally.

‡Associated with health risks and/or adverse reactions.

TABLE 4.1 IF Ratings: A to Z, *continued*

Food	Amount	IF Rating	Fat (g)	Carb (g)
Nutri-Grain Wheat	1 serving (1 cup)	−104	0	24
Oat Bran (Quaker)	1 serving (1¼ cups)	−185	3	43
Oat bran, raw	½ cup	−111	3	31
Oatmeal, dry	⅓ cup	−56	2	18
Oatmeal, made with water	1 serving (¾ cup)	−64	2	19
Oatmeal cookie	1 cookie	−76	5	17
Ocean perch, Atlantic, baked or grilled	3 oz.	195	2	0
Octopus, steamed or stewed	3 oz.	164	2	4
Ohyo (raw halibut)	1 oz.	19	1	0
Okra, boiled	½ cup, sliced	23	0	4
Olive, black	1 jumbo	4	1	0
Olive, black	¼ cup, chopped	16	4	0
Olive, green	1 jumbo	8	1	0
Olive, green	¼ cup, chopped	32	4	0
Olive oil	1 tbsp.	73	14	0
Olive oil	½ cup	583	108	0
Onion, boiled	1 medium	236	0	10
Onion, boiled	½ cup, diced	300	0	12
Onion, canned	1 medium	163	0	3
Onion, canned	½ cup, diced	286	0	5
Onion, frozen	10-oz. package	724	0	19
Onion, raw	2 tbsp., chopped	52	0	2

Food	Amount	IF Rating	Fat (g)	Carb (g)
Onion, raw	1 slice	93	0	4
Onion, raw	½ cup, sliced	150	0	6
Onion, raw	1 small	175	0	7
Onion, raw	½ cup, diced	206	0	8
Onion, raw	1 medium	278	0	11
Onion, raw	1 large	382	0	15
Onion flakes	1 tbsp.	584	0	4
Onion powder	1 tsp.	291	0	2
Orange	1 small	−10	0	11
Orange	1 cup sections	−19	0	21
Orange	1 large	−19	0	22
Orange, with peel	1 medium	−15	0	25
Orange drink mix, sugar-free‡	8 oz. (prepared)	26	0	2
Orange juice, fresh squeezed	8 oz.	−65	1	26
Orange juice, from concentrate	8 oz.	−76	0	27
Orange peel (zest), fresh	1 tbsp.	3	0	1
Orange roughy,** baked or grilled	3 oz.	44	1	0
Oregano, ground	1 tsp.	1	0	1
Oregano, fresh	2 tbsp.	2	0	1
Oyster crackers	3 crackers	−13	0	2
Oysters, Eastern, canned	1 cup	872	5	7

*High in mercury; eat only occasionally.

**Very high in mercury; avoid eating.

†May contain nitrates and nitrites; eat only occasionally.

‡Associated with health risks and/or adverse reactions.

TABLE 4.1 IF Ratings: A to Z, *continued*

Food	Amount	IF Rating	Fat (g)	Carb (g)
Oysters, Eastern (farmed), baked	3 oz. (8 medium)	327	2	6
Oysters, Eastern (farmed), raw	1 medium	48	0	1
Oysters, Eastern (wild), baked	3 oz. (8 medium)	362	2	4
Oysters, Eastern (wild), raw	1 medium	55	0	1
Oysters, Eastern (wild), raw	1 cup	732	6	10
Oysters, Eastern (wild), steamed	3 oz. (12 medium)	500	4	7
Oysters, Pacific, raw	1 large	178	1	2
Oysters, Pacific, steamed	3 oz. (3 large)	703	4	8
Palm heart, canned	1 piece	5	0	2
Palm kernel oil	1 tbsp.	−97	14	0
Palm kernel oil	½ cup	−775	109	0
Palm oil	1 tbsp.	−27	14	0
Palm oil	½ cup	−219	108	0
Pancake, prepared from mix	1 pancake	−180	2	28
Papaya	1 cup, cubed	−6	0	14
Paprika	1 tsp.	13	0	1
Parmesan cheese	1 oz.	−16	7	1
Parmesan cheese	½ cup, grated	−31	14	2
Parsley, dried	1 tbsp.	7	0	1
Parsley, fresh	2 tbsp.	40	0	0
Parsley, fresh	½ cup	157	0	2
Parsnip, boiled	½ cup, sliced	−86	0	13
Pasta shells, cooked	½ cup	−55	0	16

Food	Amount	IF Rating	Fat (g)	Carb (g)
Pasta shells, uncooked	8 oz.	−495	0	144
Pasta, corn, cooked	½ cup	−124	1	20
Pastrami†	1 oz.	0	2	0
Pâté de foie gras	1 oz.	−23	12	1
Peach	1 large	−54	0	17
Peach	1 cup, sliced	−58	0	19
Peach	1 small	−27	0	9
Peaches, canned (heavy syrup)	1 cup (with liquid)	−247	0	49
Peaches, canned (juice pack)	1 cup (with liquid)	−90	0	29
Peaches, canned (light syrup)	1 cup (with liquid)	−157	0	37
Peanut oil	1 tbsp.	−3	14	0
Peanut oil	½ cup	−23	108	0
Peanuts, dry-roasted	¼ cup	14	14	6
Peanuts, dry-roasted	4 oz.	57	56	24
Peanuts, oil-roasted	¼ cup	17	14	5
Peanuts, oil-roasted	4 oz.	67	56	21
Pear	1 cup, sliced	−73	1	25
Pear	1 medium	−74	1	25
Pears, canned (juice pack)	½ fruit	−36	0	10
Peas, canned	½ cup	−8	0	12
Peas, frozen	½ cup	4	0	10

*High in mercury; eat only occasionally.

**Very high in mercury; avoid eating.

†May contain nitrates and nitrites; eat only occasionally.

‡Associated with health risks and/or adverse reactions.

TABLE 4.1 IF Ratings: A to Z, *continued*

Food	Amount	IF Rating	Fat (g)	Carb (g)
Pecans, dry-roasted	¼ cup	64	21	4
Pecans, dry-roasted	4 oz.	258	84	15
Pecans, oil-roasted	¼ cup	45	21	4
Pecans, oil-roasted	4 oz.	180	85	15
Pecans, raw	¼ cup	53	20	4
Pecans, raw	4 oz.	210	82	16
Pepper, black, ground	1 tsp.	1	0	1
Pepper, green, boiled	½ cup, chopped	27	0	5
Pepper, green, raw	½ cup, chopped	32	0	4
Pepper, green, raw	1 medium	50	0	6
Pepper, hot banana	1 pepper	66	0	1
Pepper, hot cherry	1 pepper	33	0	1
Pepper, hot chili, dried	1 pepper	252	0	0
Pepper, Hungarian	1 pepper	63	0	2
Pepper, jalapeño, canned	1 pepper	56	0	1
Pepper, jalapeño, raw	1 pepper	55	0	1
Pepper, red chili, canned	½ cup, chopped	488	0	3
Pepper, red chili, raw	1 pepper	286	0	4
Pepper, red bell, boiled	½ cup, chopped	84	0	5
Pepper, red bell, frozen	10-oz. package	19	0	1
Pepper, red bell, raw	½ cup, chopped	90	0	5
Pepper, red bell, raw	1 medium	140	0	8

Food	Amount	IF Rating	Fat (g)	Carb (g)
Pepper, serrano, raw	1 pepper	122	0	0
Pepper, yellow bell, raw	1 pepper	159	0	12
Pepperoni†	1 oz.	−3	12	1
Perch, Atlantic, baked or grilled	3 oz.	195	2	0
Perch, white, baked or grilled	3 oz.	88	1	0
Pickle, dill	1 medium	3	0	1
Pie crust (pastry crust)	⅛ pie (single crust)	−76	8	11
Pie crust (pastry crust)	9" pie (single crust)	−608	64	88
Pignolias	¼ cup	−41	19	4
Pignolias	4 oz.	−164	78	15
Pike, Northern, baked or grilled	3 oz.	46	1	0
Pike, walleye, baked or grilled	3 oz.	112	1	0
Pimento cheese, pasteurized	1 oz.	−22	9	0
Pimentos, canned	2 tbsp., chopped	16	0	1
Pineapple, canned (water pack)	1 cup (with liquid)	−108	0	20
Pineapple, fresh	1 cup, diced	−37	1	19
Pineapple juice, canned	8 oz.	−118	0	34

TABLE 4.1 IF Ratings: A to Z, *continued*

Food	Amount	IF Rating	Fat (g)	Carb (g)
Pineapple juice, from concentrate	8 oz.	−125	0	32
Pine nuts	¼ cup	−41	19	4
Pine nuts	4 oz.	−164	78	15
Pinto beans, boiled	½ cup	−21	1	22
Pinto beans, canned	½ cup	−33	1	18
Pistachios, dry-roasted	¼ cup	26	13	8
Pistachios, dry-roasted	4 oz.	103	52	30
Pita, white	1 small	−74	0	16
Pita, whole wheat	1 small	−65	1	15
Plum	1 fruit	−25	0	9
Polish sausage†	4″ section	27	24	1
Pollack, Atlantic, baked or grilled	3 oz.	221	1	0
Pollack, walleye, baked or grilled	3 oz.	211	1	0
Pompano, baked or grilled	3 oz.	44	10	0
Poppy seed	1 tbsp.	−20	4	2
Poppy seed oil	1 tbsp.	−76	14	0
Poppy seed oil	½ cup	−607	109	0
Pork and beans	½ cup	−52	1	24
Pork and beans	16-oz. can	−185	4	83
Pork bologna	1 oz.	8	5	0
Pork breakfast strips,† grilled	2 slices	10	9	0
Pork chop (loin), center cut, braised	3 oz.	5	12	0

Food	Amount	IF Rating	Fat (g)	Carb (g)
Pork chop (loin), center cut, braised	1 lb. (uncooked weight)	10	24	0
Pork chop (loin), center cut, braised, lean portions only	3 oz.	10	7	0
Pork chop (loin), center cut, broiled or grilled	3 oz.	2	11	0
Pork chop (loin), center cut, broiled or grilled	1 lb. (uncooked weight)	10	55	0
Pork chop (loin), center cut, broiled or grilled, lean portions only	3 oz.	14	7	0
Pork chop (loin), center cut, pan-fried	1 lb. (uncooked weight)	10	19	0
Pork chop (loin), center cut, pan-fried	3 oz.	−7	14	0
Pork chop (loin), center cut, pan-fried, lean portions only	3 oz.	12	9	0
Pork chop (rib), braised	3 oz.	−5	13	0
Pork chop (rib), braised	1 lb. (uncooked weight)	−10	26	0
Pork chop (rib), braised, lean portions only	3 oz.	10	8	0
Pork chop (rib), broiled or grilled	3 oz.	1	13	0

*High in mercury; eat only occasionally.

**Very high in mercury; avoid eating.

†May contain nitrates and nitrites; eat only occasionally.

‡Associated with health risks and/or adverse reactions.

TABLE 4.1 IF Ratings: A to Z, *continued*

Food	Amount	IF Rating	Fat (g)	Carb (g)
Pork chop (rib), broiled or grilled	1 lb. (uncooked weight)	2	26	0
Pork chop (rib), broiled or grilled, lean portions only	3 oz.	17	9	0
Pork chop (rib), pan-fried	3 oz.	−7	14	0
Pork chop (rib), pan-fried	1 lb. (uncooked weight)	−14	28	0
Pork chop (rib), pan-fried, lean portions only	3 oz.	7	9	0
Pork chop (rib), roasted	3 oz.	−30	13	0
Pork chop (rib), roasted	1 lb. (uncooked weight)	−60	26	0
Pork chop (rib), roasted, lean portions only	3 oz.	−7	9	0
Pork loin roast	3 oz.	5	11	0
Pork loin roast	1 lb. (uncooked weight)	15	35	0
Pork loin roast, lean portions only	3 oz.	13	8	0
Pork ribs, country-style, braised	3 oz.	−7	18	0
Pork ribs, country-style, braised	1 lb. (uncooked weight)	−14	39	0
Pork ribs, country-style, braised, lean portions only	3 oz.	15	12	0
Pork ribs, country-style, roasted	3 oz.	−31	22	0

Food	Amount	IF Rating	Fat (g)	Carb (g)
Pork ribs, country-style, roasted	1 lb. (uncooked weight)	−62	43	0
Pork ribs, country-style, roasted, lean portions only	3 oz.	5	13	0
Pork shoulder roast, braised	3 oz.	−43	20	0
Pork shoulder roast, braised	1 lb. (uncooked weight)	−129	59	0
Pork shoulder roast, cured and roasted (picnic ham)	3 oz.	−50	18	0
Pork shoulder roast, cured and roasted (picnic ham)	1 lb. (uncooked weight)	−150	55	0
Pork shoulder roast, cured and roasted (picnic ham), lean portions only	3 oz.	−37	6	0
Pork shoulder roast, roasted	3 oz.	−45	20	0
Pork shoulder roast, roasted	1 lb. (uncooked weight)	−135	61	0
Pork spareribs, braised	3 oz.	−49	26	0
Pork spareribs, braised	1 lb. (uncooked weight)	−98	51	0
Pork tenderloin, broiled or grilled	3 oz.	13	7	0

*High in mercury; eat only occasionally.

**Very high in mercury; avoid eating.

†May contain nitrates and nitrites; eat only occasionally.

‡Associated with health risks and/or adverse reactions.

TABLE 4.1 IF Ratings: A to Z, *continued*

Food	Amount	IF Rating	Fat (g)	Carb (g)
Pork tenderloin, broiled or grilled	1 lb. (uncooked weight)	39	21	0
Pork tenderloin, broiled or grilled, lean portions only	3 oz.	16	5	0
Pork tenderloin, roasted	3 oz.	6	5	0
Pork tenderloin, roasted	1 lb. (uncooked weight)	18	15	0
Pork tenderloin, roasted, lean portions only	3 oz.	13	4	0
Porterhouse steak, broiled or grilled	3 oz.	17	22	0
Porterhouse steak, broiled or grilled	1 lb. (uncooked weight)	51	65	0
Porterhouse steak, broiled or grilled, lean portions only	3 oz.	12	10	0
Port Salut cheese	1 oz.	−13	8	0
Pot roast, braised	3 oz.	29	16	0
Pot roast, braised	1 lb. (uncooked	87	49	0
Pot roast, braised, lean portions only	3 oz.	35	6	0
Potato, baked, with skin	1 medium	−258	0	37
Potato, boiled, without skin	1 medium	−253	0	33
Potato, boiled, without skin	½ cup	−118	0	15
Potato, canned	½ cup	−68	0	15
Potato, russet, baked	1 medium	−264	0	30

Food	Amount	IF Rating	Fat (g)	Carb (g)
Potato chips	1 oz.	−110	10	15
Potato chips	8-oz. bag	−881	79	120
Poultry seasoning	1 tsp.	3	0	1
Pound cake	1 piece	−111	6	15
Preserves, apricot	1 tbsp.	−68	0	13
Pretzels, hard, regular	1 oz. (5 pretzels)	−179	1	24
Pretzels, hard, regular	8-oz. bag	−1,434	8	190
Pretzels, hard, whole wheat	1 oz. (5 pretzels)	−168	1	23
Prime rib, broiled or grilled	1 lb. (uncooked weight)	0	34	0
Prime rib, broiled or grilled	3 oz.	0	17	0
Prime rib, broiled or grilled, lean portions only	3 oz.	14	6	0
Prime rib, roasted	3 oz.	20	23	0
Prime rib, roasted	1 lb. (uncooked weight)	40	46	0
Prime rib, roasted, lean portions only	3 oz.	20	10	0
Provolone cheese	1 oz.	−23	9	1
Provolone cheese	1 cup, shredded	−77	30	2
Provolone cheese	1 cup, diced	−91	35	3
Prune, dried	1 fruit	−12	0	5

*High in mercury; eat only occasionally.

**Very high in mercury; avoid eating.

†May contain nitrates and nitrites; eat only occasionally.

‡Associated with health risks and/or adverse reactions.

TABLE 4.1 IF Ratings: A to Z, *continued*

Food	Amount	IF Rating	Fat (g)	Carb (g)
Pudding, chocolate	½ cup	−130	4	28
Pudding, vanilla	½ cup	−110	4	26
Puffed wheat	1 serving (1¼ cups)	−80	0	11
Pumpernickel bread	1 slice	−42	1	15
Pumpkin, boiled	½ cup, mashed	25	0	6
Pumpkin, canned	½ cup	15	0	10
Pumpkin pie spice	1 tsp.	0	0	1
Pumpkin seeds, hulled, raw	¼ cup	−26	13	5
Pumpkin seeds, hulled, raw	4 oz.	−102	52	20
Pumpkin seeds, hulled, roasted	¼ cup	−23	12	4
Pumpkin seeds, hulled, roasted	4 oz.	−90	48	15
Purslane, raw	1 cup	5	0	1
Queso añejo	1 oz.	−23	9	1
Queso añejo	1 cup, shredded	−92	34	5
Queso asadero	1 oz.	−21	8	1
Queso asadero	1 cup, melted	−180	69	7
Rabbit meat, stewed	3 oz.	22	3	0
Rabbit meat, stewed	1 lb. (uncooked weight)	88	12	0
Radicchio	1 cup, shredded	28	0	2
Radish, red	1 medium	1	0	0
Radish, red	½ cup sliced	7	0	2
Radish, white	½ cup, sliced	8	0	1

Food	Amount	IF Rating	Fat (g)	Carb (g)
Radish sprouts	½ cup	6	1	1
Raisin bran (Kellogg's)	1 serving (1 cup)	−215	2	47
Raisins	1 mini-box	−67	0	11
Raisins	50 raisins	−124	0	21
Raisins	1 cup, not packed	−694	1	115
Raisins	1 cup, packed	−789	1	131
Ranch dressing	2 tbsp.	−38	16	2
Ranch dressing, fat-free	2 tbsp.	0	0	0
Rapeseed oil	1 tbsp.	72	14	0
Rapeseed oil	½ cup	580	109	0
Raspberries	10 berries	2	0	3
Raspberries	1 cup	9	1	15
Raspberries	1 pint	23	2	37
Red cabbage, boiled	½ cup, shredded	17	0	5
Red cabbage, raw	1 cup, shredded	36	0	5
Red bell pepper, boiled	½ cup, chopped	84	0	5
Red pepper, frozen	10-oz. package	190	1	13
Red pepper, ground	1 tsp.	509	0	1
Red pepper, raw	½ cup, chopped	90	0	5
Red pepper, raw	1 medium	140	0	8

*High in mercury; eat only occasionally.

**Very high in mercury; avoid eating.

†May contain nitrates and nitrites; eat only occasionally.

‡Associated with health risks and/or adverse reactions.

TABLE 4.1 IF Ratings: A to Z, *continued*

Food	Amount	IF Rating	Fat (g)	Carb (g)
Red snapper, baked or grilled	3 oz.	125	1	0
Red snapper, raw	1 oz.	37	0	0
Rhubarb, fresh	1 cup, diced	18	0	6
Rhubarb, frozen	1 cup	16	0	7
Rib eye steak, broiled or grilled, lean portions only	3 oz.	3	8	0
Rib roast (beef), broiled or grilled	3 oz.	6	24	0
Rib roast (beef), broiled or grilled	1 lb. (uncooked weight)	12	45	0
Rib roast (beef), broiled or grilled, lean portions only	3 oz.	−5	11	0
Rib roast (beef), roasted	3 oz.	11	25	0
Rib roast (beef), roasted	1 lb. (uncooked weight)	22	49	0
Rib roast (beef), roasted, lean portions only	3 oz.	12	11	0
Rice, brown long-grain, cooked	½ cup	−103	1	22
Rice, brown long-grain, uncooked	½ cup	−206	2	44
Rice, white long-grain, cooked	½ cup	−108	0	22
Rice, white long-grain, uncooked	½ cup	−216	0	44
Rice, white parboiled (converted), cooked	½ cup	−123	0	22

Food	Amount	IF Rating	Fat (g)	Carb (g)
Rice, white parboiled (converted), uncooked	½ cup	−246	0	44
Rice, white short-grain, cooked	½ cup	−172	0	27
Rice, white short-grain, uncooked	½ cup	−344	0	54
Rice, sushi-style, cooked	½ cup	−145	0	18
Rice bran, raw	½ cup	−16	12	29
Rice bran oil	1 tbsp.	−12	14	0
Rice bran oil	½ cup	−97	109	0
Rice cake, plain	1 piece	−57	0	7
Rice Chex	1 serving (1¼ cups)	−176	0	27
Rice Krispies	1 serving (1¼ cups)	−202	0	28
Rice noodles, cooked	½ cup	−80	0	22
Ricotta, part-skim	½ cup	−7	10	6
Ricotta, part-skim	16 oz.	−28	40	24
Ricotta, whole-milk	½ cup	−35	16	4
Ricotta, whole-milk	16 oz.	−140	64	15
Rockfish, Pacific, baked or grilled	3 oz.	188	2	0
Roe	1 tbsp.	139	1	0
Romaine lettuce	1 cup, shredded	61	0	2
Romano cheese	1 oz.	−19	8	1

*High in mercury; eat only occasionally.

**Very high in mercury; avoid eating.

†May contain nitrates and nitrites; eat only occasionally.

‡Associated with health risks and/or adverse reactions.

TABLE 4.1 IF Ratings: A to Z, *continued*

Food	Amount	IF Rating	Fat (g)	Carb (g)
Romano cheese	½ cup grated	−34	14	2
Roquefort cheese	1 oz.	−22	9	1
Rosemary, dried	1 tsp.	1	0	1
Rosemary, fresh	2 tbsp.	0	0	0
Roughy,** baked or grilled	3 oz.	44	1	0
Russian dressing	2 tbsp.	−34	16	4
Russian dressing, low-fat	2 tbsp.	−2	2	14
Rutabaga, boiled	½ cup, mashed	16	0	11
Rye bread	1 slice	−63	1	15
Rye crispbread	1 cracker	−49	0	8
Rye crispbread	1 cup, crushed	−268	1	45
Saba* (raw mackerel)	1 oz.	268	4	0
Sablefish, baked or grilled	3 oz.	685	17	0
Sablefish, smoked	1 oz.	233	6	0
Safflower oil, high-linoleic	1 tbsp.	−89	14	0
Safflower oil, high-linoleic	½ cup	−709	109	0
Safflower oil, high-oleic	1 tbsp.	98	14	0
Safflower oil, high-oleic	½ cup	788	109	0
Saffron	1 tsp.	0	0	0
Sage, ground	1 tsp.	3	0	0
Salad dressing, blue cheese	2 tbsp.	−32	16	2
Salad dressing, blue cheese, low-fat	2 tbsp.	−6	2	0
Salad dressing, French	2 tbsp.	−54	20	0
Salad dressing, French, low-fat	2 tbsp.	−4	4	8

Food	Amount	IF Rating	Fat (g)	Carb (g)
Salad dressing, imitation mayonnaise	1 tbsp.	−1	0	1
Salad dressing, Italian	2 tbsp.	−16	8	4
Salad dressing, Italian, low-fat	2 tbsp.	−14	6	2
Salad dressing, mayonnaise, low-fat	1 tbsp.	−10	5	4
Salad dressing, mayonnaise, low-fat	½ cup	−80	40	29
Salad dressing, mayonnaise-type (Miracle Whip)	1 tbsp.	−26	11	1
Salad dressing, mayonnaise-type (Miracle Whip)	½ cup	−208	87	4
Salad dressing, mayonnaise-type (Miracle Whip), low-fat	1 tbsp.	−8	3	3
Salad dressing, mayonnaise-type (Miracle Whip), low-fat	½ cup	−64	21	27
Salad dressing, oil and vinegar	2 tbsp.	−38	16	0
Salad dressing, ranch	2 tbsp.	−38	16	2
Salad dressing, ranch, low-fat	2 tbsp.	0	0	0
Salad dressing, Russian	2 tbsp.	−34	16	4
Salad dressing, Russian, low-fat	2 tbsp.	−2	2	14

*High in mercury; eat only occasionally.

**Very high in mercury; avoid eating.

†May contain nitrates and nitrites; eat only occasionally.

‡Associated with health risks and/or adverse reactions.

TABLE 4.1 IF Ratings: A to Z, *continued*

Food	Amount	IF Rating	Fat (g)	Carb (g)
Salami, cooked†	1 oz.	8	6	1
Salmon, Atlantic (farmed), baked or grilled	3 oz.	−180	11	0
Salmon, Atlantic (farmed), raw	1 oz.	−61	3	0
Salmon, Atlantic (wild), baked or grilled	3 oz.	493	7	0
Salmon, Atlantic (wild), raw	1 oz.	127	2	0
Salmon, chinook, baked or grilled	3 oz.	581	11	0
Salmon, chinook, raw	1 oz.	228	3	0
Salmon, chinook, smoked	1 oz.	72	1	0
Salmon, chinook, smoked	1 cup	334	6	0
Salmon, chum, baked or grilled	3 oz.	331	4	0
Salmon, chum, canned	3 oz.	447	5	0
Salmon, chum, canned	15-oz. can	2,235	23	0
Salmon, chum, raw	1 oz.	86	1	0
Salmon, coho (farmed), baked or grilled	3 oz.	455	7	0
Salmon, coho (farmed), raw	1 oz.	141	2	0
Salmon, coho (wild), poached	3 oz.	451	6	0
Salmon, coho, (wild), raw	1 oz.	119	2	0
Salmon, pink, baked or grilled	3 oz.	469	4	0
Salmon, pink, canned	3 oz.	661	5	0
Salmon, pink, canned	15-oz. can	3,308	27	0
Salmon, pink, raw	1 oz.	122	1	0

Food	Amount	IF Rating	Fat (g)	Carb (g)
Salmon, smoked	1 oz.	72	1	0
Salmon, sockeye, baked or grilled	3 oz.	518	9	0
Salmon, sockeye, canned	3 oz.	192	7	0
Salmon, sockeye, canned	15-oz. can	964	33	0
Salmon, sockeye, raw	1 oz.	145	2	0
Salsa, tomato-based	¼ cup	52	0	4
Salt pork†	2 oz.	−133	183	0
Saltine	1 cracker	−13	0	2
Saltines	1 cup, crushed	−319	8	50
Sardines, canned in oil	3-oz. can	470	11	0
Sardines, canned in tomato sauce	3-oz. can	380	9	1
Sausage links, pork and beef†	1 sausage	5	5	0
Sausage links, pork†	1 sausage	−28	7	0
Sausage patty, pork and beef†	1 patty	−23	10	1
Savoy cabbage, boiled	½ cup, shredded	13	0	4
Savoy cabbage, raw	1 cup, shredded	40	0	4
Scallion, raw	2 tbsp., chopped	33	0	1
Scallion, raw	1 large	68	0	2
Scallops, bay, raw	1 scallop	16	0	0

*High in mercury; eat only occasionally.

**Very high in mercury; avoid eating.

†May contain nitrates and nitrites; eat only occasionally.

‡Associated with health risks and/or adverse reactions.

TABLE 4.1 IF Ratings: A to Z, *continued*

Food	Amount	IF Rating	Fat (g)	Carb (g)
Scallops, bay, steamed	3 oz. (12 scallops)	139	1	0
Scallops, sea, steamed	3 oz. (5 scallops)	139	1	0
Sea bass,* baked or grilled	3 oz.	331	2	0
Sea bass,* raw	1 oz.	88	1	0
Sea trout,* baked or grilled	3 oz.	12	4	0
Sea trout,* raw	1 oz.	6	1	0
Seaweed, agar	2 tbsp.	2	0	1
Seaweed, Irish moss	2 tbsp.	10	0	1
Seaweed, kelp	2 tbsp.	5	0	1
Seaweed, lavar	2 tbsp.	16	0	1
Seaweed, wakame	2 tbsp.	15	0	1
Serrano pepper, raw	1 pepper	122	0	0
Sesame oil	1 tbsp.	−20	14	0
Sesame oil	½ cup	−162	109	0
Sesame seeds	2 tbsp.	−8	10	3
Sesame seeds	4 oz.	−12	15	4
Shad, baked or grilled	3 oz.	37	15	0
Shallot	2 tbsp., chopped	52	0	3
Shallot, dried	1 tbsp.	3	0	1
Shea nut oil	1 tbsp.	−9	14	0
Shea nut oil	½ cup	−75	109	0
Shortbread cookie	1 cookie	−27	2	5
Shortening	1 tbsp.	−40	13	0
Shortening	½ cup	−323	103	0

Food	Amount	IF Rating	Fat (g)	Carb (g)
Short ribs (beef), braised	3 oz.	12	36	0
Short ribs (beef), braised	1 lb. (uncooked weight)	24	73	0
Short ribs (beef), braised, lean portions only	3 oz.	2	15	0
Shredded wheat, original	1 serving (2 biscuits)	−230	1	37
Shredded wheat, spoon size	1 serving (1 cup)	−230	1	37
Shrimp, canned	3 oz.	162	2	1
Shrimp, canned	6-oz. can	323	3	2
Shrimp, raw	1 large	13	0	0
Shrimp, steamed or boiled	1 large	6	0	0
Shrimp, steamed or boiled	3 oz. (15 shrimp)	95	1	0
Sirloin strip, broiled or grilled	3 oz.	10	13	0
Sirloin strip, broiled or grilled	1 lb.	36	47	0
Sirloin strip, broiled or grilled, lean portions only	3 oz.	17	6	0
Sirloin strip, pan-fried, lean portions only	3 oz.	−4	9	0
Sirloin tip, broiled or grilled	3 oz.	18	5	0

*High in mercury; eat only occasionally.

**Very high in mercury; avoid eating.

†May contain nitrates and nitrites; eat only occasionally.

‡Associated with health risks and/or adverse reactions.

TABLE 4.1 IF Ratings: A to Z, *continued*

Food	Amount	IF Rating	Fat (g)	Carb (g)
Sirloin tip, broiled or grilled	1 lb. (uncooked weight)	54	15	0
Sirloin tip, broiled or grilled, lean portions only	3 oz.	22	5	0
Sirloin tip, roasted	3 oz.	15	11	0
Sirloin tip, roasted	1 lb. (uncooked weight)	45	35	0
Sirloin tip, roasted, lean portions only	3 oz.	11	5	0
Skipjack tuna, baked or grilled	3 oz.	139	1	0
Skipjack tuna, raw	1 oz.	38	0	0
Skirt steak, broiled or grilled	3 oz.	20	10	0
Skirt steak, broiled or grilled	1 lb. (uncooked weight)	60	31	0
Skirt steak, broiled or grilled, lean portions only	3 oz.	4	12	0
Smacks (Kellogg's)	1 serving (¾ cup)	−131	1	24
Smelt, rainbow, baked or grilled	3 oz.	337	3	0
Snap beans, boiled	½ cup	14	0	5
Snap beans, canned	½ cup	12	0	3
Snap beans, frozen	½ cup	9	0	5
Snap beans, raw	½ cup	15	0	4
Snapper, baked or grilled	3 oz.	125	1	0
Snickers candy bar	1 fun-size bar	−38	3	10

Food	Amount	IF Rating	Fat (g)	Carb (g)
Snickers candy bar	1 bar	−144	11	37
Snow peas, raw	1 cup	52	0	7
Snow peas, boiled	½ cup	36	0	6
Sockeye, baked or grilled	3 oz.	518	9	0
Sockeye, canned	3 oz.	192	7	0
Sockeye, canned	15-oz. can	964	33	0
Sole, baked or grilled	3 oz.	204	1	0
Sole, raw	1 oz.	25	0	0
Sour cream	1 tbsp.	−9	3	1
Sour cream	½ cup	−73	24	5
Sour cream	16 oz.	−290	96	20
Sour cream, reduced-fat	1 tbsp.	−5	2	1
Sour cream, reduced-fat	½ cup	−40	15	5
Sour cream, reduced-fat	16 oz.	−160	60	20
Sourdough bread	1 slice	−261	2	33
Soybean lecithin oil	1 tbsp.	−40	14	0
Soybean lecithin oil	½ cup	−323	109	0
Soybean oil	1 tbsp.	−33	14	0
Soybean oil	½ cup	−264	109	0
Soybeans, boiled	½ cup	−7	8	8
Soy milk	8 oz.	−9	5	4
Soy sauce	1 tbsp.	1	0	1
Soy sauce	¼ cup	4	0	4

*High in mercury; eat only occasionally.

**Very high in mercury; avoid eating.

†May contain nitrates and nitrites; eat only occasionally.

‡Associated with health risks and/or adverse reactions.

TABLE 4.1 IF Ratings: A to Z, *continued*

Food	Amount	IF Rating	Fat (g)	Carb (g)
Spaghetti, cooked	½ cup	−49	0	20
Spaghetti, uncooked	8 oz.	−392	0	160
Spaghetti, whole wheat, cooked	½ cup	−33	0	19
Spaghetti, whole wheat, uncooked	8 oz.	−264	0	152
Spaghetti squash, boiled	½ cup	4	0	5
Spareribs (pork), braised	3 oz.	−49	26	0
Spareribs (pork), braised	1 lb. (uncooked weight)	−98	51	0
Spearmint, dried	1 tsp.	1	0	0
Spearmint, fresh	2 tbsp.	3	0	1
Special K	1 serving (1 cup)	−34	0	22
Spinach, boiled	½ cup	241	0	3
Spinach, boiled	1 lb. (uncooked weight)	1,325	0	18
Spinach, canned	½ cup	261	1	4
Spinach, frozen	½ cup	276	0	5
Spinach, frozen	10-oz. package	640	1	11
Spinach, raw	1 cup (loosely packed)	80	0	1
Spinach, raw	1 lb.	1,200	0	15
Splenda	1 tsp.	0	0	0
Split peas, boiled	½ cup	−23	0	21
Split pea soup	1 cup	−102	2	30
Split pea soup	16-oz. can	−181	4	53

Food	Amount	IF Rating	Fat (g)	Carb (g)
Split pea soup with ham	1 cup	−77	4	27
Split pea soup with ham	16-oz. can	−143	8	50
Sponge cake	1 piece	−110	1	23
Spring onion	2 tbsp., chopped	33	0	1
Spring onion	1 large	68	0	2
Spring water	8 oz.	0	0	0
Sprouts, alfalfa	½ cup	4	0	1
Sprouts, mung bean	½ cup	8	0	3
Sprouts, radish	½ cup	6	1	1
Squash, spaghetti, boiled	½ cup	4	0	5
Squash, summer, boiled	½ cup, sliced	9	0	4
Squash, summer, raw	1 cup, sliced	20	0	4
Squid, fried	3 oz.	245	6	7
Squid, raw	1 oz.	72	0	1
Strawberries, fresh	1 cup, sliced	28	0	12
Strawberries, fresh	10 medium berries	22	0	9
Strawberries, fresh	1 pint	67	1	28
Strawberries, frozen	1 cup, thawed	16	0	20
Strawberries, pureed	1 cup	31	0	13
Striped bass,* baked or grilled	3 oz.	421	3	0
Striped mullet, baked or grilled	3 oz.	86	4	0

*High in mercury; eat only occasionally.

**Very high in mercury; avoid eating.

†May contain nitrates and nitrites; eat only occasionally.

‡Associated with health risks and/or adverse reactions.

TABLE 4.1 IF Ratings: A to Z, *continued*

Food	Amount	IF Rating	Fat (g)	Carb (g)
Stuffing prepared from mix	½ cup	−149	8	19
Sturgeon, baked or grilled	3 oz.	103	4	0
Sturgeon, smoked	3 oz.	52	4	0
Sugar, brown	1 tbsp., packed	−93	0	14
Sugar, brown	½ cup, packed	−746	0	110
Sugar, granulated	1 tsp.	−29	0	4
Sugar, granulated	½ cup	−725	0	107
Sugar, powdered	1 tsp.	−14	0	2
Sugar, powdered	½ cup	−339	0	50
SugarTwin	1 tsp.	0	0	0
Summer sausage†	1 oz.	13	8	1
Summer squash, boiled	½ cup, sliced	9	0	4
Summer squash, raw	1 cup, sliced	20	0	4
Sunflower oil	1 tbsp.	−3	14	0
Sunflower oil	½ cup	−27	109	0
Sunflower oil, high-linoleic	1 tbsp.	−75	14	0
Sunflower oil, high-linoleic	½ cup	−598	109	0
Sunflower seeds, dry-roasted	¼ cup	−41	14	7
Sunflower seeds, dry-roasted	4 oz.	−163	56	27
Suzuki* (raw sea bass)	1 oz.	88	1	0
Sweet'n Low	1 packet	0	0	0
Sweet potato, boiled	1 medium	210	0	27
Sweet potato, boiled	½ cup, mashed	228	0	29
Swiss chard, raw	1 cup, chopped	94	0	1
Swiss chard, boiled	½ cup	185	0	5

Food	Amount	IF Rating	Fat (g)	Carb (g)
Swiss chard, boiled	1 lb. (uncooked weight)	1,018	0	28
Swiss cheese	1 oz.	−22	8	1
Swiss cheese	1 cup, shredded	−88	31	4
Swiss cheese	1 cup, diced	−104	36	4
Swiss cheese	1 cup, melted	−191	67	8
Swiss cheese food, pasteurized	1 oz.	−17	7	1
Swordfish,** baked or grilled	3 oz.	309	4	0
Swordfish,** raw	1 oz.	78	1	0
Tabasco sauce	1 tsp.	370	0	0
Taco shell, baked	1 medium	−61	3	8
Tai (raw snapper)	1 oz.	37	0	0
Tamarind	1 fruit	0	0	1
Taro leaf, raw	1 cup	37	0	2
Taro shoots, raw	½ cup, sliced	5	0	1
Tarragon, ground	1 tsp.	1	0	1
T-bone steak, broiled or grilled	3 oz.	14	19	0
T-bone steak, broiled or grilled	1 lb. (uncooked weight)	28	38	0
T-bone steak, broiled or grilled, lean portions only	3 oz.	3	8	0

*High in mercury; eat only occasionally.

**Very high in mercury; avoid eating.

†May contain nitrates and nitrites; eat only occasionally.

‡Associated with health risks and/or adverse reactions.

TABLE 4.1 IF Ratings: A to Z, *continued*

Food	Amount	IF Rating	Fat (g)	Carb (g)
Tea, black	8 oz.	2	0	1
Tea, black, decaf	8 oz.	2	0	1
Tea, instant, decaf	8 oz.	0	0	0
Tea, instant, sugar-free‡	8 oz.	0	0	1
Tea, instant, with lemon	8 oz.	0	0	1
Tea biscuit	1 cookie	−22	1	4
Thyme, fresh	1 tbsp.	3	0	1
Thyme, ground	1 tsp.	7	0	1
Tilefish,** baked or grilled	3 oz.	272	4	0
Tilsit cheese	1 oz.	−19	7	1
Tomatillo, raw	1 medium	3	0	2
Tomato, green	1 small	19	0	5
Tomato, Italian (plum)	1 medium	12	0	2
Tomato, orange	1 medium	14	0	3
Tomato, orange	1 cup, chopped	20	0	5
Tomato, red	1 cup, chopped	35	0	7
Tomato, red	1 large	52	0	10
Tomato, sun-dried	1 piece	1	0	1
Tomato, sun-dried	½ cup	14	0	14
Tomato, yellow	1 cup, chopped	14	1	4
Tomato, yellow	1 large	21	1	6
Tomatoes, canned	1 cup	20	0	9
Tomatoes, canned	28-oz. can	62	0	27
Tomatoes, cherry	1 cup	15	0	6

Food	Amount	IF Rating	Fat (g)	Carb (g)
Tomatoes, pureed	1 cup	40	1	23
Tomatoes, pureed	28-oz. can	120	3	69
Tomatoes, stewed	1 cup	20	0	16
Tomatoes, stewed	28-oz. can	62	0	50
Tomato juice	8 oz.	45	0	10
Tomato soup, condensed, prepared with water	1 cup	−25	2	17
Tongue (beef), simmered or braised	1 lb. (uncooked weight)	85	93	0
Tongue (beef), simmered or braised	3 oz.	−17	19	0
Top blade roast (beef), braised	3 oz.	21	21	0
Top blade roast (beef), braised	1 lb. (uncooked weight)	63	65	0
Top blade roast (beef), braised, lean portions only	3 oz.	25	11	0
Top blade steak (beef), broiled or grilled	3 oz.	25	10	0
Top blade steak (beef), broiled or grilled	1 lb. (uncooked weight)	75	30	0
Top blade steak (beef), broiled or grilled, lean portions only	3 oz.	26	9	0
Tortilla, corn	6" tortilla	−48	1	11
Tortilla, wheat flour	6" tortilla	−30	2	16

*High in mercury; eat only occasionally.

**Very high in mercury; avoid eating.

†May contain nitrates and nitrites; eat only occasionally.

‡Associated with health risks and/or adverse reactions.

TABLE 4.1 IF Ratings: A to Z, *continued*

Food	Amount	IF Rating	Fat (g)	Carb (g)
Tortilla, wheat flour	10" tortilla	−69	5	36
Tortilla chips, plain	1 oz.	−91	7	18
Tortilla chips, plain	8-oz. bag	−728	60	143
Total cereal	1 serving (¾ cup)	43	1	23
Tripe, simmered or braised	3 oz.	−37	3	2
Tripe, simmered or braised	1 lb. (uncooked weight)	−187	17	8
Trout (freshwater), baked or grilled	3 oz.	202	7	0
Trout (saltwater),* baked or grilled	3 oz.	12	4	0
Trout, rainbow (farmed), baked or grilled	3 oz.	439	6	0
Trout, rainbow (wild), baked or grilled	3 oz.	310	5	0
Tuna, bluefin,* baked or grilled	3 oz.	591	5	0
Tuna, bluefin,* raw	1 oz.	154	1	0
Tuna, light, canned in oil	3 oz.	107	7	0
Tuna, light, canned in oil	6-oz. can	214	14	0
Tuna, light, canned in water	3 oz.	133	1	0
Tuna, light, canned in water	6-oz. can	265	1	0
Tuna, skipjack, baked or grilled	3 oz.	139	1	0
Tuna, skipjack, raw	1 oz.	38	0	0
Tuna, white,* canned in water	3 oz.	347	3	0

Food	Amount	IF Rating	Fat (g)	Carb (g)
Tuna, white,* canned in water	6-oz. can	694	5	0
Tuna, yellowfin,* raw	1 oz.	31	0	0
Tuna, yellowfin, baked or grilled	3 oz.	118	1	0
Turkey, dark meat, roasted	1 cup	−283	10	0
Turkey bologna†	1 oz.	−15	4	1
Turkey breast (pre-basted), roasted, with skin	3 oz.	−45	3	0
Turkey breast (pre-basted), roasted, with skin	1 breast	−915	59	0
Turkey breast, roasted, with skin	3 oz.	−106	6	0
Turkey breast, roasted, with skin	1 breast	−2,155	128	0
Turkey breast, sliced (packaged)	1 oz.	11	1	1
Turkey giblets, simmered	3 oz.	−75	10	1
Turkey ham†	1 oz.	−16	1	1
Turkey hot dog†	1 sausage	−8	8	1
Turkey pastrami†	1 oz.	−16	1	1
Turkey roll (luncheon meat)†	1 oz.	−33	2	0
Turkey salami†	1 oz.	−11	3	0
Turkey wing, roasted, with skin	1 wing	−226	23	0
Turmeric	1 tsp.	501	0	0
Turnip, boiled	½ cup, mashed	9	0	6

*High in mercury; eat only occasionally.

**Very high in mercury; avoid eating.

†May contain nitrates and nitrites; eat only occasionally.

‡Associated with health risks and/or adverse reactions.

TABLE 4.1 IF Ratings: A to Z, *continued*

Food	Amount	IF Rating	Fat (g)	Carb (g)
Turnip greens, boiled	½ cup	212	0	4
Twix candy bar	1 bar	−129	14	37
Unagi (freshwater eel)	1 oz.	15	4	0
Vanilla wafer	1 cookie	−28	1	4
Vanilla wafers	1 cup, crushed	−373	15	56
Veal kidney	3 oz.	−108	5	0
Veal kidney	1 lb. (uncooked weight)	−540	24	0
Veal loin, braised	3 oz.	−91	15	0
Veal loin, braised	1 lb. (uncooked weight)	−364	58	0
Veal loin, braised, lean portions only	3 oz.	−101	8	0
Veal loin, roasted	3 oz.	−71	10	0
Veal loin, roasted	1 lb. (uncooked weight)	−768	113	0
Veal loin, roasted, lean portions only	3 oz.	−71	6	0
Veal shank, braised	3 oz.	−41	5	0
Veal shank, braised	1 lb. (uncooked weight)	−61	8	0
Veal shank, braised, lean portions only	3 oz.	−45	4	0
Veal shoulder, braised	3 oz.	−55	9	0
Veal shoulder, braised	1 lb. (uncooked weight)	−348	56	0

Food	Amount	IF Rating	Fat (g)	Carb (g)
Veal shoulder, roasted	3 oz.	−71	7	0
Veal shoulder, roasted	1 lb. (uncooked weight)	−213	22	0
Veal shoulder, roasted, lean portions only	3 oz.	−66	6	0
Veal sirloin, braised	3 oz.	−61	11	0
Veal sirloin, braised	1 lb. (uncooked weight)	−183	34	0
Veal sirloin, braised, lean portions only	3 oz.	−60	6	0
Veal sirloin, roasted	3 oz.	−51	9	0
Veal sirloin, roasted	1 lb. (uncooked weight)	−153	27	0
Veal sirloin, roasted, lean portions only	3 oz.	−61	5	0
Vegetarian bacon	1 strip	−6	3	1
Vegetarian breakfast patty	1 patty	−6	3	4
Vegetarian burger	1 patty	49	4	7
Vegetarian hot dog	1 sausage	−8	7	2
Vegetarian meat substitute	3 oz.	−6	9	5
Vienna sausage†	1 sausage	7	3	0
Vinegar, cider	1 tbsp.	0	0	0
Vinegar, distilled	1 tbsp.	0	0	0
Waffle, frozen	1 waffle	−85	2	12

*High in mercury; eat only occasionally.

**Very high in mercury; avoid eating.

†May contain nitrates and nitrites; eat only occasionally.

‡Associated with health risks and/or adverse reactions.

TABLE 4.1 IF Ratings: A to Z, *continued*

Food	Amount	IF Rating	Fat (g)	Carb (g)
Walleye pike, baked or grilled	3 oz.	112	1	0
Walleye pollack, baked or grilled	3 oz.	211	1	0
Walnut oil	1 tbsp.	−25	14	0
Walnut oil	½ cup	−200	110	0
Walnuts, black	1 oz.	−39	17	3
Walnuts, black	1 cup, chopped	−174	74	12
Walnuts, English	1 oz.	−38	18	4
Walnuts, English	1 cup, chopped	−162	78	16
Water chestnuts, canned	½ cup, sliced	3	0	9
Watercress	1 cup, chopped	44	0	0
Watermelon	1 cup, diced	−62	0	11
Wheat germ oil	1 tbsp.	−53	14	0
Wheat germ oil	½ cup	−421	109	0
Wheaties	1 serving (1 cup)	−103	1	24
Whitefish, baked or grilled	3 oz.	421	6	0
Whitefish, smoked	1 oz.	31	0	0
Whiting, baked or grilled	3 oz.	219	1	0
Worcestershire sauce	1 tbsp.	2	0	4
Yam, baked	½ cup, cubed	−52	0	19
Yeast, baking	1 packet (2 tsp.)	40	0	3
Yellow cake with vanilla frosting	1 piece	−163	9	38

Food	Amount	IF Rating	Fat (g)	Carb (g)
Yellowfin tuna,* raw	1 oz.	31	0	0
Yellowfin tuna, baked or grilled	3 oz.	118	1	0
Yogurt, low-fat, fruit flavors	1 cup (8 oz.)	−144	3	46
Yogurt, low-fat, plain	1 cup (8 oz.)	−17	4	18
Yogurt, nonfat, fruit flavors	1 cup (8 oz.)	−130	0	46
Yogurt, nonfat, plain	1 cup (8 oz.)	−4	0	17
Yogurt, whole-milk, plain	1 cup (8 oz.)	−31	8	11
Zucchini, boiled	½ cup, sliced	19	0	4
Zucchini, raw	1 cup, chopped	22	0	4
Zucchini, raw	1 medium	33	0	6

*High in mercury; eat only occasionally.

**Very high in mercury; avoid eating.

†May contain nitrates and nitrites; eat only occasionally.

‡Associated with health risks and/or adverse reactions.

TABLE 4.2 IF Ratings by Category

Category Guide

Food	Typical Serving	IF Rating	Fat (g)	Carb (g)
Fruits (See **Beverages** for fruit juices.)				
Acerola cherries	10 cherries	340	0	4
Apple, fresh	1 medium	−62	1	21
Apple, dried	4 rings	−40	0	16
Apricot, canned (light syrup)	2 halves	−60	0	14
Apricot, dried	2 halves	−8	0	4
Apricot, fresh	1 fruit	−7	0	4
Banana	1 medium	−118	1	28
Blueberries	½ cup	−11	0	10
Cantaloupe	1 cup	21	0	11
Cherries, sweet	10 cherries	−16	0	10

Food	Typical Serving	IF Rating	Fat (g)	Carb (g)
Date, dried	1 fruit	−26	0	6
Fig, dried	1 fruit	−27	0	5
Fruit cocktail, canned (water pack)	½ cup	−43	0	10
Grapefruit, pink	½ fruit	1	0	9
Grapefruit, white	½ fruit	−1	0	10
Grapes, red or green, seedless	15 grapes	−57	0	15
Grapes, red or green, with seeds	15 grapes	−61	0	16
Guava	1 fruit	35	1	8
Kiwi	1 fruit	−14	0	13
Kumquat, with peel	1 fruit	4	0	3
Lemon, without peel	1 fruit	21	0	8
Lime, without peel	1 fruit	10	0	7
Mango	1 fruit	−106	1	35
Mulberries	10 berries	0	0	0
Orange	1 large	−19	0	22
Papaya	½ cup, cubed	−3	0	7
Peach	1 large	−54	0	17
Peaches, canned (heavy syrup)	½ cup (with liquid)	−123	0	25
Peaches, canned (juice pack)	½ cup (with liquid)	−45	0	15
Peaches, canned (light syrup)	½ cup (with liquid)	−78	0	19
Pear	1 medium	−74	1	25
Pears, canned (juice pack)	½ fruit	−36	0	10

TABLE 4.2 IF Ratings by Category, *continued*

Food	Typical Serving	IF Rating	Fat (g)	Carb (g)
Pineapple, canned (water pack)	½ cup (with liquid)	−54	0	10
Pineapple, fresh	½ cup, diced	−19	1	10
Plum	1 fruit	−25	0	9
Prune, dried	1 fruit	−12	0	5
Raisins	1 mini-box	−67	0	11
Raspberries	½ cup	5	1	8
Rhubarb, fresh	½ cup, diced	9	0	3
Rhubarb, frozen	½ cup, diced	8	0	4
Strawberries	10 medium berries	22	0	9
Tamarind	1 fruit	0	0	1
Watermelon	1 cup, diced	−62	0	11

Vegetables (See **Beverages** for juices.)

Food	Typical Serving	IF Rating	Fat (g)	Carb (g)
Alfalfa sprouts	½ cup	4	0	1
Artichoke, boiled	1 artichoke	25	0	13
Artichoke hearts, boiled	½ cup	17	0	9
Arugula, raw	1 cup (loosely packed)	16	0	0
Asparagus, boiled	½ cup	55	0	4
Asparagus, canned	½ cup	53	1	3
Asparagus, frozen	½ cup	87	0	4
Aubergine, cooked	½ cup, cubed	2	0	4
Avocado, raw	½ cup, mashed	105	17	10
Bamboo shoots, canned	½ cup, sliced	1	0	1
Bean sprouts	½ cup	8	0	3
Beet greens, raw	1 cup, chopped	68	0	2

Food	Typical Serving	IF Rating	Fat (g)	Carb (g)
Beets, canned	½ cup, sliced	−23	0	6
Belgian endive	1 cup	8	0	4
Bok choy, raw	1 cup, shredded	67	0	2
Borage, raw	1 cup, chopped	16	1	3
Broccoli, boiled	½ cup	73	0	4
Broccoli, frozen	½ cup	55	0	5
Broccoli, raw	½ cup, diced	25	0	2
Brussels sprouts, boiled	½ cup	61	0	6
Brussels sprouts, frozen	½ cup	83	0	8
Butter beans, canned	½ cup	−19	0	20
Cabbage, green, boiled	½ cup, shredded	18	0	3
Cabbage, green, raw	1 cup, shredded	26	0	4
Cabbage, red, boiled	½ cup, shredded	17	0	5
Cabbage, red, raw	1 cup, shredded	36	0	5
Cabbage, savoy, boiled	½ cup, shredded	13	0	4
Cabbage, savoy, raw	1 cup, shredded	40	0	4
Carrots, canned	½ cup, sliced	72	0	4
Carrots, frozen	½ cup, sliced	112	0	6
Carrots, raw	½ cup, sliced	60	0	6
Cauliflower, boiled	½ cup	19	0	3
Cauliflower, raw	½ cup	15	0	2

TABLE 4.2 IF Ratings by Category, *continued*

Food	Typical Serving	IF Rating	Fat (g)	Carb (g)
Celery, boiled	1 cup, diced	34	0	6
Celery, raw	½ cup, diced	10	0	2
Chili pepper, red, canned	¼ cup, chopped	244	0	2
Chili pepper, red, raw	1 pepper	286	0	4
Chinese cabbage, boiled	½ cup, shredded	11	0	1
Chinese cabbage, raw	1 cup, shredded	67	0	2
Collard greens, boiled	½ cup, chopped	205	0	5
Collard greens, raw	1 cup, chopped	83	0	2
Corn, frozen	½ cup	−62	1	17
Corn, white, canned	½ cup, drained	−72	1	15
Corn, yellow, canned	½ cup, drained	−108	1	32
Corn on cob, boiled	1 ear	−111	1	22
Courgette, boiled	½ cup, sliced	19	0	4
Courgette, raw	1 cup, chopped	22	0	4
Cucumber, raw, with peel	½ cup, sliced	4	0	2
Dandelion greens, boiled	½ cup, chopped	92	0	3
Dandelion greens, raw	½ cup, chopped	76	0	5
Edamame, boiled	½ cup, shelled	−7	8	8
Eggplant, cooked	½ cup, cubed	2	0	4

Food	Typical Serving	IF Rating	Fat (g)	Carb (g)
Endive, raw	1 cup, chopped	52	0	2
Fennel bulb, raw	1 cup, sliced	10	0	6
French fries, fast-food	1 small order	−213	16	34
French fries, frozen	10 fries	−86	4	16
Garlic, raw	1 clove	111	0	1
Green beans, boiled	½ cup	15	0	5
Green beans, canned	½ cup	12	0	3
Green beans, frozen	½ cup	10	0	5
Green beans, raw	½ cup	15	0	4
Jerusalem artichoke, raw	½ cup, sliced	5	0	15
Kale, boiled	½ cup, chopped	232	0	4
Kelp, raw	2 tbsp.	5	0	1
Kohlrabi, boiled	½ cup, sliced	23	0	6
Leek, boiled	½ cup, chopped	134	0	4
Lettuce, Bibb	1 cup, shredded	22	0	1
Lettuce, Boston	1 cup, shredded	43	0	1
Lettuce, butterhead	1 cup, shredded	43	0	1
Lettuce, iceberg	1 cup, shredded	13	0	2
Lettuce, leaf	1 cup, shredded	52	0	1
Lettuce, romaine	1 cup, shredded	61	0	2

TABLE 4.2 IF Ratings by Category, *continued*

Food	Typical Serving	IF Rating	Fat (g)	Carb (g)
Lima beans, baby, boiled	½ cup	−28	0	18
Lima beans, large, boiled	½ cup	−19	0	20
Mung bean sprouts	½ cup	8	0	3
Mung beans, boiled	½ cup	−9	0	19
Mushroom, canned	½ cup, sliced	5	0	4
Mushroom, cremini	1 mushroom	4	0	1
Mushroom, enoki	1 mushroom	1	0	0
Mushroom, oyster	1 mushroom	4	0	1
Mushroom, straw, canned	½ cup	17	1	4
Mushroom, white	½ cup, sliced	4	0	1
Mustard greens, boiled	½ cup, chopped	117	0	1
Napa cabbage, boiled	½ cup, shredded	14	0	1
Okra, boiled	½ cup, sliced	23	0	4
Onion, boiled	½ cup, diced	300	0	12
Onion, canned	½ cup, diced	286	0	5
Onion, frozen	½ cup, diced	203	0	5
Onion, raw	½ cup, diced	206	0	8
Palm hearts, canned	1 piece	5	0	2
Parsnip, boiled	½ cup, sliced	−86	0	13
Peas, canned	½ cup	−8	0	12
Peas, frozen	½ cup	4	0	10
Pepper, banana, raw	1 pepper	65	0	2
Pepper, green, boiled	½ cup, chopped	27	0	5
Pepper, green, raw	1 cup, chopped	63	0	7

Food	Typical Serving	IF Rating	Fat (g)	Carb (g)
Pepper, Hungarian	1 pepper	63	0	2
Pepper, jalapeño, canned	1 pepper	56	0	1
Pepper, jalapeño, raw	1 pepper	55	0	1
Pepper, red bell, boiled	½ cup, chopped	84	0	5
Pepper, red bell, frozen	½ cup, chopped	100	1	7
Pepper, red bell, raw	½ cup, chopped	90	0	5
Pepper, serrano, raw	1 pepper	122	0	0
Pepper, yellow bell, raw	1 pepper	159	0	12
Pimento, canned	2 tbsp., chopped	16	0	1
Potato, boiled, without skin	½ medium	−127	0	17
Potato, baked, with skin	½ medium	−129	0	19
Potato, canned	½ cup	−68	0	15
Potato, russet, baked	½ medium	−132	0	19
Pumpkin, boiled	½ cup, mashed	25	0	6
Pumpkin, canned	½ cup	15	0	10
Purslane, raw	1 cup	5	0	1
Radicchio	1 cup, shredded	28	0	2
Radish sprouts	½ cup	6	1	1
Radish, red	½ cup, sliced	7	0	2
Radish, white	½ cup, sliced	8	0	1
Rutabaga, boiled	½ cup, mashed	16	0	11
Scallion, raw	1 large	68	0	2

TABLE 4.2 IF Ratings by Category, *continued*

Food	Typical Serving	IF Rating	Fat (g)	Carb (g)
Seaweed, agar	2 tbsp.	2	0	1
Seaweed, Irish moss	2 tbsp.	10	0	1
Seaweed, kelp	2 tbsp.	5	0	1
Seaweed, lavar	2 tbsp.	16	0	1
Seaweed, wakame	2 tbsp.	15	0	1
Shallot	2 tbsp., chopped	52	0	3
Snap beans, boiled	½ cup	15	0	5
Snap beans, canned	½ cup	12	0	3
Snap beans, frozen	½ cup	10	0	5
Snap beans, raw	½ cup	15	0	4
Snow peas, raw	½ cup	26	0	4
Snow peas, boiled	½ cup	36	0	6
Soybeans, boiled	½ cup	−7	8	8
Spaghetti squash, boiled	½ cup	4	0	5
Spinach, boiled	½ cup	241	0	3
Spinach, canned	½ cup	261	1	4
Spinach, frozen	½ cup	276	0	5
Spinach, raw	1 cup (loosely packed)	80	0	1
Summer squash, boiled	½ cup, sliced	9	0	4
Summer squash, raw	1 cup, sliced	20	0	4
Sweet potato, boiled	1 medium	210	0	27
Sweet potato, boiled	½ cup, mashed	228	0	29
Swiss chard, boiled	½ cup	185	0	5
Swiss chard, raw	1 cup, chopped	94	0	1

Food	Typical Serving	IF Rating	Fat (g)	Carb (g)
Taro leaf, raw	1 cup	37	0	2
Taro shoots, raw	½ cup, sliced	5	0	1
Tomatillo, raw	1 medium	3	0	2
Tomato, green	1 small	19	0	5
Tomato, Italian (plum)	1 medium	12	0	2
Tomato, orange	1 cup, chopped	20	0	5
Tomato, red	1 cup, chopped	35	0	7
Tomato, sun-dried	1 piece	1	0	1
Tomato, yellow	1 medium	21	1	6
Tomatoes, canned	1 cup	20	0	9
Tomatoes, cherry	1 cup	15	0	6
Tomatoes, stewed	1 cup	20	0	16
Turnip, boiled	½ cup, mashed	9	0	6
Turnip greens, boiled	½ cup	212	0	4
Water chestnut, canned	½ cup, sliced	3	0	9
Watercress	1 cup, chopped	44	0	0
Yam, baked	½ cup, cubed	−52	0	19
Zucchini, boiled	½ cup, sliced	19	0	4
Zucchini, raw	1 cup, chopped	22	0	4

Beans and Legumes

Food	Typical Serving	IF Rating	Fat (g)	Carb (g)
Baked beans	½ cup	−65	0	27
Baked beans, with pork	½ cup	−52	1	24

TABLE 4.2 IF Ratings by Category, *continued*

Food	Typical Serving	IF Rating	Fat (g)	Carb (g)
Black beans, boiled	½ cup	−11	0	20
Black-eyed peas, boiled	½ cup	−12	0	18
Broad beans, boiled	½ cup	−74	0	17
Butter beans, boiled	½ cup	−19	0	20
Chick-peas, boiled	½ cup	−39	2	22
Edamame, boiled	½ cup, shelled	−7	8	9
Fava beans, boiled	½ cup	−74	0	17
Garbanzo beans, boiled	½ cup	−39	2	22
Green beans, boiled	½ cup	14	0	5
Green beans, canned	½ cup	11	0	3
Green beans, frozen	½ cup	9	0	5
Green beans, raw	½ cup	14	0	4
Kidney beans, light, boiled	½ cup	−6	0	20
Kidney beans, dark, boiled	½ cup	−4	0	20
Lentils, boiled	½ cup	6	0	20
Lima beans, baby, boiled	½ cup	−28	0	9
Lima beans, large, boiled	½ cup	−19	0	20
Mung bean sprouts	½ cup	8	0	3
Mung beans, boiled	½ cup	−9	0	19
Navy beans, canned	½ cup	−51	1	27
Pinto beans, boiled	½ cup	−21	1	22
Pinto beans, canned	½ cup	−33	1	18
Snap beans, boiled	½ cup	14	0	5
Snap beans, canned	½ cup	11	0	3
Snap beans, frozen	½ cup	9	0	5
Snap beans, raw	½ cup	14	0	4

Food	Typical Serving	IF Rating	Fat (g)	Carb (g)
Soybeans, boiled	½ cup	−7	8	9
Split peas, boiled	½ cup	−23	0	21

Eggs and Egg Products

Food	Typical Serving	IF Rating	Fat (g)	Carb (g)
Egg	1 large	−43	5	0
Egg, duck	1 egg	−163	10	1
Egg, goose	1 egg	−290	19	2
Egg, quail	1 egg	−6	1	0
Egg, turkey	1 egg	−62	9	1
Egg, whole, dried	1 tbsp.	−14	2	0
Egg substitute, frozen	¼ cup (equiv. to 1 egg)	−7	7	2
Egg substitute, liquid	¼ cup (equiv. to 1 egg)	14	2	0
Egg white	1 large	5	0	0
Egg white, dried	1 tbsp.	17	0	1
Egg yolk	1 large	−48	5	1
Egg yolk, dried	1 tbsp.	−16	2	0

Cheese

Food	Typical Serving	IF Rating	Fat (g)	Carb (g)
American, pasteurized	1 oz.	−23	9	0
Blue	1 oz.	−22	8	1
Brick	1 oz.	−21	8	1
Brie	1 oz.	−16	8	0
Camembert	1 oz.	−14	7	0
Cheddar	1 oz.	−26	9	0
Cheddar, low-fat	1 oz.	−1	3	1
Cheese food, cold pack	1 oz.	−16	7	2

TABLE 4.2 IF Ratings by Category, *continued*

Food	Typical Serving	IF Rating	Fat (g)	Carb (g)
Colby	1 oz.	−23	9	1
Colby, low-fat	1 oz.	−1	3	1
Cottage cheese, 1% fat	½ cup	9	1	3
Cottage cheese, 2% fat	½ cup	7	2	4
Cottage cheese, creamed	½ cup	−4	5	3
Cottage cheese, nonfat	½ cup	14	0	2
Cream cheese	1 oz.	−31	10	1
Cream cheese, nonfat	1 oz.	2	0	1
Cream cheese, reduced-fat	1 oz.	−21	7	1
Edam	1 oz.	−18	8	0
Feta	1 oz.	−20	6	1
Fontina	1 oz.	−21	8	0
Goat, hard	1 oz.	−45	10	1
Goat, semisoft	1 oz.	−39	8	1
Goat, soft	1 oz.	−26	6	0
Gouda	1 oz.	−19	8	1
Gruyère	1 oz.	−17	9	0
Limburger	1 oz.	−14	8	0
Monterey Jack	1 oz.	−22	9	0
Mozzarella, part-skim	1 oz.	−11	5	1
Mozzarella, whole-milk	1 oz.	−10	6	1
Muenster	1 oz.	−22	8	0
Neufchâtel	1 oz.	−21	7	1
Parmesan	1 oz.	−16	7	1
Pimento cheese, pasteurized	1 oz.	−22	9	0
Port Salut	1 oz.	−13	8	0

Food	Typical Serving	IF Rating	Fat (g)	Carb (g)
Provolone	1 oz.	−23	9	1
Queso añejo	1 oz.	−23	9	1
Queso asadero	1 oz.	−21	8	1
Ricotta, part-skim	½ cup	−7	10	6
Ricotta, whole-milk	½ cup	−35	16	4
Romano	1 oz.	−19	8	1
Roquefort	1 oz.	−22	9	1
Swiss	1 oz.	−22	8	1
Swiss cheese food, pasteurized	1 oz.	−17	7	1
Tilsit	1 oz.	−19	7	1

Dairy Products (See also **Cheese**.)

Food	Typical Serving	IF Rating	Fat (g)	Carb (g)
Cottage cheese, 1% fat	½ cup	9	1	3
Cottage cheese, 2% fat	½ cup	7	2	4
Cottage cheese, creamed	½ cup	−4	5	3
Cottage cheese, nonfat	½ cup	14	0	2
Cream, half-and-half	1 tbsp.	−5	2	1
Cream, heavy (whipping)	1 tbsp.	−18	6	0
Cream, light (table)	1 tbsp.	−15	5	0
Cream cheese	1 oz.	−31	10	1
Cream cheese, nonfat	1 oz.	2	0	1
Cream cheese, reduced-fat	1 oz.	−21	7	1
Ice cream, chocolate	½ cup	−127	7	19
Ice cream, chocolate, premium	½ cup	−91	13	15
Ice cream, vanilla	½ cup	−124	8	17

TABLE 4.2 IF Ratings by Category, *continued*

Food	Typical Serving	IF Rating	Fat (g)	Carb (g)
Ice cream, vanilla, light	½ cup	−102	4	20
Ice cream, vanilla, premium	½ cup	−165	17	24
Ice milk, vanilla	½ cup	−80	3	15
Milk, chocolate	1 cup	−116	8	26
Milk, chocolate, low-fat	1 cup	−80	3	26
Milk, nonfat dry powder	¼ cup	−35	0	16
Milk, skim	1 cup	−28	0	12
Milk, sweetened condensed	1 tbsp.	−66	2	10
Milk, whole	1 cup	−45	8	11
Neufchâtel cheese	1 oz.	−21	7	1
Sour cream	1 tbsp.	−9	3	1
Sour cream, reduced-fat	1 tbsp.	−5	2	1
Sour half-and-half	1 tbsp.	−5	2	1
Soy milk	1 cup	−9	5	4
Yogurt, low-fat, fruit flavors	1 cup	−144	3	46
Yogurt, low-fat, plain	1 cup	−17	4	18
Yogurt, nonfat, fruit flavors	1 cup	−130	0	46
Yogurt, nonfat, plain	1 cup	−4	0	17
Yogurt, whole-milk, plain	1 cup	−31	8	11
Fish (See also **Fish: Sushi.**)				
Anchovy, canned in oil	1 oz.	297	3	0
Arctic char (farmed)	3 oz.	622	10	0
Bass, freshwater, baked or grilled	3 oz.	167	4	0
Bass, sea,* baked or grilled	3 oz.	331	2	0

*High in mercury; eat only occasionally.

Food	Typical Serving	IF Rating	Fat (g)	Carb (g)
Bass, striped,* baked or grilled	3 oz.	421	3	0
Bluefin tuna,* baked or grilled	3 oz.	591	5	0
Bluefish,* baked or grilled	3 oz.	439	5	0
Carp, baked or grilled	3 oz.	41	6	0
Catfish (farmed), baked or grilled	3 oz.	59	7	0
Catfish (wild), baked or grilled	3 oz.	46	2	0
Caviar, black and red	1 tbsp.	421	3	1
Chum, baked or grilled	3 oz.	331	4	0
Chum, canned	3 oz.	447	5	0
Cisco, smoked	3 oz.	447	10	0
Clams, canned	3 oz.	169	2	4
Clams, raw	3 oz. (5 medium)	55	1	2
Clams, steamed	3 oz. (9 small)	190	2	4
Cod, Atlantic, baked or grilled	3 oz.	71	1	0
Cod, Atlantic, canned	3 oz.	71	1	0
Cod, Atlantic, dried and salted	1 oz.	74	1	0
Cod, Pacific, baked or grilled	3 oz.	129	1	0
Coho (farmed), baked or grilled	3 oz.	455	7	0
Coho (wild), poached	3 oz.	451	6	0

*High in mercury; eat only occasionally.

TABLE 4.2 IF Ratings by Category, *continued*

Food	Typical Serving	IF Rating	Fat (g)	Carb (g)
Crab, Alaska king, steamed or boiled	3 oz.	60	1	0
Crab, blue, canned	3 oz.	127	1	0
Crab, blue, steamed or boiled	3 oz.	171	1	0
Crab, imitation	3 oz.	238	1	9
Crayfish (farmed), steamed or boiled	3 oz.	47	1	0
Crayfish (wild), steamed or boiled	3 oz.	55	1	0
Cuttlefish, steamed	3 oz.	146	1	1
Eel, baked or grilled	3 oz.	44	13	0
Fish sticks, frozen	1 stick	0	3	7
Flounder, baked or grilled	3 oz.	204	1	0
Grouper,** baked or grilled	3 oz.	83	1	0
Haddock, baked or grilled	3 oz.	100	1	0
Haddock, smoked	1 oz.	34	1	0
Halibut, Atlantic,* baked or grilled	3 oz.	78	3	0
Halibut, Greenland,* baked or grilled	3 oz.	493	15	0
Halibut, Pacific,* baked or grilled	3 oz.	78	3	0
Herring, Atlantic, baked or grilled	3 oz.	790	10	0
Herring, Atlantic, kippered	1 oz.	289	4	0
Jack mackerel, baked or grilled	3 oz.	686	9	0

*High in mercury; eat only occasionally.   **Very high in mercury; avoid eating.

Food	Typical Serving	IF Rating	Fat (g)	Carb (g)
King mackerel,** baked or grilled	3 oz.	214	2	0
Lobster, Maine,* steamed or boiled	3 oz.	80	1	1
Lox, smoked	1 oz.	72	1	0
Mackerel, Atlantic, baked or grilled	3 oz.	512	15	0
Mackerel, jack, canned	3 oz.	465	5	0
Mackerel, king,** baked or grilled	3 oz.	214	2	0
Mackerel, Pacific, baked or grilled	3 oz.	686	9	0
Mahimahi, baked or grilled	3 oz.	91	1	0
Mullet, baked or grilled	3 oz.	86	4	0
Mussels, blue, raw	3 oz. (5 medium)	167	2	3
Mussels, blue, steamed	3 oz. (8 medium)	293	4	6
Octopus, steamed or stewed	3 oz.	164	2	4
Orange roughy,** baked or grilled	3 oz.	44	1	0
Oysters, Eastern (farmed), baked	3 oz. (8 medium)	327	2	6
Oysters, Eastern (farmed), raw	3 oz. (6 medium)	292	1	5
Oysters, Eastern (wild), baked	3 oz. (8 medium)	362	2	4
Oysters, Eastern (wild), raw	3 oz. (6 medium)	331	2	3

*High in mercury; eat only occasionally.   **Very high in mercury; avoid eating.

TABLE 4.2 IF Ratings by Category, *continued*

Food	Typical Serving	IF Rating	Fat (g)	Carb (g)
Oysters, Eastern (wild), steamed	3 oz. (12 medium)	500	4	7
Oysters, Pacific, raw	3 oz. (2 large)	356	2	4
Oysters, Pacific, steamed	3 oz. (3 large)	703	4	8
Perch, Atlantic, baked or grilled	3 oz.	195	2	0
Perch, white, baked or grilled	3 oz.	88	1	0
Pike, Northern, baked or grilled	3 oz.	46	1	0
Pike, walleye, baked or grilled	3 oz.	112	1	0
Pollack, Atlantic, baked or grilled	3 oz.	221	1	0
Pollack, walleye, baked or grilled	3 oz.	211	1	0
Pompano, baked or grilled	3 oz.	44	10	0
Red snapper, baked or grilled	3 oz.	125	1	0
Rockfish, Pacific, baked or grilled	3 oz.	188	2	0
Roe	1 tbsp.	176	1	0
Roughy,** baked or grilled	3 oz.	44	1	0
Sablefish, baked or grilled	3 oz.	685	17	0
Sablefish, smoked	1 oz.	233	6	0
Salmon, Atlantic (farmed), baked or grilled	3 oz.	−180	11	0
Salmon, Atlantic (wild), baked or grilled	3 oz.	493	7	0

**Very high in mercury; avoid eating.

Food	Typical Serving	IF Rating	Fat (g)	Carb (g)
Salmon, chinook, baked or grilled	3 oz.	581	11	0
Salmon, chinook, smoked	1 oz.	72	1	0
Salmon, chum, baked or grilled	3 oz.	331	4	0
Salmon, chum, canned	3 oz.	447	5	0
Salmon, coho (farmed), baked or grilled	3 oz.	455	7	0
Salmon, coho (wild), poached	3 oz.	451	6	0
Salmon, pink, baked or grilled	3 oz.	469	4	0
Salmon, pink, canned	3 oz.	661	5	0
Salmon, smoked	1 oz.	72	1	0
Salmon, sockeye, baked or grilled	3 oz.	518	9	0
Salmon, sockeye, canned	3 oz.	192	7	0
Sardines, canned in oil	3 oz.	470	11	0
Sardines, canned in tomato sauce	3 oz.	380	9	1
Scallops, bay, steamed	3 oz. (12 scallops)	139	1	0
Scallops, sea, steamed	3 oz. (5 scallops)	139	1	0
Sea bass,* baked or grilled	3 oz.	331	2	0
Sea trout,* baked or grilled	3 oz.	12	4	0
Shad, baked or grilled	3 oz.	37	15	0
Shrimp, canned	3 oz.	162	2	1

*High in mercury; eat only occasionally.

TABLE 4.2 IF Ratings by Category, *continued*

Food	Typical Serving	IF Rating	Fat (g)	Carb (g)
Shrimp, steamed or boiled	3 oz. (15 shrimp)	95	1	0
Skipjack tuna, baked or grilled	3 oz.	139	1	0
Smelt, rainbow, baked or grilled	3 oz.	337	3	0
Snapper, baked or grilled	3 oz.	125	1	0
Sockeye, baked or grilled	3 oz.	518	9	0
Sockeye, canned	3 oz.	192	7	0
Sole, baked or grilled	3 oz.	204	1	0
Squid, fried	3 oz.	245	6	7
Striped bass,* baked or grilled	3 oz.	421	3	0
Striped mullet, baked or grilled	3 oz.	86	4	0
Sturgeon, baked or grilled	3 oz.	103	4	0
Sturgeon, smoked	1 oz.	17	1	0
Swordfish,** baked or grilled	3 oz.	309	4	0
Tilefish,** baked or grilled	3 oz.	272	4	0
Trout, freshwater, baked or grilled	3 oz.	202	7	0
Trout, rainbow (farmed), baked or grilled	3 oz.	439	6	0
Trout, rainbow (wild), baked or grilled	3 oz.	310	5	0
Trout, saltwater,* baked or grilled	3 oz.	12	4	0

*High in mercury; eat only occasionally.   **Very high in mercury; avoid eating.

Food	Typical Serving	IF Rating	Fat (g)	Carb (g)
Tuna, bluefin,* baked or grilled	3 oz.	591	5	0
Tuna, light, canned in oil	3 oz.	107	7	0
Tuna, light, canned in water	3 oz.	133	1	0
Tuna, skipjack, baked or grilled	3 oz.	139	1	0
Tuna, white,* canned in water	3 oz.	347	3	0
Tuna, yellowfin,* baked or grilled	3 oz.	118	1	0
Walleye pike, baked or grilled	3 oz.	112	1	0
Walleye pollack, baked or grilled	3 oz.	211	1	0
Whitefish, baked or grilled	3 oz.	421	6	0
Whitefish, smoked	1 oz.	31	0	0
Whiting, baked or grilled	3 oz.	219	1	0
Yellowfin tuna,* baked or grilled	3 oz.	118	1	0

Fish: Sushi

Food	Typical Serving	IF Rating	Fat (g)	Carb (g)
Abalone, raw	1 oz.	20	0	2
Ama-ebi	1 large	13	0	0
Anago	1 oz.	15	4	0
Awabi	1 oz.	20	0	2
Bluefin tuna,* raw	1 oz.	154	1	0
Bonito	1 oz.	38	0	0
Clam, raw	1 medium	11	0	0

*High in mercury; eat only occasionally.

TABLE 4.2 IF Ratings by Category, *continued*

Food	Typical Serving	IF Rating	Fat (g)	Carb (g)
Crab, imitation	1 oz.	79	0	3
Ebi	1 large	6	0	0
Eel, baked or grilled	1 oz.	15	4	0
Flounder, raw	1 oz.	25	0	0
Halibut, raw	1 oz.	19	1	0
Hamaguri	1 medium	11	0	0
Hawara	1 oz.	177	2	0
Hirame	1 oz.	25	0	0
Hotate-gai	1 medium	16	0	0
Ika	1 oz.	72	0	1
Ikura	1 tbsp.	139	1	0
Kajiki**	1 oz.	78	1	0
Kamaboko	1 oz.	79	0	3
Karei	1 oz.	25	0	0
Katsuo	1 oz.	38	0	0
Mackerel, Pacific, raw	1 oz.	177	2	0
Mackerel, king,** raw	1 oz.	268	4	0
Maguro: Refer to specific type of tuna.				
Masu*	1 oz.	6	1	0
Ohyo	1 oz.	19	1	0
Oyster, Eastern (farmed), raw	1 medium	48	0	1
Oyster, Eastern (wild), raw	1 medium	55	0	1
Oyster, Pacific, raw	1 large	178	1	2
Red snapper, raw	1 oz.	37	0	0

*High in mercury; eat only occasionally.   **Very high in mercury; avoid eating.

Food	Typical Serving	IF Rating	Fat (g)	Carb (g)
Roe	1 tbsp.	139	1	0
Saba**	1 oz.	268	4	0
Sake: Refer to specific type of salmon.				
Salmon, Atlantic (farmed), raw	1 oz.	−61	3	0
Salmon, Atlantic (wild), raw	1 oz.	127	2	0
Salmon, chinook, raw	1 oz.	228	3	0
Salmon, chum, raw	1 oz.	86	1	0
Salmon, coho (farmed), raw	1 oz.	141	2	0
Salmon, coho (wild), raw	1 oz.	119	2	0
Salmon, pink, raw	1 oz.	122	1	0
Salmon, sockeye, raw	1 oz.	145	2	0
Scallop, raw	1 medium	16	0	0
Sea bass,* raw	1 oz.	88	1	0
Sea trout,* raw	1 oz.	6	1	0
Shrimp, raw	1 large	13	0	0
Shrimp, steamed or boiled	1 large	6	0	0
Skipjack tuna, raw	1 oz.	38	0	0
Sole, raw	1 oz.	25	0	0
Squid, raw	1 oz.	72	0	1
Suzuki*	1 oz.	88	1	0
Swordfish,** raw	1 oz.	78	1	0
Tai	1 oz.	37	0	0
Tuna, bluefin,* raw	1 oz.	154	1	0
Tuna, skipjack, raw	1 oz.	38	0	0

*High in mercury; eat only occasionally.   **Very high in mercury; avoid eating.

TABLE 4.2 IF Ratings by Category, *continued*

Food	Typical Serving	IF Rating	Fat (g)	Carb (g)
Tuna, yellowfin,* raw	1 oz.	31	0	0
Unagi	1 oz.	15	4	0
Yellowfin tuna,* raw	1 oz.	31	0	0

Poultry

Food	Typical Serving	IF Rating	Fat (g)	Carb (g)
Chicken breast, roasted, meat only	3 oz.	−14	3	0
Chicken breast, roasted, with skin	3 oz.	−23	7	0
Chicken breast, stewed, with skin	3 oz.	−21	6	0
Chicken drumstick, battered and fried, with skin	3 oz.	−60	13	7
Chicken drumstick, roasted, with skin	3 oz.	−57	10	0
Chicken drumstick, stewed, with skin	3 oz.	−52	9	0
Chicken spread, canned	2 oz.	5	10	2
Chicken thigh, battered and fried, with skin	3 oz.	−82	16	9
Chicken thigh, fried, meat only	3 oz.	−97	11	2
Chicken thigh, roasted, with skin	3 oz.	−77	13	0
Chicken thigh, stewed, with skin	3 oz.	−74	12	0
Cornish game hen, roasted	3 oz.	−115	3	0
Duck, roasted, meat only	3 oz.	14	10	0
Duck, roasted, with skin	3 oz.	26	24	0

*High in mercury; eat only occasionally.

Food	Typical Serving	IF Rating	Fat (g)	Carb (g)
Goose, roasted, meat only	3 oz.	20	11	0
Goose, roasted, with skin	3 oz.	38	19	0
Ground turkey, cooked	3 oz.	−60	11	0
Turkey breast, roasted, with skin	3 oz.	−106	6	0
Turkey breast (pre-basted), roasted, with skin	3 oz.	−45	3	0
Turkey thigh, roasted, meat only	3 oz.	−170	6	0
Meat: Beef and Veal				
Bottom round, roasted	3 oz.	19	10	0
Bottom round, roasted, lean portions only	3 oz.	3	6	0
Brisket, braised	3 oz.	17	27	0
Brisket, braised, lean portions only	3 oz.	10	11	0
Corned beef brisket	3 oz.	42	11	0
Corned beef, canned	3 oz.	41	13	0
Cube steak, braised	3 oz.	18	8	0
Cube steak, braised, lean portions only	3 oz.	11	7	0
Cube steak, roasted, lean portions only	3 oz.	12	6	0
Delmonico steak, broiled or grilled, lean portions only	3 oz.	3	8	0
Eye of round, roasted	3 oz.	21	8	0
Eye of round, roasted, lean portions only	3 oz.	23	3	0

TABLE 4.2 IF Ratings by Category, *continued*

Food	Typical Serving	IF Rating	Fat (g)	Carb (g)
Filet mignon, broiled or grilled	3 oz.	10	15	0
Filet mignon, broiled or grilled, lean portions only	3 oz.	13	7	0
Filet mignon, roasted	3 oz.	−8	22	0
Filet mignon, roasted, lean portions only	3 oz.	−21	10	0
Flank steak, broiled or grilled	3 oz.	−8	8	0
Flank steak, braised	3 oz.	23	14	0
Ground beef, 80% lean, baked	3 oz.	−14	14	0
Ground beef, 80% lean, broiled or grilled	3 oz.	−5	15	0
Ground beef, 80% lean, pan-fried	3 oz.	−30	16	0
Ground beef, 90% lean, baked	3 oz.	−6	9	0
Ground beef, 90% lean, broiled or grilled	3 oz.	−7	10	0
Ground beef, 90% lean, pan-fried	3 oz.	−17	15	0
Ground beef, 95% lean, baked	3 oz.	−4	5	0
Ground beef, 95% lean, broiled or grilled	3 oz.	−7	6	0
Ground beef, 95% lean, pan-broiled	3 oz.	−5	5	0
Ground beef, 95% lean, pan-fried	3 oz.	−9	14	0

Food	Typical Serving	IF Rating	Fat (g)	Carb (g)
Ground veal, broiled or grilled	3 oz.	−57	6	0
London broil, braised	3 oz.	12	10	0
London broil, braised, lean portions only	3 oz.	11	5	0
London broil, broiled or grilled	3 oz.	15	8	0
London broil, broiled or grilled, lean portions only	3 oz.	12	4	0
New York strip, broiled or grilled	3 oz.	6	17	0
New York strip, broiled or grilled, lean portions only	3 oz.	5	8	0
Porterhouse steak, broiled or grilled	3 oz.	17	22	0
Porterhouse steak, broiled or grilled, lean portions only	3 oz.	12	10	0
Pot roast, braised	3 oz.	29	16	0
Pot roast, braised, lean portions only	3 oz.	35	6	0
Prime rib, broiled or grilled	3 oz.	0	17	0
Prime rib, broiled or grilled, lean portions only	3 oz.	14	6	0
Prime rib, roasted	3 oz.	20	23	0
Prime rib, roasted, lean portions only	3 oz.	20	10	0
Rib roast, broiled or grilled	3 oz.	6	24	0
Rib roast, broiled or grilled, lean portions only	3 oz.	−5	11	0

TABLE 4.2 IF Ratings by Category, *continued*

Food	Typical Serving	IF Rating	Fat (g)	Carb (g)
Rib roast, roasted	3 oz.	11	25	0
Rib roast, roasted, lean portions only	3 oz.	12	11	0
Rib eye steak, broiled or grilled, lean portions only	3 oz.	3	8	0
Shank, simmered	3 oz.	27	12	0
Shank, simmered, lean portions only	3 oz.	30	5	0
Short ribs, braised	3 oz.	12	36	0
Short ribs, braised, lean portions only	3 oz.	2	15	0
Sirloin strip, broiled or grilled	3 oz.	10	13	0
Sirloin strip, broiled or grilled, lean portions only	3 oz.	17	6	0
Sirloin strip, pan-fried, lean portions only	3 oz.	−4	9	0
Sirloin tip, broiled or grilled	3 oz.	18	5	0
Sirloin tip, broiled or grilled, lean portions only	3 oz.	22	5	0
Sirloin tip, roasted	3 oz.	15	11	0
Sirloin tip, roasted, lean portions only	3 oz.	11	5	0
Skirt steak, broiled or grilled	3 oz.	20	10	0
Skirt steak, broiled or grilled, lean portions only	3 oz.	4	12	0
T-bone steak, broiled or grilled	3 oz.	14	19	0

Food	Typical Serving	IF Rating	Fat (g)	Carb (g)
T-bone steak, broiled or grilled, lean portions only	3 oz.	3	8	0
Top blade roast, braised	3 oz.	21	21	0
Top blade roast, braised, lean portions only	3 oz.	25	11	0
Top blade steak, broiled or grilled	3 oz.	25	10	0
Top blade steak, broiled or grilled, lean portions only	3 oz.	26	9	0
Veal loin, braised	3 oz.	−91	15	0
Veal loin, braised, lean portions only	3 oz.	−101	8	0
Veal loin, roasted	3 oz.	−71	10	0
Veal loin, roasted, lean portions only	3 oz.	−71	6	0
Veal shank, braised	3 oz.	−41	5	0
Veal shank, braised, lean portions only	3 oz.	−45	4	0
Veal shoulder, braised	3 oz.	−55	9	0
Veal shoulder, roasted	3 oz.	−71	7	0
Veal shoulder, roasted, lean portions only	3 oz.	−66	6	0
Veal sirloin, braised	3 oz.	−61	11	0
Veal sirloin, braised, lean portions only	3 oz.	−60	6	0
Veal sirloin, roasted	3 oz.	−51	9	0
Veal sirloin, roasted, lean portions only	3 oz.	−61	5	0

TABLE 4.2 IF Ratings by Category, *continued*

Food	Typical Serving	IF Rating	Fat (g)	Carb (g)
Meat: Lamb				
Ground lamb, broiled or grilled	3 oz.	−24	17	0
Leg (Australian), broiled or grilled	3 oz.	−13	10	0
Leg (Australian), broiled or grilled, lean portions only	3 oz.	−7	7	0
Leg (Australian), roasted	3 oz.	−17	13	0
Leg (Australian), roasted, lean portions only	3 oz.	−4	7	0
Leg (domestic), roasted	3 oz.	−17	14	0
Leg (domestic), roasted, lean portions only	3 oz.	4	7	0
Leg (New Zealand), roasted	3 oz.	−13	13	0
Leg (New Zealand), roasted, lean portions only	3 oz.	−15	6	0
Loin (Australian), broiled or grilled	3 oz.	−16	10	0
Loin (Australian), broiled or grilled, lean portions only	3 oz.	−11	7	0
Loin (domestic), roasted	3 oz.	−43	20	0
Loin (domestic), roasted, lean portions only	3 oz.	−30	8	0
Loin chop (Australian), broiled or grilled	3 oz.	−19	12	0
Loin chop (Australian), broiled or grilled, lean portions only	3 oz.	−9	7	0
Loin chop (domestic), broiled or grilled	3 oz.	−31	20	0

Food	Typical Serving	IF Rating	Fat (g)	Carb (g)
Loin chop (domestic), broiled or grilled, lean portions only	3 oz.	−5	8	0
Loin chop (New Zealand), broiled or grilled	3 oz.	−31	20	0
Loin chop (New Zealand), broiled or grilled, lean portions only	3 oz.	−19	7	0
Rib (Australian), roasted	3 oz.	−26	17	0
Rib (Australian), roasted, lean portions only	3 oz.	−14	10	0
Rib (domestic), broiled or grilled	3 oz.	−76	23	0
Rib (domestic), broiled or grilled, lean portions only	3 oz.	−57	11	0
Rib (domestic), roasted	3 oz.	−50	23	0
Rib (domestic), roasted, lean portions only	3 oz.	−38	11	0
Rib (New Zealand), roasted	3 oz.	−38	22	0
Rib (New Zealand), roasted, lean portions only	3 oz.	−20	9	0
Shank (Australian), roasted	3 oz.	−16	12	0
Shank (Australian), roasted, lean portions only	3 oz.	−3	6	0
Shank (domestic), roasted	3 oz.	−2	11	0
Shank (domestic), roasted, lean portions only	3 oz.	16	6	0
Shoulder (Australian), roasted	3 oz.	−33	18	0
Shoulder (Australian), roasted, lean portions only	3 oz.	−18	11	0

TABLE 4.2 IF Ratings by Category, *continued*

Food	Typical Serving	IF Rating	Fat (g)	Carb (g)
Shoulder (domestic), braised	3 oz.	−54	21	0
Shoulder (domestic), braised, lean portions only	3 oz.	−38	14	0
Shoulder (domestic), broiled or grilled	3 oz.	−39	16	0
Shoulder (domestic), broiled or grilled, lean portions only	3 oz.	−32	9	0
Shoulder (domestic), roasted	3 oz.	−43	17	0
Shoulder (domestic), roasted, lean portions only	3 oz.	−27	9	0
Shoulder (New Zealand), braised	3 oz.	−34	22	0
Shoulder (New Zealand), braised, lean portions only	3 oz.	−23	13	0
Meat: Pork				
Ground pork, cooked	3 oz.	−31	17	0
Ham, canned	3 oz.	45	13	0
Ham, canned, extra-lean	3 oz.	26	4	0
Ham, roasted	3 oz.	28	8	0
Ham, roasted, extra-lean	3 oz.	28	5	1
Loin chop, center cut, braised	3 oz.	5	12	0
Loin chop, center cut, braised, lean portions only	3 oz.	10	7	0
Loin chop, center cut, broiled or grilled	3 oz.	2	11	0

Food	Typical Serving	IF Rating	Fat (g)	Carb (g)
Loin chop, center cut, broiled or grilled, lean portions only	3 oz.	14	7	0
Loin chop, center cut, pan-fried	3 oz.	−7	14	0
Loin chop, center cut, pan-fried, lean portions only	3 oz.	12	9	0
Loin roast	3 oz.	5	11	0
Loin roast, lean portions only	3 oz.	13	8	0
Rib chop, braised	3 oz.	−5	13	0
Rib chop, braised, lean portions only	3 oz.	10	8	0
Rib chop, broiled or grilled	3 oz.	1	13	0
Rib chop, broiled or grilled, lean portions only	3 oz.	17	9	0
Rib chop, pan-fried	3 oz.	−7	14	0
Rib chop, pan-fried, lean portions only	3 oz.	7	9	0
Rib chop, roasted	3 oz.	−30	13	0
Rib chop, roasted, lean portions only	3 oz.	−7	9	0
Ribs, country-style, braised	3 oz.	−7	18	0
Ribs, country-style, braised, lean portions only	3 oz.	15	12	0
Ribs, country-style, roasted	3 oz.	−31	22	0
Ribs, country-style, roasted, lean portions only	3 oz.	5	13	0
Salt pork	2 oz.	−33	45	0
Shoulder roast, braised	3 oz.	−43	20	0

TABLE 4.2 IF Ratings by Category, *continued*

Food	Typical Serving	IF Rating	Fat (g)	Carb (g)
Shoulder roast, cured and roasted (picnic ham)	3 oz.	−50	18	0
Shoulder roast, cured and roasted, lean portions only	3 oz.	−37	6	0
Shoulder roast, roasted	3 oz.	−45	20	0
Spareribs, braised	3 oz.	−49	26	0
Tenderloin, broiled or grilled	3 oz.	13	7	0
Tenderloin, broiled or grilled, lean portions only	3 oz.	16	5	0
Tenderloin, roasted	3 oz.	6	5	0
Tenderloin, roasted, lean portions only	3 oz.	13	4	0
Meat: Game				
Bison, roasted	3 oz.	−20	2	0
Boar, roasted	3 oz.	−70	4	0
Caribou, roasted	3 oz.	−99	4	0
Deer, roasted	3 oz.	1	3	0
Goat, roasted	3 oz.	−42	3	0
Moose, roasted	3 oz.	−53	1	0
Rabbit, stewed	3 oz.	22	3	0
Meat: Organ and Variety				
Beef brain, simmered or braised	3 oz.	−357	9	0
Beef heart, simmered or braised	3 oz.	−155	4	0

Food	Typical Serving	IF Rating	Fat (g)	Carb (g)
Beef kidney, simmered or braised	3 oz.	−131	4	0
Beef liver, braised	3 oz.	−6	4	3
Beef liver, pan-fried	3 oz.	−12	4	4
Beef lung, braised	3 oz.	−130	3	0
Beef tongue, simmered or braised	3 oz.	−17	19	0
Beef tripe, simmered or braised	3 oz.	−37	3	2
Chicken giblets, simmered	3 oz.	−93	8	1
Chicken liver pâté	1 oz.	18	8	0
Chicken livers, simmered	3 oz.	−258	6	1
Goose liver pâté	1 oz.	−16	11	1
Pâté de foie gras (goose)	1 oz.	−23	12	1
Pork chitterlings, simmered	3 oz.	−124	17	0
Turkey giblets, simmered	3 oz.	−75	10	1
Veal kidney	3 oz.	−108	5	0

Meat: Cured and Processed†

Food	Typical Serving	IF Rating	Fat (g)	Carb (g)
Bacon, Canadian-style, grilled	2 slices	17	4	1
Bacon, pan-fried	2 strips	−8	7	0
Beef jerky	1 oz.	11	1	1
Bologna, beef	1 slice	9	8	1
Bologna, low-fat	1 slice	8	6	1
Bologna, pork	1 slice	8	5	0
Bologna, turkey	1 slice	−15	4	1

†May contain nitrates and nitrites; eat only occasionally.

TABLE 4.2 IF Ratings by Category, *continued*

Food	Typical Serving	IF Rating	Fat (g)	Carb (g)
Bratwurst	1 sausage	−51	25	2
Braunschweiger	1 slice	28	8	1
Chorizo	1 sausage	−19	23	1
Corned beef	1 slice	14	4	0
Ham, canned, extra-lean	1 slice	9	1	0
Ham, canned, regular	1 slice	15	4	0
Ham, roasted	1 slice	9	2	0
Ham luncheon meat	1 slice	0	2	1
Ham luncheon meat, extra-lean	1 slice	8	1	1
Hot dog, turkey	1 sausage	−8	8	1
Italian sausage	1 sausage	23	18	3
Kielbasa	4″ section	30	23	2
Knackwurst	1 sausage	21	20	2
Lebanon bologna	1 slice	13	3	0
Liverwurst	1 slice	23	8	1
Pastrami	1 slice	0	2	0
Pastrami, turkey	1 slice	−16	1	1
Pepperoni	15 slices	−3	12	1
Polish sausage	4″ section	27	24	1
Salami, cooked	1 slice	8	6	1
Salami, hard	1 slice	16	8	1
Salami, turkey	1 slice	−11	3	0
Sausage links	1 sausage	−28	7	0
Sausage patty	1 patty	−23	10	1
Summer sausage	1 oz.	13	8	1

Food	Typical Serving	IF Rating	Fat (g)	Carb (g)
Turkey ham	1 slice	−16	1	1
Turkey roll (luncheon meat)	1 slice	−33	2	0
Vienna sausage	1 sausage	7	3	0
Meatless Alternatives				
Bacon, vegetarian	2 strips	−12	6	2
Breakfast patty, vegetarian	1 patty	−6	3	4
Burger crumbles, vegetarian	3 oz.	−6	9	5
Burger, vegetarian	1 patty	49	4	7
Frankfurter, vegetarian	1 sausage	−8	7	2
Breads and Pastries (See also **Desserts**.)				
Bagel, plain	1 bagel	−186	1	30
Banana bread	1 slice	−151	6	33
Bread, French	1 slice	−261	2	33
Bread, gluten-free	1 slice	−133	6	19
Bread, mixed-grain	1 slice	−33	1	12
Bread, pumpernickel	1 slice	−42	1	15
Bread, rye	1 slice	−63	1	15
Bread, sourdough	1 slice	−261	2	33
Bread, Vienna	1 slice	−261	2	33
Bread, white	1 slice	−77	1	13
Bread, whole wheat	1 slice	−72	1	13
Croissant	1 croissant	−179	12	26
Doughnut, plain, cake	1 doughnut	−171	10	23
English muffin	1 muffin	−173	1	26
Hamburger bun	1 roll	−113	2	21

TABLE 4.2 IF Ratings by Category, *continued*

Food	Typical Serving	IF Rating	Fat (g)	Carb (g)
Hot dog bun	1 roll	−113	2	21
Kaiser roll	1 roll	−185	2	30
Muffin, blueberry	1 small	−179	4	32
Muffin, oat bran	1 small	−164	5	32
Pancake, prepared from mix	1 pancake	−180	2	28
Pie crust (pastry crust)	1 piece (single crust)	−76	8	11
Pita, white	1 small	−74	0	16
Pita, whole wheat	1 small	−65	1	15
Stuffing prepared from mix	½ cup	−149	8	19
Taco shell, baked	1 medium	−61	3	8
Tortilla, corn	6″ tortilla	−48	11	1
Tortilla, flour	10″ tortilla	−69	36	5
Tortilla, flour	6″ tortilla	−30	2	16
Waffle, frozen	1 waffle	−110	3	15

Cereal

Food	Typical Serving	IF Rating	Fat (g)	Carb (g)
All-Bran, Extra Fiber	½ cup	4	1	23
All-Bran Bran Buds	⅓ cup	50	1	24
Bran flakes	¾ cup	9	1	23
Cheerios	1 cup	−81	2	23
Corn Chex	1 cup	−151	0	26
Cornflakes	1 cup	−182	0	24
Cream of Wheat, instant	¾ cup	−122	0	24
Cream of Wheat, regular	¾ cup	−135	0	20
Crispix	1 cup	−149	0	25
Grape-Nuts	⅓ cup	−219	1	35

Food	Typical Serving	IF Rating	Fat (g)	Carb (g)
Grape-Nuts Flakes	¾ cup	−144	1	24
Just Right	1 cup	−172	2	45
Life	¾ cup	−52	1	25
Muesli, no sugar added	⅓ cup	−41	4	14
Multi-Bran Chex	1 cup	−118	1	41
Nutri-Grain Wheat	1 cup	−104	0	24
Oat Bran (Quaker)	1¼ cups	−185	3	43
Oatmeal, made with water	¾ cup	−64	2	19
Oats, rolled	⅓ cup, dry	−49	2	17
Puffed wheat	1¼ cups	−80	0	11
Raisin bran	1 cup	−215	2	47
Rice Chex	1¼ cups	−176	0	27
Rice Krispies	1¼ cups	−202	0	28
Shredded wheat, original	2 biscuits	−230	1	37
Shredded wheat, spoon size	1 cup	−230	1	37
Special K	1 cup	−34	0	22
Total	¾ cup	43	1	23
Wheaties	1 cup	−103	1	24

Pasta and Grains

Food	Typical Serving	IF Rating	Fat (g)	Carb (g)
Barley, cooked	½ cup	−39	0	22
Cornmeal, yellow	½ cup	−279	2	47
Couscous, cooked	½ cup	−91	0	18
Kasha (buckwheat)	½ cup	−73	1	17
Macaroni elbows, cooked	½ cup	−76	0	20
Macaroni shells, cooked	½ cup	−55	0	16

TABLE 4.2 IF Ratings by Category, *continued*

Food	Typical Serving	IF Rating	Fat (g)	Carb (g)
Millet, cooked	½ cup	−135	1	21
Oat bran, raw	½ cup	−111	3	31
Oatmeal, dry	½ cup	−84	3	27
Pasta, corn, cooked	½ cup	−124	1	20
Rice bran, raw	½ cup	−16	12	29
Rice noodles, cooked	½ cup	−80	0	22
Rice, brown long-grain, cooked	½ cup	−103	1	22
Rice, white long-grain, cooked	½ cup	−108	0	22
Rice, white parboiled (converted), cooked	½ cup	−123	0	22
Rice, white short-grain, cooked	½ cup	−172	0	27
Rice, white, sushi-style	½ cup	−145	0	18
Spaghetti, cooked	½ cup	−49	0	20
Spaghetti, whole wheat, cooked	½ cup	−33	0	19

Fats and Oils

Food	Typical Serving	IF Rating	Fat (g)	Carb (g)
Almond oil	1 tbsp.	62	14	0
Apricot kernel oil	1 tbsp.	33	13	0
Avocado oil	1 tbsp.	66	14	0
Butter	1 tbsp.	−45	12	0
Butter, whipped	1 tbsp.	−25	8	0
Butter flavoring, powdered	1 tsp.	0	0	1
Butter oil	1 tbsp.	−42	13	0
Canola oil	1 tbsp.	72	14	0

Food	Typical Serving	IF Rating	Fat (g)	Carb (g)
Cocoa butter oil	1 tbsp.	−39	14	0
Coconut oil	1 tbsp.	−112	14	0
Cod liver oil	1 tbsp.	1,028	14	0
Corn oil	1 tbsp.	−49	14	0
Cottonseed oil	1 tbsp.	−92	14	0
Fish oil, salmon	1 tbsp.	1,889	14	0
Grape seed oil	1 tbsp.	−84	14	0
Hazelnut oil	1 tbsp.	85	14	0
Lard	1 tbsp.	−3	13	0
Margarine, liquid, soybean oil	1 tbsp.	−44	11	0
Margarine, corn	1 tbsp.	−25	11	0
Margarine, corn and soy, 80% fat	1 tbsp.	−14	11	0
Margarine, soy	1 tbsp.	−19	11	0
Margarine, soy and cottonseed	1 tbsp.	3	11	0
Margarine, sunflower	1 tbsp.	−52	11	0
Margarine, tub, 40% fat	1 tbsp.	−3	6	0
Margarine, tub, 60% fat	1 tbsp.	−5	8	0
Margarine, tub, 70% fat	1 tbsp.	−5	10	0
Margarine, tub, nonfat	1 tbsp.	−3	0	1
Margarine-butter blend	1 tbsp.	−26	11	0
Olive oil	1 tbsp.	73	14	0
Palm kernel oil	1 tbsp.	−97	14	0
Palm oil	1 tbsp.	−27	14	0

TABLE 4.2 IF Ratings by Category, *continued*

Food	Typical Serving	IF Rating	Fat (g)	Carb (g)
Peanut oil	1 tbsp.	−3	14	0
Poppy seed oil	1 tbsp.	−76	14	0
Rapeseed oil	1 tbsp.	72	14	0
Rice bran oil	1 tbsp.	−12	14	0
Safflower oil, high-linoleic	1 tbsp.	−89	14	0
Safflower oil, high-oleic	1 tbsp.	98	14	0
Sesame oil	1 tbsp.	−20	14	0
Shea nut oil	1 tbsp.	−9	14	0
Shortening	1 tbsp.	−40	13	0
Soybean lecithin oil	1 tbsp.	−40	14	0
Soybean oil	1 tbsp.	−33	14	0
Sunflower oil	1 tbsp.	−3	14	0
Sunflower oil, high-linoleic	1 tbsp.	−75	14	0
Walnut oil	1 tbsp.	−25	14	0
Wheat germ oil	1 tbsp.	−53	14	0

Nuts and Seeds

Food	Typical Serving	IF Rating	Fat (g)	Carb (g)
Almond butter	2 tbsp.	82	19	7
Almonds, dry-roasted	¼ cup	57	15	5
Almonds, oil-roasted	¼ cup	56	16	5
Almonds, raw	¼ cup	54	14	6
Almonds, raw, blanched	¼ cup	54	14	6
Brazil nuts, raw	¼ cup	175	19	3
Cashews, dry-roasted	¼ cup	26	13	9
Cashews, oil-roasted	¼ cup	23	14	9
Filberts, blanched	¼ cup	118	17	5

Food	Typical Serving	IF Rating	Fat (g)	Carb (g)
Filberts, dry-roasted	¼ cup	107	18	5
Flaxseed	2 tbsp.	26	8	8
Hazelnuts, blanched	¼ cup	118	17	5
Hazelnuts, dry-roasted	¼ cup	107	18	5
Hickory nuts, raw	¼ cup	28	18	5
Linseed	2 tbsp.	26	8	8
Macadamia nuts, dry-roasted	¼ cup	137	22	4
Macadamia nuts, raw	¼ cup	133	21	4
Peanuts, dry-roasted	¼ cup	14	14	6
Peanuts, oil-roasted	¼ cup	17	14	5
Pecans, dry-roasted	¼ cup	64	21	4
Pecans, oil-roasted	¼ cup	45	21	4
Pecans, raw	¼ cup	53	20	4
Pignolias	¼ cup	−41	19	4
Pine nuts	¼ cup	−41	19	4
Pistachios, dry-roasted	¼ cup	26	13	8
Poppy seeds	2 tbsp.	−40	8	4
Pumpkin seeds, hulled, raw	¼ cup	−26	13	5
Pumpkin seeds, hulled, roasted	¼ cup	−23	12	4
Sesame seeds	2 tbsp.	−8	10	3
Sunflower seeds, dry-roasted	¼ cup	−41	14	7
Walnuts, black	¼ cup	−43	18	3
Walnuts, English	¼ cup	−40	20	4

TABLE 4.2 IF Ratings by Category, *continued*

Food	Typical Serving	IF Rating	Fat (g)	Carb (g)
Herbs and Spices				
Allspice, ground	1 tsp.	0	0	1
Aniseed	1 tsp.	2	0	1
Basil, dried	1 tsp.	8	0	1
Basil, fresh	2 tbsp.	9	0	0
Bay leaf, dried	1 tsp.	0	0	0
Black pepper, ground	1 tsp.	1	0	1
Capers	1 tbsp.	1	0	0
Caraway seed	1 tbsp.	6	1	3
Cardamom, ground	1 tsp.	1	0	1
Cayenne, ground	1 tsp.	509	0	1
Celery seed	1 tbsp.	10	2	3
Chervil, dried	1 tsp.	1	0	0
Chili pepper, dried	1 pepper	252	0	0
Chili pepper, red, canned	¼ cup	244	0	2
Chili pepper, red, raw	1 pepper	286	0	4
Chili powder	1 tbsp.	230	0	4
Chives, dried	1 tbsp.	1	0	0
Chives, fresh	2 tbsp.	24	0	0
Cilantro, dried	1 tbsp.	12	0	1
Cilantro, fresh	¼ cup	7	0	0
Cinnamon, ground	1 tsp.	1	0	2
Cloves, ground	1 tsp.	1	0	1
Coriander seed	1 tbsp.	8	1	3
Cumin, ground	1 tsp.	4	0	1

Food	Typical Serving	IF Rating	Fat (g)	Carb (g)
Cumin seed	1 tbsp.	9	1	3
Curry powder	1 tbsp.	378	1	4
Dill, dried	1 tsp.	0	0	1
Dill, fresh	¼ cup	2	0	0
Dill seed	1 tsp.	2	0	1
Fennel seed	1 tbsp.	6	1	3
Garlic, raw	1 clove	111	0	1
Garlic powder	1 tsp.	440	0	2
Ginger, ground	1 tsp.	501	0	1
Gingerroot, fresh	1 tbsp.	390	0	0
Hot chili, dried	1 pepper	252	0	0
Hungarian pepper, raw	1 pepper	63	0	2
Jalapeño pepper, raw	1 pepper	55	0	1
Lemongrass, fresh	2 tbsp.	2	0	3
Lemon peel (zest), fresh	1 tbsp.	4	0	1
Mace, ground	1 tsp.	0	1	1
Marjoram, dried	1 tsp.	2	0	0
Mint, dried	1 tsp.	1	0	0
Mint, fresh	2 tbsp.	3	0	1
Mustard seed	1 tbsp.	37	3	4
Nutmeg, ground	1 tsp.	−5	1	1
Onion flakes	1 tbsp.	584	0	4
Onion powder	1 tsp.	291	0	2
Orange peel (zest), fresh	1 tbsp.	3	0	1
Oregano, fresh	2 tbsp.	2	0	1

TABLE 4.2 IF Ratings by Category, *continued*

Food	Typical Serving	IF Rating	Fat (g)	Carb (g)
Oregano, ground	1 tsp.	1	0	1
Paprika	1 tsp.	13	0	1
Parsley, dried	1 tbsp.	7	0	1
Parsley, fresh	2 tbsp.	40	0	0
Pepper, Hungarian, raw	1 pepper	63	0	2
Pepper, jalapeño, raw	1 pepper	55	0	1
Pepper, red chili, canned	¼ cup	244	0	2
Pepper, red chili, raw	1 pepper	286	0	4
Pepper, serrano, raw	1 pepper	122	0	0
Poppy seed	1 tbsp.	−20	4	2
Poultry seasoning	1 tsp.	3	0	1
Pumpkin pie spice	1 tsp.	0	0	1
Red pepper, ground	1 tsp.	509	0	1
Rosemary, dried	1 tsp.	1	0	1
Rosemary, fresh	2 tbsp.	0	0	0
Saffron	1 tsp.	0	0	0
Sage, ground	1 tsp.	3	0	0
Serrano pepper, raw	1 pepper	122	0	0
Shallot, dried	1 tbsp.	3	0	1
Shallot, raw	2 tbsp.	52	0	3
Spearmint, dried	1 tsp.	1	0	0
Spearmint, fresh	2 tbsp.	3	0	1
Tarragon, ground	1 tsp.	1	0	1
Thyme, fresh	1 tbsp.	3	0	1
Thyme, ground	1 tsp.	7	0	1
Turmeric	1 tsp.	501	0	0

Food	Typical Serving	IF Rating	Fat (g)	Carb (g)
Ingredients				
Baking powder, double-acting	1 tsp.	0	0	1
Baking soda	1 tsp.	0	0	0
Beef bouillon, dehydrated	1 cube	1	0	1
Beef broth/bouillon, canned	1 cup (8 oz.)	2	1	0
Capers	1 tbsp.	1	0	0
Chicken bouillon, dehydrated	1 cube	0	1	1
Chicken broth or stock	1 cup (8 oz.)	2	1	1
Chocolate milk powder	2 tbsp. (to make 1 cup)	−101	1	19
Corn syrup	¼ cup	−396	0	58
Cream of tartar	½ tsp.	0	0	1
Fish stock	1 cup (8 oz.)	64	2	0
Gelatin, dry, unflavored	100 grams	15	0	0
Honey	¼ cup	−380	0	168
Lemon juice	1 tbsp.	3	0	1
Lime juice	1 tbsp.	3	0	2
Maple syrup (100% pure)	¼ cup	−280	0	52
Milk, nonfat dry	¼ cup	−35	0	16
Milk, sweetened condensed	¼ cup	−263	7	42
Sugar, brown	¼ cup (packed)	−373	0	55
Sugar, white granulated	¼ cup	−363	0	54
Sugar, white powdered	¼ cup	−170	0	25
Vinegar, cider	1 tbsp.	0	0	0
Vinegar, distilled	1 tbsp.	0	0	0

TABLE 4.2 IF Ratings by Category, *continued*

Food	Typical Serving	IF Rating	Fat (g)	Carb (g)
Yeast, baking	1 packet (2 tsp.)	40	0	3
Sweeteners				
Brown sugar	1 tbsp., packed	−93	0	14
Equal‡	1 packet	0	0	0
Honey	1 tbsp.	−95	0	17
Maple syrup (100% pure)	1 tbsp.	−70	0	13
Splenda	1 tsp.	0	0	0
SugarTwin‡	1 tsp.	0	0	0
Sugar, granulated	1 tbsp.	−87	0	12
Sugar, powdered	1 tbsp.	−51	0	8
Sweet'n Low‡	1 packet	0	0	0
Sauces, Dressings, and Condiments				
Banana pepper, hot, pickled	1 pepper	66	0	1
Blue cheese dressing	2 tbsp.	−32	16	2
Blue cheese dressing, low-fat	2 tbsp.	−6	2	0
Cherry pepper, hot, pickled	1 pepper	33	0	1
French dressing	2 tbsp.	−54	20	0
French dressing, low-fat	2 tbsp.	−4	4	8
Horseradish, prepared	1 tsp.	1	0	1
Hot sauce (Tabasco)	1 tsp.	370	0	0
Italian dressing	2 tbsp.	−16	8	4
Italian dressing, low-fat	2 tbsp.	−14	6	2

‡Some artificial sweeteners have been associated with health risks or adverse reactions.

Food	Typical Serving	IF Rating	Fat (g)	Carb (g)
Jalapeño pepper, canned	1 pepper	56	0	1
Jam, various fruit	1 tbsp.	−67	0	14
Marmalade, orange	1 tbsp.	−62	0	13
Mayonnaise	1 tbsp.	−33	12	0
Mayonnaise, imitation	1 tbsp.	−1	0	1
Mayonnaise, reduced-fat	1 tbsp.	−12	5	1
Mayonnaise, tofu	1 tbsp.	−10	5	1
Miracle Whip	1 tbsp.	−26	11	1
Miracle Whip, light	1 tbsp.	−8	3	3
Mustard, prepared	1 tsp.	3	0	0
Olive, black	1 jumbo	4	1	0
Olive, green	1 jumbo	8	1	0
Pepper, hot banana	1 pepper	66	0	1
Pepper, hot cherry	1 pepper	33	0	1
Pepper, jalapeño, canned	1 pepper	56	0	1
Pickle, dill	1 medium	3	0	1
Preserves, apricot	1 tbsp.	−68	0	13
Ranch dressing	2 tbsp.	−38	16	2
Ranch dressing, fat-free	2 tbsp.	0	0	0
Russian dressing	2 tbsp.	−34	16	4
Russian dressing, low-fat	2 tbsp.	−2	2	14
Salad dressing, oil and vinegar	2 tbsp.	−38	16	0
Salsa	¼ cup	52	0	4
Soy sauce	1 tbsp.	1	0	1
Worcestershire sauce	1 tbsp.	2	0	4

TABLE 4.2 IF Ratings by Category, *continued*

Food	Typical Serving	IF Rating	Fat (g)	Carb (g)
Crackers, Cookies, and Chips				
Corn chips	1 oz.	−116	9	16
Graham cracker	1 cracker	−37	1	5
Melba toast	1 toast	−13	0	2
Oatmeal cookie	1 cookie	−76	5	17
Oyster crackers	3 crackers	−27	0	3
Potato chips	1 oz.	−110	10	15
Pretzels, hard, regular	1 oz. (5 pieces)	−179	1	24
Pretzels, hard, whole wheat	1 oz. (5 pieces)	−168	1	23
Rice cake, plain	1 piece	−57	0	7
Rye crispbread	1 cracker	−49	0	8
Saltine	1 cracker	−13	0	2
Shortbread	1 cookie	−27	2	5
Tea biscuit	1 cookie	−22	1	4
Tortilla chips, plain	1 oz.	−86	7	18
Vanilla wafer	1 cookie	−28	1	4
Candy				
Chocolate chips	1 cup	−598	52	99
Chocolate kisses	10 kisses	−166	14	28
Fruit leather	1 roll	−61	0	12
Fruit leather snack	1 oz.	−136	0	24
Jelly beans	10 small	−80	0	10
Jelly beans	10 large	−204	0	26

Food	Typical Serving	IF Rating	Fat (g)	Carb (g)
Mars almond bar	1 bar	−190	12	31
Milk chocolate	1 miniature bar	−19	2	4
Milk chocolate	1 bar	−156	13	26
Snickers	1 fun-size bar	−38	3	10
Snickers	1 bar	−144	11	37
Twix	1 bar	−129	14	37
Desserts				
Banana bread	1 slice	−151	6	33
Cake, angel food	1 piece	−183	0	29
Cake, chocolate with chocolate frosting	1 piece	−115	11	35
Cake, yellow with vanilla frosting	1 piece	−163	9	38
Fruit leather snack	1 oz.	−136	0	24
Fruit leather roll	1 small	−61	0	12
Ice cream, chocolate	½ cup	−127	7	19
Ice cream, chocolate, premium	½ cup	−91	13	15
Ice cream, vanilla	½ cup	−124	8	17
Ice cream, vanilla, light	½ cup	−102	4	20
Ice cream, vanilla, premium	½ cup	−165	17	24
Ice milk, vanilla	½ cup	−80	3	15
Jello, sugar-free‡	½ cup	6	0	1
Pie crust	1 piece (single crust)	−76	8	11

‡Some artificial sweeteners have been associated with health risks or adverse reactions.

269

TABLE 4.2 IF Ratings by Category, *continued*

Food	Typical Serving	IF Rating	Fat (g)	Carb (g)
Pound cake	1 piece	−111	6	15
Pudding, chocolate	½ cup	−130	4	28
Pudding, vanilla	½ cup	−110	4	26
Sponge cake	1 piece	−110	1	23

Beverages

Food	Typical Serving	IF Rating	Fat (g)	Carb (g)
Apple juice, canned or bottled	8 oz.	−72	0	29
Apple juice, from concentrate	8 oz.	−84	0	28
Carrot juice	8 oz.	396	0	22
Club soda, seltzer	12 oz.	1	0	0
Coca-Cola Classic	12 oz.	−215	0	41
Coffee, brewed	8 oz.	0	0	1
Coffee, brewed, decaf	8 oz.	0	0	0
Coffee, instant	8 oz.	0	0	1
Coffee, instant, decaf	8 oz.	0	0	1
Coffee, instant, with chicory	8 oz.	0	0	1
Coffee substitute (grain-based), instant	8 oz.	1	0	2
Cranberry juice cocktail	8 oz.	−150	0	36
Diet Coke‡	12 oz.	0	0	0
Espresso	1 oz.	0	0	0
Gatorade sport drink mix	8 oz.	−119	0	15
Grapefruit juice, from concentrate	8 oz.	−76	0	24

‡Some artificial sweeteners have been associated with health risks or adverse reactions.

Food	Typical Serving	IF Rating	Fat (g)	Carb (g)
Iced tea, from powdered mix, sugar-free‡	8 oz.	0	0	0
Lemonade, from frozen concentrate	8 oz.	−166	0	26
Lemonade, from powdered mix, sugar-free‡	8 oz.	3	0	1
Lemon-lime soda, sugar-free‡	12 oz.	0	0	0
Milk, chocolate	1 cup	−116	8	26
Milk, chocolate, low-fat	1 cup	−80	3	26
Milk, low-fat (1%)	8 oz.	−33	2	12
Milk, nonfat (skim)	8 oz.	−28	0	12
Milk, reduced-fat (2%)	8 oz.	−41	5	11
Milk, whole	8 oz.	−45	8	11
Orange drink mix, sugar-free‡	8 oz.	26	0	2
Orange juice, freshly squeezed	8 oz.	−65	1	26
Orange juice, from concentrate	8 oz.	−76	0	27
Pineapple juice, canned	8 oz.	−118	0	34
Pineapple juice, from concentrate	8 oz.	−125	0	32
Soy milk	8 oz.	−9	5	4
Tea, black	8 oz.	2	0	1
Tea, black, decaf	8 oz.	2	0	1
Tea, herbal	8 oz.	1	0	0

‡Some artificial sweeteners have been associated with health risks or adverse reactions.

TABLE 4.2 IF Ratings by Category, *continued*

Food	Typical Serving	IF Rating	Fat (g)	Carb (g)
Tea, instant, decaf	8 oz.	0	0	0
Tea, instant, sugar-free‡	8 oz.	0	0	1
Tea, instant, with lemon	8 oz.	0	0	1
Tomato juice	8 oz.	45	0	10
Water, bottled	8 oz.	0	0	0
Wine, nonalcoholic	4 oz.	0	0	0

‡ Some artificial sweeteners have been associated with health risks or adverse reactions.

Selected References

Adam, O. 2003. Dietary fatty acids and immune reactions in synovial tissue. *European Journal of Medical Research* 20 (8) (August): 381–87.

Ali, M. 1995. Mechanism by which garlic (*Allium sativum*) inhibits cyclooxygenase activity: Effect of raw versus boiled garlic extract on the synthesis of prostanoids. *Prostaglandins Leukotrienes and Essential Fatty Acids* 53 (6) (December): 397–400.

Ali, M., M. Afzal, R. A. Hassan, A. Farid, and J. F. Burka. 1990. Comparative study of the in vitro synthesis of prostaglandins and thromboxanes in plants belonging to Liliaceae family. *General Pharmacology* 21 (3): 273–76.

Ali, M., T. Bordia, and T. Mustafa. 1999. Effect of raw versus boiled aqueous extract of garlic and onion on platelet aggregation. *Prostaglandins Leukotrienes and Essential Fatty Acids* 60 (1) (January): 43–47.

Ariga, T., K. Tsuj, T. Seki, T. Moritomo, and J. I. Yamamoto. 2000. Antithrombotic and antineoplastic effects of phyto-organosulfur compounds. *Biofactors* 13 (1–4): 251–55.

Batirel, H. F., S. Aktan, C. Aykut, B. C. Yegen, and T. Coskun. 1996. The effect of aqueous garlic extract on the levels of arachidonic acid metabolites (leukotriene C4 and prostaglandin E2) in rat forebrain after ischemia-reperfusion injury. *Prostaglandins Leukotrienes and Essential Fatty Acids* 54 (4) (April): 289–92.

Bordia, A., S. K. Verma, and K. C. Srivastava. 1998. Effect of garlic (*Allium sativum*) on blood lipids, blood sugar, fibrinogen and fibrinolytic activity in patients with coronary artery disease. *Prostaglandins Leukotrienes and Essential Fatty Acids* 58 (4) (April): 257–63.

Brand-Miller, J. C. 2004. Glycemic index in relation to coronary disease. *Asia Pacific Journal of Clinical Nutrition* 13 (Suppl.): S3.

Chainani-Wu, N. 2003. Safety and anti-inflammatory activity of curcumin: a component of turmeric (*Curcuma longa*). *Journal of Alternative and Complementary Medicine* 9 (1) (February): 161–68.

Chrysohoou, C., D. B. Panagiotakos, C. Pitsavos, U. N. Das, and C. Stefanadis. 2004. Adherence to the Mediterranean diet attenuates inflammation and coagulation process in healthy adults: The ATTICA Study. *Journal of the American College of Cardiology* 44 (1) (July 7): 152–58.

Conner, E. M., and M. B. Grisham. 1996. Inflammation, free radicals, and antioxidants. *Nutrition* 12 (4) (April): 274–77.

Darlington, L. G., and T. W. Stone. 2001. Antioxidants and fatty acids in the amelioration of rheumatoid arthritis and related disorders. *British Journal of Nutrition* 85 (3) (March): 251–69.

Dillon, S. A., G. M. Lowe, D. Billington, and K. Rahman. 2002. Dietary supplementation with aged garlic extract reduces plasma and urine concentrations of 8-iso-prostaglandin F(2 alpha) in smoking and nonsmoking men and women. *Journal of Nutrition* 132 (2) (February): 168–71.

Engler, M. M., M. B. Engler, et al. 2003. Antioxidant vitamins C and E improve endothelial function in children with hyperlipidemia: Endothelial assessment of risk from lipids in youth (EARLY) trial. *Circulation* 108 (September 2): 1059–63.

Erlinger, T. P., et al. 2001. Relationship between systemic markers of inflammation and serum beta-carotene levels. *Archives of Internal Medicine* 161 (15) (August 13–27): 1903–8.

Ferretti, A., G. J. Nelson, P. C. Schmidt, D. S. Kelley, G. Bartolini, and V. P. Flanagan. 1997. Increased dietary arachidonic acid enhances the synthesis of vasoactive eicosanoids in humans. *Lipids* 32 (4) (April): 435–39.

Foster-Powell, K., J. C. Brand-Miller, and S. H. A. Holt. 2002. International table of glycemic index and glycemic load values. *American Journal of Clinical Nutrition* 76: 5–56.

Friedman, A. N., L. G. Hunsicker, J. Selhub, and A. G. Bostom. 2004. Clinical and nutritional correlates of C-reactive protein in type 2 diabetic nephropathy. *Atherosclerosis* 172 (1) (January): 121–25.

Grimble, R. F. 1994. Nutritional antioxidants and the modulation of inflammation: Theory and practice. *New Horizons* 2 (2) (May): 175–85.

———. 1997. Effect of antioxidative vitamins on immune function with clinical applications. *International Journal for Vitamin and Nutrition Research* 67 (5): 312–20.

———. 1998. Nutritional modulation of cytokine biology. *Nutrition* 14 (7–8) (July–August): 634–40.

Grimble, R. F., and P. S. Tappia. 1998. Modulation of pro-inflammatory cytokine biology by unsaturated fatty acids. *Zeitschrift für Ernährungswissenschaft* 37 (Suppl. 1): 57–65.

Hodge, G., S. Hodge, and P. Han. 2002. *Allium sativum* (garlic) suppresses leukocyte inflammatory cytokine production in vitro: Potential therapeutic use in the treatment of inflammatory bowel disease. *Cytometry* 48 (4) (August 1): 209–15.

Joe, B., and B. R. Lokesh. 1997. Effect of curcumin and capsaicin on arachidonic acid metabolism and lysosomal enzyme secretion by rat peritoneal macrophages. *Lipids* 32 (11) (November): 1173–80.

Kelley, D. S. 2001. Modulation of human immune and inflammatory responses by dietary fatty acids. *Nutrition* 17 (7–8) (July–August): 669–73.

Kelley, D. S., P. C. Taylor, G. J. Nelson, and B. E. Mackey. 1998. Arachidonic acid supplementation enhances synthesis of eicosanoids without suppressing immune functions in young healthy men. *Lipids* 33 (2) (February): 125–30.

Kelley, D. S., P. C. Taylor, G. J. Nelson, P. C. Schmidt, et al. 1999. Docosahexaenoic acid ingestion inhibits natural killer cell activity and production of inflammatory mediators in young healthy men. *Lipids* 34 (4) (April): 317–24.

Krest, I., and M. Keusgen. 1999. Quality of herbal remedies from *Allium sativum*: Differences between alliinase from garlic powder and fresh garlic. *Planta Medica* 65 (2) (March): 139–43.

Langlois, M., et al. 2001. Serum vitamin C concentration is low in peripheral arterial disease and is associated with inflammation and severity of atherosclerosis. *Circulation* 103 (14) (April 10): 1863–68.

Liu, S., J. E. Manson, et al. 2002. Relation between a diet with a high glycemic load and plasma concentrations of high-sensitivity C-reactive protein in middle-aged women. *American Journal of Clinical Nutrition* 75 (3) (March): 492–98.

Makheja, A. N., and J. M. Bailey. 1990. Antiplatelet constituents of garlic and onion. *Agents and Actions* 29 (3–4) (March): 360–63.

Makheja, A. N., J. Y. Vanderhoek, and J. M. Bailey. 1979. Effects of onion (*Allium cepa*) extract on platelet aggregation and thromboxane synthesis. *Prostaglandins and Medicine* 2 (6) (June): 413–24.

Mangoni, A. A., R. Arya, E. Ford, B. Asonganyi, et al. 2003. Effects of folic acid supplementation on inflammatory and thrombogenic markers in chronic smokers: A randomised controlled trial. *Thrombosis Research* 110 (1) (April 15): 13–17.

Mayland, C., K. R. Allen, T. J. Degg, and M. Bennet. 2004. Micronutrient concentrations in patients with malignant disease: Effect of the inflammatory response. *Annals of Clinical Biochemistry* 41 (pt. 2) (March): 138–41.

Meydani, M. 2001. Nutrition interventions in aging and age-associated disease. *Annals of the New York Academy of Sciences* 928 (April): 226–35.

Mozaffarian, D., T. Pischon, S. E. Hankinson, et al. 2004. Dietary intake of trans fatty acids and systemic inflammation in women. *American Journal of Clinical Nutrition* 79: 606–12.

Reddi, K., B. Henderson, et al. 1995. IL-6 production by lipopolycaccharide-stimulated human fibroblasts is potently inhibited by vitamin K compounds. *Cytokine* 7 (3) (April): 287–90.

Srivas, K. C. 1984. Effects of aqueous extracts of onion, garlic and ginger on platelet aggregation and metabolism of arachidonic acid in the blood vascular system: In vitro study. *Prostaglandins Leukotrienes and Medicine* 13 (2) (February): 227–35.

Srivastava, K. C. 1984. Aqueous extracts of onion, garlic and ginger inhibit platelet aggregation and alter arachidonic acid metabolism. *Biomedica Biochimica ACTA* 43 (8–9): S335–46.

Srivastava, K. C., and O. D. Tyagi. 1993. Effects of a garlic-derived principle (ajoene) on aggregation and arachidonic acid metabolism in human blood platelets. *Prostaglandins Leukotrienes and Essential Fatty Acids* 49 (2) (August): 587–95.

Ullegaddi, R., H. J. Powers, and S. E. Gariballa. 2004. B-group vitamin supplementation mitigates oxidative damage after acute ischaemic stroke. *Clinical Science (London)* 107 (5) (November): 477–84.

U.S. Department of Agriculture, Agricultural Research Service. 2004. USDA National Nutrient Database for Standard Reference, Release 17.

Upritchard, J. E. 2000. Effect of supplementation with tomato juice, vitamin E, and vitamin C on LDL oxidation and products of inflammatory activity in type 2 diabetes. *Diabetes Care* 23 (6) (June): 733–38.

Wegge, J. K., C. K. Roberts, T. H. Ngo, and R. J. Barnard. 2004. Effect of diet and exercise intervention on inflammatory and adhesion molecules in postmenopausal women on hormone replacement therapy and at risk for coronary artery disease. *Metabolism* 53 (3) (March): 377–81.

Yxfeldt, A., S. Wallberg-Jonsson, J. Hultdin, and S. Rantapaa-Dahlqvist. 2003. Homocysteine in patients with rheumatoid arthritis in relation to inflammation and B-vitamin treatment. *Scandanavian Journal of Rheumatology* 32 (4): 205–10.

Index

About the Author

A noted nutrition researcher, author, and trained chef, Monica Reinagel has written and edited numerous books, articles, and other publications on health, nutrition, and diet. Previous books include *Secrets of Evening Primrose Oil* and *The Life Extension Revolution: The New Science of Growing Older Without Aging*, with Philip Miller, M.D.

Monica Reinagel is the creator of the IF Rating™ system, a scientific method for determining the inflammatory effects of foods. Visit her online health and nutrition resource at www.stayhealthy-livewell.com.

About the Consulting Editor

Julius N. Torelli, M.D., is director of the Integrative Cardiology Center in High Point, North Carolina, where he specializes in preventive cardiology and emphasizes the importance of an anti-inflammatory diet. He is a fellow of the American College of Cardiology. Dr. Torelli's articles and abstracts have appeared in the *American Journal of Cardiology* and the *Journal of the American Society of Echocardiography*, among others. He is the author of *Beyond Cholesterol*.